101

IRISH RECORDS
YOU MUST HEAR
BEFORE YOU DIE

101

IRISH RECORDS
YOU MUST HEAR
BEFORE YOU DIE

TONY CLAYTON-LEA

LIB
ERT
IES

First published in 2011 by
Liberties Press
Guinness Enterprise Centre | Taylor's Lane | Dublin 8
Tel: +353 (1) 415 1224
www.libertiespress.com | info@libertiespress.com

Distributed in the United States by
Dufour Editions | PO Box 7 | Chester Springs | Pennsylvania 19425

Trade enquiries to Gill & Macmillan Distribution
Hume Avenue | Park West | Dublin 12
T: +353 (1) 500 9534 | F: +353 (1) 500 9595 | E: sales@gillmacmillan.ie

Distributed in the UK by
Turnaround Publisher Services
Unit 3 | Olympia Trading Estate | Coburg Road | London N22 6TZ
T: +44 (0) 20 8829 3000 | E: orders@turnaround-uk.com

Copyright © Tony Clayton-Lea, 2011

The author has asserted his moral rights.

ISBN: 978-1-907593-34-5
2 4 6 8 10 9 7 5 3 1
A CIP record for this title is available from the British Library.

Cover design by Graham Thew
Internal design by Sin É Design
Printed by Cambrian Printers Ltd, Aberystwyth

To the latest member of the Clayton-Lea family – Hayley, who, as the old song goes, was born with a smile on her face.

Van Morrison – © Jill Furmanovsky courtesy of rockarchive.com

ACKNOWLEDGEMENTS

If it hadn't been for the following people, it would have been far more difficult to have started and finished this book, so thumbs up to the following:

Rosemary Collier, of the Arts Council, for the publisher tips . . . Declan Burke for the heads-up on Liberties Press . . . Siobhan Long for the traditional music advice . . . Stephen Kennedy for the Engine Alley vinyl . . . Gary Sheehan for delivering a few albums . . . Steve Averill and Elvera Butler for digging out archived record covers . . . Dave O'Grady for several contact numbers . . . EMI Ireland's Head of Media, Pete Murphy, and Universal Ireland's Head of Press, Chantal Hourihan, for sending out a few 'old' albums . . . Liberties Press people, Seán O'Keeffe and Dan Bolger, who, rather surprisingly, just let me get on with it.

A bucket full of respect is directed towards *The Irish Times* and several people there, who, over the years, have commissioned me to write features and reviews that have assisted in the gathering of what some people might dismiss as useless information, but which for me is an essential aspect of not just my day job but my life (cultural and otherwise). So, giddy high-fives to editors Anthea McTeirnan, Shane Hegarty, Hugh Linehan, Conor Goodman and Gerry Smyth.

A shed load of thanks must go to all of the songwriters and musicians who very generously gave of their time to talk and email for the book. (Unless otherwise stated, by the way, all quotes are from interviews conducted by myself.) Particular thanks to Ann Scott and Gemma Hayes, who each assisted beyond the call of duty!

Last, and as always, by no means least, much love to Angela, Sarah and the two Pauls, without whom . . .

Julie Feeney – © Bryan O'Brien/*The Irish Times.*

INTRODUCTION

This book is not a definitive history of Irish music. Neither is it 'the story of or behind' the featured albums or singles.

It is instead a very personal trawl through music from the magnificent, the great, the good, the lost, the who-the-hell-are-they?, the forgotten and the fondly recalled. Some names you will recognise immediately; other names you might not be too familiar with. All, however, have one crucial fact in common: they have made records and written songs that join the dots between the head and the heart, that connect the ambiguous to the tangible.

The lines between the dots might occasionally be crooked, and the connections may occasionally fracture, but as day follows night you can guarantee that each and every one of them make sense in a world that too often doesn't know its ass from its elbow.

Beg your pardon? What's that? You have already scanned the list of 101 records before landing on this page, and discovered in the process that your own favorite album or single is missing?

That record would be number 102, then . . .

Tony Clayton-Lea
November 2011

MayKay from Fight Like Apes / Bell X1 / Damien Rice / Glen Hansard / Sinéad O'Connor / Gary Lightbody of Snow Patrol / Gavin Friday / Bob Geldof / The Cranberries.

A HOUSE

I AM THE GREATEST (1991)

DAVE COUSE

'All art is quite useless, according to Oscar Wilde. It may well be useless, but there is a lot of fun, turmoil, joy, hardship, elation, disappointment, surprises, self-belief, self-doubt, mistakes, bad judgement calls, love, misguided trust, friendships born, friendships die, delusion, hope, sweat, laughter, camaraderie, confusion, isolation, big ideals, letdowns and blow-ups along the way. *I Am The Greatest* was all of these and more.'

FERGAL BUNBURY

'*I Am The Greatest*? Three weeks of sleeping on the floor of a squat in Camberwell, missing meals and playing the guitar. I can smell the cheap beer, I can taste the duty-free cigarettes, I can feel the sticky carpet, and I am happy. It was great to be alive. Whenever I'm gone, you could reconstruct part of my DNA from this album. If you wanted to.'

Snatching victory from the jaws of defeat is something that put-upon rock bands always aim for but rarely achieve. Following A House's 1988 major-label debut, *On Our Big Fat Merry Go Round*, and its 1990 follow-up, *I Want Too Much*, they were dropped (unceremoniously, of course). It was presumed, even by the band's most fervent fans, that following the distinct lack of commercial success of *I Want Too Much*, they would split. Yet with no obvious contingency plans for a new record deal, A House came back with a bang, helped out by the indie label Setanta (itself a refuge for many an Irish band in the eighties and nineties), with *I Am The Greatest*.

For a while, without doubt, A House *were* the greatest; indeed, some would say they were the best Irish band of the past thirty years, leapfrogging over the usual suspects by virtue of their uncompromising nature, provocative lyrical stance and perversely discordant approach. The band was idiosyncratic before this became fashionable and profitable, and seemed to take perverse delight in rubbing people up the wrong way. Which is to say, the right way . . .

Sometimes, of course, the memories are stronger and more resonant than the music, but the impact of songs as emotionally strong and raw as 'You're Too Young', 'When I First Saw You', 'I Am Afraid', 'I Lied' and the spoken-word title track is such that, as a listener, you're left wondering how many more uncompromising songs you can take. For his many sins, lead singer and main songwriter Dave Couse (see page 56 for the entry on his solo album, *Genes*) is one of the few Irish lyricists who can be credited with dredging the depths of his own vulnerabilities and mixing in his work a blend of the hurtful and heartfelt.

But there's more. 'Endless Art', a shopping-list litany of deceased cultural figures and icons, is a deadpan rock-minimalist classic that still engages on every level; while 'Take It Easy on Me' spirals in and out and through the head, leaving in its trail slivers of doubt and casual machismo.

'Whatever happened to good music?' asks Couse in the spoken-word title track. 'You know, in the days when you could feel it? It was almost sexual, sending shivers up your spine.'

Whatever happened to good music? Good question; the answer is right here.

Released: 1991
Record Label: Setanta Records, Parlophone (UK), Radioactive Records (US)
Producer: Edwyn Collins
Recorded at: The Elephant Studios, London
Sleeve Design: Julie Blair Carter (design), Amelia Stein and Kevin Westenberg (photography)

Tracks:
1 I Don't Care **3:45**
2 You're Too Young **3:24**
3 Endless Art **3:02**
4 When I First Saw You **1:54**
5 Take It Easy on Me **4:01**
6 I Am Afraid **3:53**
7 Blind Faith **2:43**

8 I Lied **3:55**
9 Creatures of Craze **3:57**
10 How Strong Is Love **4:29**
11 Slipping Away **2:49**
12 I Wanted Too Much **2:27**
13 I Am the Greatest **4:32**

AFRO CELT SOUND SYSTEM

VOLUME 1: SOUND MAGIC (1996)

SIMON EMMERSON

'When we first emerged a few Irish critics and musicians on the trad scene "got it", but most tried to marginalise us as an irrelevancy or joke. It was the same with large aspects of the UK world music scene – we simply didn't fit into their own territorial and proscriptive definitions of "authenticity" . . . With the risk of sounding rather pompous, I think that Afro Celts clearly shows the paucity of words and the poverty of language in trying to capture a mercurial and dynamic process that creates radical and progressive musical forms. We make music for the global village but not music to "globalise" the village.'

Brace yourself, Brigid! Shove the pig into the yard, Seamus! Break open the Buckfast! Put the kettle on, remove the chairs, and make way for – well, for what exactly? How about something like this: a mayhem-fuelled mash-up of piping-hot traditional Irish music, possessed-by-poltergeists African rhythms, spiralling techno, trip-hop, *sean nós* singing and a no-holds-barred, volatile musical mugging?

If Moving Hearts (see page 134) set some form of an agenda for the meshing of Irish traditional music with other forms and genres, then Afro Celt Sound System added to that loosely conceived blueprint by virtue of their unadulterated and often mind-blowing fusion techniques. Following time in the early nineties spent in Senegal making an album with African musician Baaba Maal, Simon Emmerson was intrigued by the similarities between a particular African melody and a traditional Irish tune. On his return to the UK, he struck up a conversation with Irish uilleann piper Davy Spillane, who expounded the theory behind the belief that nomadic Celts lived in Africa prior to migrating to Western Europe. Theoretically spurious or otherwise, Emmerson was excited enough by the notion of fusing the two musics, and so he engineered rehearsals between members of Baaba Maal's band and traditional Irish musicians to see what might happen.

The result was as exciting as it was original, but what placed a succulent cherry on top of a substantial cake was Emmerson's addition of dance/techno/electronics beats. Between the beats, jigs, reels, grooves and workouts (created by a group of people who didn't speak the same language), *Volume 1: Sound Magic* was released to, at first, an overwhelming amount of WTF head-scratching.

It was, without question, a new hybrid, and an album where intelligent production, an interesting concept and, especially, intuitive musicianship (take a bow Emmerson, James McNally, Masamba Diop, Ronan Browne, Myrdhin, Davy Spillane, Kauwding Cissokho and Iárla Ó Lionáird) took hold of the listener and made them face – without sunglasses or factor 30 sun lotion – a series of startlingly bright global musical configurations.

It starts with 'Saor/Free' (blissfully, expectantly seductive; question: is this the person for me?) and ends with 'Saor Reprise' (shagged-out afterglow; answer: no). In between are standout tracks such as 'Sure-As-Not/Sure-As-Knot', 'Whirl-Y-Reel 1', 'Whirl-Y-Reel 2', 'House of the Ancestors' and 'Eistigh Liomsa Sealad'. With each of these (and the rest of it), you are cuffed to the fringes of a magic carpet that weaves this way and that, dips and wiggles, equal parts vertiginous and depth-charged.

Can't tell the difference between a bodhrán and a djembe? A nyatiti and a kora? A doudouk and a sintar? Not everyone can. The most important aspect of a record as astonishing as this is that it doesn't matter.

Released: 1996
Record Label: Real World Records
Producer: Ron Aslan, Jo Bruce, Simon
Emmerson, Martin Russell
Recorded at: Real World Studios, Wiltshire
(England)
Sleeve Design: Tristan Manco (graphic
design), Jamie Reid (paintings)

Tracks:
1 Saor (Free)/News From Nowhere **8:21**
2 Whirl-Y-Reel 1 **7:21**
3 Inion (Daughter) **4:15**
4 Sure-As-Not/Sure-As-Knot **9:58**
5 Nil Cead Againn Dul Abhaile **7:20**
6 Dark Moon, High Tide **4:12**
7 Whirl-Y-Reel 2 **5:27**

8 House of the Ancestors **8:01**
9 Eistigh Liomsa Sealad (Listen to Me)/
   Saor Reprise **10:53**

ASH

FREE ALL ANGELS (2001)

TIM WHEELER

'We are definitely not a lads' band, and that was a good balance for Charlotte because she's a bit of a tomboy. There's a feminine side to our band, anyway, so that worked, too. The songs are romantic to a degree, a little indie Venus among the power chords. Where does the romance and reflection come from? I suppose we're faggy straight blokes. That's just the way we are: nerdy, introspective guys who read Kerouac more than *Playboy*. Maybe that comes from my mum – she always pushed books my way. Rick was a straight-A student into politics and history – as well as being something of an idiot savant, which is possibly why he used to drink so much to compensate for not being able to deal with his intellect.'

For a band that flings out nuggets of granite-hard rock, Ash aren't very blokey; and therein lies the emblematic problem with them. They make – sometimes generally, sometimes quite specifically – superb punk/pop music, but oft-times their image is betrayed by their intelligence and upbringing. And their best songs are a bit soppy, aren't they? Brilliant, yes, and rolling from left to right with a pronounced swagger, but they are covered in hand-holding, eye-catching love-bites nonetheless.

You forget, though, how young they were when this Downpatrick trio started out in the early nineties. In 1994, while still studying for their A-levels, Tim Wheeler, Mark Hamilton and Rick McMurray released their pop/punk mini-album, *Trailer*. It's fair to say that, thereafter, the teenagers took to the rock 'n' roll lifestyle with unfettered glee. (The envelope that contained Wheeler's A-level results was opened live on BBC Radio 1.) By 1997, English guitarist Charlotte Hatherly had joined them, and their sound swiftly matured from that of teenage Green Day wannabes to a band in their early twenties eager to adopt a more elaborate sound that was still inspired by punk, yet was more open to outside influences.

In the case of *Free All Angels* – written mostly in 1999 by Wheeler, during a six-month bender, and recorded in 2000 on the island of Majorca – those influences amounted to The Beach Boys, Phil Spector, sunshine, romance, sandy shores, sex and sangria. 'Shining Light' was the first single from an album full of them, and introduced the band's newly fashioned sugar-rush retro-pop to a new audience. Ash weren't about redefining pop/punk music, but for sheer exuberance alone they were pretty much untouchable.

Several years later, Ash would go on to announce the death of the album, and release on a monthly basis a series of download-only singles (gathered together a short time later on, yes, the albums *A-Z Vols 1* and *2*, each released in 2010), but on *Free All Angels* they had all their ducks lined up neatly: eminently punchy, ricocheting, melodic and zinging guitar-pop songs that pledge allegiance to neither simpering singer-songwriters nor the fusion of rap and rock (nor any other fusion, for that matter).

Listen to *Free All Angels* for unadulterated Ash: a trim, lean unit that relinquishes twenty-something cynicism for teenage dreams. Hard to beat.

Released: 2001
Record Label: Infectious Records
Producer: Owen Morris, Ash
Recorded at: El Cortijo, Puerto Banus; The Wool Hall, Beckingham and Rak Studios, London
Sleeve Design: The Deceptikons, Jim Fitzpatrick

Tracks:
1 Walking Barefoot **4:13**
2 Shining Light **5:09**
3 Burn Baby Burn **3:29**
4 Candy **4:52**
5 Cherry Bomb **3:16**
6 Submission **3:32**
7 Someday **4:31**
8 Pacific Palisades **1:57**
9 Shark **3:18**
10 Sometimes **4:04**
11 Nicole **3:26**
12 There's a Star **4:20**
13 World Domination **2:17**

ASLAN

'THIS IS' (1986)

CHRISTY DIGNAM

'No matter what happens, or doesn't happen, or didn't happen, "This Is" will always be a testament to what we did. It's a great song, I know it's a great song, and I'd rather have it on my repertoire than the combined albums, and monies, of the records of Westlife and Boyzone. Success is the writing of that song, and no matter what we did or didn't achieve on an international stage, it's irrelevant in the light of that.'

Meat Loaf was right: rock 'n' roll dreams can come true. Formed in the early eighties, the Ballymun/Finglas band started with a cross on their back in that they weren't middle class enough for some, and too working class for others. Such was the social temperature of Dublin at the time that the impression in certain sections of the media was that the band, in between making some very decent rock music, robbed cars, lived in slum flats and took drugs. 'No one ever questioned where Hothouse Flowers came from,' mused the band's roguish lead singer, Christy Dignam, some years later.

No matter. In 1986, despite the fact that their rehearsal space, adjoining Dublin Airport, hosted the remnants of a pig sty, Aslan were looking, and playing, as if they knew that great things would land at their feet. You know how some bands make you feel that they own the stage? Well, in their prime, Aslan made you feel that they owned the venue. Rock 'n' roll dreams for five working-class geezers were surely about to come true: rapturously received shows, recording BBC Radio 1 sessions, winning Most Promising New Act gongs, signing to EMI, releasing a debut album (*Feel No Shame*, 1988), watching it hit the number one spot, turning from silver to gold.

Following stylistic changes from fast to mellow, 'This Is' started off in 1986 as one song on a three-song demo that was recorded in a small studio a spit away from the River Liffey. The demo was shopped around, hustled, optimistically bragged about, cautiously hoped for. One of the first stops along the road to selling it was U2-owned Mother Records, which was set up by the band to assist other Irish acts. At a meeting in the Docker's pub, down by the quays close to where the Mother/U2 offices were, Aslan's Dignam and Joe Jewell were told by Bono that he didn't think 'This Is' was good enough. An offer of a loan of a four-track recording machine to help them with their songwriting was politely refused. We can all suffer from lack of judgement, and make a wrong call; Bono's incorrect decision only galvanised Aslan further.

The song is a classic example of honesty and decency, a truthful reflection of changing social conventions ('this is the face of a teenage mother, this is the child she bears'), conflict with religion ('these are the feet of a punished pilgrim') and working-class toil ('these are the hands of a tired man', which directly references Dignam's father, who was an upholsterer with Ireland's national bus company). It wasn't just the lyrics, though; the words were copper-fastened to a melody, a chorus and a fade-out that were made for stadiums and arenas.

At the heel of the hunt, Aslan never made it to the venues that many of their champions had wished for them, and their best-hoped-for rock 'n' roll dreams occasionally turned into nightmares. But 'This Is', borne out of acute, innate observation of social change, a great burden of responsibility, and the failings of the Catholic hierarchy, remains what it has always been: a terrific pop song.

Released: 1986
Record Label: EMI Ireland, Capitol Records
Producer: Mick Glossop
Recorded at: Westland Studios, Dublin;
Terminal 24/Townhouse 3, London
Sleeve Design: Works Associates,
Steve Averill
Duration: 5:24

AUTAMATA

MY SANCTUARY (2004)

KEN MCHUGH

'I originally sent around four or five demo tracks from the album to record labels, and I was quite surprised with the response. Labels like Warp, Virgin and 4AD all liked different tracks and were suggesting that I duplicate the sound on the ones that they liked and ditch the others . . . I chose in the end to set up my own label to release the album and not compromise my vision and how I wanted the album to be . . . I was pretty much just making music for myself – it was my way of escaping the world into my own space, having fun, dancing around – and that's why I called it *My Sanctuary*.'

It happens: you're so skilled at grappling with different genres – in this instance, trip-hop, electronica, electro-acoustic, electro-pop – that the very same record companies which tripped over themselves to get your name on the dotted line are now wondering how in the name of Thor they can market you. To which producer and tune-maker extraordinaire Ken McHugh (who *is* Autamata) responded: tough.

McHugh's obsession with music began as a child, when, as a member of Mayo-based trad/folk act the McHugh Family, he travelled around Ireland playing pubs and lounges. As he grew older, his interest in music continued via a course in sound engineering. It was this that set McHugh off on a career of multi-tracking, producing and composing. His controlling instincts and a growing awareness that, sometimes, human beings let you down dictated his work patterns. In short, he taught himself everything there was to know about samplers and, later, how to make a record by himself.

On *My Sanctuary*, all of the music is written, played and (heavily) programmed by McHugh. (He also produced, arranged and engineered it.) If this makes him seem like a self-obsessed dictator, fretting about how to make things work and sound, consumed with the creation of melodies, then so be it. Frankly, such dedication is fine by us when the results are so fresh. Of course, because McHugh fusses around so much with genres, you're wrong-footed from the start. But what a start: 'Fragments' is one of those jaunty slivers of superbly crafted electronica that just settles itself nicely into your system. It's followed by 'Jive County', a loping tune with a piece of straw in its mouth that seems in no hurry to reach a conclusion – and the only track on the album sung by McHugh. It is here that the album transcends its limitations.

Although *My Sanctuary* was originally conceived as a purely instrumental album, McHugh allowed his controlling instincts to be infiltrated and splintered by lyricists/vocalists Cathy Davey (see separate entry, page 62) and Carol Keogh, whose contributions to the album are no mere background – they give the pretty but sometimes detached music a sense of tenderness. Davey sings on two tracks (the ordinary 'Let's Normalise', and the astonishing 'Jellyman'), but Keogh takes the weight of the remainder, playing a blinder on the likes of 'Out of This', 'Onward' and 'Postscript'. One of the most unfairly overlooked Irish female vocalists of her generation, Keogh is by turns beautifully subtle ('Out of This'), unaffected ('Onward') and flawless ('Postscript'). So it's the music. And the vocals. And the surprises ('To Be a Robot'). And the fun 'n' games ('Little Green Men'). And the unabashed, unapologetic, utterly charismatic smartness of it all.

Ah, but what's this peeking around the corner? One more surprise? In 'Hide and Seek's running time there is a concealed track that is as cute a coda as you can imagine.

autamata
MY SANCTUARY

Released: 2004
Record Label: RG Records
Producer: Ken McHugh
Recorded at: Area 51 Studio, Dublin
Sleeve Design: Martin Yates (cover photo),
Rob Crane (design)

Tracks:
1 Fragments **3:46**
2 Jive County **4:25**
3 Out of This **5:00**
4 Registered User **3:43**
5 Little Green Men **4:19**
6 Let's Normalise **4:38**
7 Jellyman **3:39**

8 To Be a Robot **5:17**
9 Onward **4:08**
10 Postscript **5:24**
11 Hide and Seek **12:48**
12 Plainsong **2:26**

BELL X1
MUSIC IN MOUTH (2003)

PAUL NOONAN

'Music in Mouth was when we found our feet, I think, having moved on from the dizzy excitement of making our first record and just being delighted to be there. It was recorded in some really characterful places – Ridge Farm in Surrey, in what used to be Queen's rehearsal barn, and the Fallout Shelter in London, where a lot of the early Island records were made. We were living in the Fawlty Towers-eque Chiswick Hotel, and were living it large in London town . . . ha! The writing was, I suppose, a mix of being young men in the world, and me having recently gone through a pretty wrenching personal loss . . . "they say that her beauty was Music in Mouth".'

It's all very well to rise from the ashes of a once hotly tipped band, but it's another thing altogether to succeed so resoundingly that, after a while, no one wants to talk about the previous band. The former band in this case was Juniper (which had in its ranks Damien Rice – see page 168), which in the mid-nineties were trumpeted in some quarters as ones to watch. Unsurprisingly, Juniper fell by the wayside, scuttled by creative differences and egos, and led the way for a new kind of band toting a new kind of sound.

Bell X1 (named after the first aeroplane to break the sound barrier) released their debut album, *Neither Am I*, in 2000. So far, so humdrum. Three years later, however, *Music in Mouth* came out, and the difference in artistic scope and creative weight was little short of astonishing.

In an interesting development, and a shock to begrudgers everywhere, this time Bell X1 refused to think inside a closed box. The result was a collection of pop/rock songs that weren't actually pop/rock, but some kind of curious and compelling hybrid that filched from the forms but had a unique identity of its own.

Regardless of how well the album travelled – the song 'Eve, the Apple of My Eye' was used to soundtrack a lesbian kiss in American TV show *The OC*, and the result of such lip-lock exposure meant greater awareness for the band in the US than the UK/Europe – there was an acute sense of cultural placement in *Music in Mouth*. With nods to Irish political history (Maud Gonne), Irish towns (Knock), religion (the Garden of Eden) and – in what has to be a first – a reference to Chris de Burgh, the album couldn't have been created by any band other than an Irish one. And a very smart one, at that.

The self-assurance throughout is as solid as a rock, and as a lyricist-singer, Paul Noonan excels. From cute observations ('I'd say you'd like children but you couldn't eat a whole one', 'Alphabet Soup') to elegant writing ('Sometimes early in the morning, I watch her breathing rise and fall. I've spilled in drunk beside her in the stillness of dawn. See how her hair spills over like frayed ends of twine, all wild and wrapped around her like these wandering arms of mine', 'West of Her Spine'), Noonan places his head and heart side by side with music that is detailed, deft and stuffed with personality.

Released: 2003
Record Label: Island Records, Universal
Producer: Jamie Cullum, Roger Bechirian
Recorded at: Ridge Farm, Dorking, Surrey;
The Fallout Shelter, London; Nix Place,
Dublin; Westland Studios, Dublin
Sleeve Design: Scott Burnett

Tracks:
1 Snakes and Snakes **4:00**
2 Alphabet Soup **4:56**
3 Daybreak **5:12**
4 Eve, the Apple of My Eye **5:37**
5 Next To You **3:59**
6 West Of Her Spine **3:23**
7 Bound For Boston Hill **4:52**
8 Tongue **5:23**
9 White Water Song **2:42**
10 In Every Sunflower **5:53**
11 I'll See Your Heart And I'll Raise You
   Mine **5:09**
12 Eve, the Apple of My Eye (single
   version) **4:06**

THE BLADES
RAYTOWN REVISITED (1985)

PAUL CLEARY

'The writing process was still the same as when I was in The Blades. And still as painful – without wishing to sound like a luvvie about it. But once you have one or two songs written, I suppose you have to finish it. There is no mystery to it, as such, although some songwriters might like to think there is. I certainly had that feeling of writing songs again, but whether that's a good or bad feeling, I'm not sure. My main guiding point, lyrically, for this album was not to be too obvious or too vague.'

Question: when is an album not an album? Answer: when it's *Raytown Revisited*. Released by independent Dublin label Reekus Records (an early champion of this Dublin band), *Raytown Revisited* isn't a bona fide studio album but rather a compilation of singles tracks, solo tracks and B-sides (ask your grandfather) put together by Reekus following the dropping of The Blades by Elektra America.

Let's backtrack. Formed in 1977, from the working-class Dublin area of Ringsend, The Blades were originally a trio of Paul Cleary, his older brother, Lar Cleary, and Pat Larkin. They wrote short, direct, unaffected punk/pop/Stax-influenced songs and wore thrifty sharp suits. So far, so The Jam.

From the late seventies, however, it was clear from their live shows (which included a never-bettered residency at Dublin pub the Magnet and a stint of Tuesday-night support slots with U2 at Dublin's Baggot Inn) that not only were the band destined for much bigger things, but their singer and songwriter, Paul Cleary, was shaping up to be as fine a pop tunesmith and lyric writer as Ireland had ever produced. Indeed, it is not by any stretch of the imagination (nor, indeed, by something as critically risky as fond recollection) to state that the band's first five singles (1980's 'Hot for You', 1981's 'Ghost of a Chance', 1982's 'The Bride Wore White' and 'Revelations of Heartbreak', and 1983's 'Downmarket') constitute the first Golden Age of Irish rock music. If

that sounds a tad too speculative for you (or even too fondly recalled), then how about the best home run ever by an Irish rock band?

With the exception of 'Downmarket' (which is on the jettisoned Elektra album, *The Last Man in Europe*, released in 1986, and featuring different – but just as high-quality – musicians), all of the aforementioned songs are here, as well as most of their respective B-sides ('The Reunion', 'Animation', 'Rules of Love'; just to complicate matters, the B-side to 'Downmarket' – 'You Never Ask' – is also included).

The Blades spit up in 1986, just prior to *The Last Man In Europe* being unleashed on an indifferent public. In jig time, Cleary formed another band, The Partisans, which in 1987 released a mini-album, *Impossible*. And then? Nothing until a Paul Cleary solo album in 2001 (see separate entry, page 48).

After that? Well, how about an appearance in a Nike soccer television ad ('Before and After Ronaldo'), wherein a bedroom poster advertising The Blades at the Baggot Inn is displayed among other past icons of brilliance that include Copernicus, Newton and Galileo. The ad was made in South America under the creative execution of F/Nazca Saatchi & Saatchi. From Rinsgend to Rio? You couldn't make it up . . .

Released: 1985
Record Label: Reekus Records
Producer: Various
Recorded at: Various studios, Dublin and London
Sleeve Design: Steve Averill (Creative Dept Ltd)

Tracks:
1 Ghost of a Chance **3:26**
2 Animation **2:50**
3 Muscle Men **2:44**
4 Stranger Things Have Happened **3:19**
5 The Rules of Love **3:04**
6 Hot for You **2:17**
7 Some People Smile **2:50**

8   The Bride Wore White **3:15**
9   Revelation of Heartbreak **3:36**
10 Those Were the Days **4:09**
11 You Never Ask **2:29**
12 Too Late **4:40**
13 The Reunion **2:58** **(2000 reissue)**
14 Tell Me Lies **3:27** **(2000 reissue)**
15 Fool Me **2:49** **(2000 reissue)**

BOOMTOWN RATS
A TONIC FOR THE TROOPS (1978)

BOB GELDOF

'The Boomtown Rats were one of maybe ten bands – [including] The Sex Pistols, The Clash, The Ramones, The Jam, The Stranglers, Talking Heads, Elvis Costello, Blondie – who substantially changed what music was in the seventies. I think, too, in retrospect, that were it not for those ten bands, you would not have had the bands subsequent to that . . . All of us existed for identical reasons, and one basic premise: that whatever was happening in pop music was shite.'

Well, it was either this or their 1977 debut – honestly, it was a tough call. Their self-titled debut has an appealing frankness and acidic purity about it that still stands up – all that snotty arrogance, supreme self-confidence, fuck-off assertiveness, utter mouthiness and occasional unashamed chauvinism was corralled into a revved-up R&B/punk collection of songs that delivered Bob Geldof and his mates (Pete Briquette, Johnny Fingers, Gerry Cott, Simon Crowe) into the gaping gob of greedily grasped commercial success. They would never get as close to the core of Dublin, however, as they did in the debut's 'Neon Heart', and Geldof would never again write something as brilliantly, disgracefully, youthfully self-centered as 'Lookin' After No. 1'. (Just think of the irony now behind Geldof penning lyrics as selfish as 'don't give me "love thy neighbour", don't give me charity, don't give me "peace and love" or "the good Lord above", you only get in my way with your stupid ideas'.)

With A Tonic For The Troops, The Boomtown Rats left Ireland and provincialism behind; it really seemed that with pop songs as sturdy and intelligent as 'Like Clockwork', '(I Never Loved) Eva Braun', 'She's So Modern' and 'Rat Trap' – and with so eloquent and outrageously charming a front man – that they could become the first mouthy rock act from Ireland to capture the hearts and money of people the world over.

In what was back then a truly subversive moment (Geldof ripping up a photo of John Travolta and Olivia Newton John on Top Of The Pops), the possibilities seemed credible and without limit: 'Rat Trap' was the first UK number one for an Irish rock band, the album spent almost a full year in the UK charts, and Geldof was a true rock star – in strictly comparative Irish terms, he had buckets more charisma than Van Morrison, more ambition in his fingertips than Rory Gallagher had in his body, and more strategic planning than the (admittedly) very canny Phil Lynott.

As well as all these factors, the songs on A Tonic For The Troops were mixed for transistor radios – the true sonic test of a good pop tune. Of course, whatever punk rock credibility they'd had from before (which is to say, not that much) disappeared completely when they started having hits – which was something the band defiantly wanted. Was A Tonic For The Troops opportunistic? More than likely. Was it a belligerent exercise in queue-jumping self-service? Without doubt. Was it the most intelligent new-wave pop album ever released by an Irish band? Absolutely.

Next stop America, then? Dear me, no – not for the first time would Geldof's mouth get him into trouble . . .

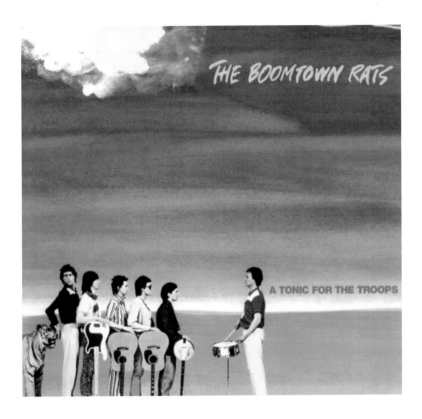

Released: 1978
Record Label: Ensign Records (UK),
Columbia Records (US)
Producer: Robert John 'Mutt' Lange
Recorded at: Relight Studios, Holland;
Dieter Dierks Studios, Stommeln,
Koln, Germany
Sleeve Design: Fin Costello (covers,
portraits), Chuck Loyola (design)

Tracks:
1 Like Clockwork **3:43**
2 Blind Date **3:21**
3 (I Never Loved) Eva Braun **4:37**
4 She's So Modern **2:56**
5 Don't Believe What You Read **3:07**
6 Living In An Island **4:10**
7 Me And Howard Hughes **3:11**
8 Can't Stop **2:19**

9 (Watch Out For) The Normal People
  2:53
10 Rat Trap **5:10**

THE BOTHY BAND

OLD HAG YOU HAVE KILLED ME (1976)

DÓNAL LUNNY

'The Bothy Band was in full flight when we made this, our second album. The first title that we seriously considered for it was "Is There A Bar On Mars?" – we even had artwork! – and I sometimes wonder how much it would have changed things if we'd gone with that title. We did a lot of layering on some tracks – "Fionnghuala" has each of our voices recorded at least four times along with the definitive take. There were dozens of us on "Calum Sgaire"; triple bodhráns on "Music In The Glen"; lots of Kevin Burke's fiddle on "Tiochfaidh an Samhradh". We had three days to mix the album; four tracks each day. On the departure day, photographers from Polydor wanted to get a picture of us in the dawn mist, so we had to get up at 4 AM. Micheál and I returned to the studio like a pair of zombies to finish the last mix. The genial engineer, Fritz Fryer – who helped to give the mixes energy and projection – finished splicing the master together around 11 AM; our Transit van was ticking over outside with everybody dozing on board, and our tour manager, P. J. Curtis, frothing at the wheel because we were due on stage at the Cambridge Festival that afternoon – a four-hour drive away. We made it.'

Formed in the mid-seventies by Dónal Lunny (who at around this time had founded the Irish record label Mulligan, on which this album was first released), The Bothy Band eased their way into the community with 1975's self-titled debut album. The configuration of the band is what made it so different from the norm: Lunny was joined by Matt Molloy (flute, whistle), Paddy Keenan (uileann pipes), Paddy Glackin (fiddle; replaced by Kevin Burke, who appears on this album), Tony McMahon (accordion, who does not appear here) and siblings Mícheál Ó Domhnaill and Tríona Ní Dhomhnaill.

It kicks off in fine fettle with a set of three reels – 'Music in the Glen', 'The Humours of Scarriff' and 'Poll an Madra Uisce' – that is thrust skywards by a blend of fiddle, whistle, bodhrán, pipes, and what appears to be an irrepressible force of nature. It continues in similar nature with the reel 'Farewell to Erin', where propulsion forms an unbreakable bond of fidelity with fierce, precision playing. Further tracks, such as 'The Ballintore Fancy' (equal parts luminous and alluring), 'The Maid of Coolmore' (sung by Tríona, a beguiling, genteel

song from the extensive collection of her aunt, Nellí Ní Dhomhnaill), and '16 Come Next Sunday' (another song from the Nellí Ní Dhomhnaill collection, also sung by Tríona, in suitably arresting fashion) attest to the band's virtuosic trawl of moods and flavors. Yet even these are surpassed by the title set, which, with its harmonic infusion of clavinet, uileann pipes and fiddle across the titular double jig, the single jig 'The Hag in the Kilt' and the closing double jig 'Morrisons', blows the roof clean off the house.

Some say that The Bothy Band invented contemporary traditional music. Others argue that they are the ultimate Irish traditional group. We'll leave these debates to the historians. What we'll note here, however (for the record, naturally), is that *Old Hag You Have Killed Me* is an album performed with much vim, vigour and charm – a collection of songs and tunes that, despite the band's mere few years in existence and its unwanted wealth of financial and managerial issues, were recorded in the spirit of generosity and the key of F-U-N.

Released: 1976
Record Label: Polydor (UK), Green Linnet Records (US), Mulligan Records (Ireland)
Producer: Mícheál Ó Domhnaill, Dónal Lunny
Recorded at: Rockfield Studios, Monmouth, South Wales
Sleeve Design: Jill Mumford, Wadewood, Paddy Keenan (photography)

Tracks:
1 Music in the Glen **3:20**
2 Fionnghuala **1:27**
3 The Kid on the Mountain **3:44**
4 Farewell to Erin **3:21**
5 Tiochfaidh an Samhradh (Summer Will Come) **5:37**
6 The Laurel Tree **3:16**
7 16 Come Next Sunday **2:58**

8 Old Hag You Have Killed Me **4:14**
9 Calum Sgaire **3:28**
10 The Ballintore Fancy **3:34**
11 The Maid of Coolmore **3:29**
12 Michael Gorman's **4:13**

PAUL BRADY
HARD STATION (1981)

PAUL BRADY

'At around the end of the seventies I began to be quite surprised at the length of time I had spent in traditional music, excluding all else – from '74 through to '79/'80. At that point I was coming back to the same crossroads in traditional music once too often, really, and was feeling an urge to reconnect with the music that I had been involved with and loved in the sixties. I wanted to find out if I could develop within that form of music, and if I had anything to say. So *Hard Station* was the culmination of a year's forced head change . . . It was a challenge, lyrically; I was coming of age, emotionally – I was at the end of my twenties, I was married with two kids, and I was really starting to feel the need to express emotions through songs . . . I don't listen to the album all that often, but when I do I tend to feel it stands up.'

A chronicler of mid-life turmoil, Paul Brady is a master of the tough acoustic guitar song. From the 1960s onwards, from R&B rocker to folk mainstay and back again to an adult rock format, he has sailed through the clatter and clamour of intense emotions and domestic and political upheaval. 'He's put into all that folk contingent,' Bono has said of Brady, 'but he's got a much darker energy and intensity. He takes the rose-tinted sheen off everything. He's the white knuckle behind the ballad.'

If anyone captures that experimental time in the sixties when the lines and attitudes between traditional Irish and rock music were intersecting (and therefore interesting), it is Brady. His teenage years were spent dodging Dublin-based university studies, opting instead for Dublin's reverberating R&B boom, and playing in highly regarded beat groups The Inmates, Rootzgroup, The Kult and Rockhouse. He never got to finish his Arts Degree – in his last year of college he was asked to relinquish his much-loved beat-group posturing and join The Johnstons, Ireland's premier ballad group of the time. Despite moderate success in America and Britain (where they were deemed credible enough to be guests at London's Singer's Club, inner sanctum of the UK folk scene), the band imploded. A short period of time in the acclaimed traditional Irish Planxty (see page 150) followed, and then a stint of what Brady terms

the 'vagabond gypsy existence', wherein he and former Planxty member Andy Irvine would travel and play gigs whenever they were asked.

By the end of the seventies, Brady decided that there wasn't much of a future for him in traditional music. He knew he loved it, but he also knew that it didn't need him. He had somewhere else to go, anyway. That somewhere else was writing songs for himself, the first attempts at concentrated and objective self-discovery. The results of Brady's process of forging an identity were made public on his first rock-oriented album of the eighties, *Hard Station* – a singularly Irish record (sensibilities, sentiments, topics) through and through.

It is an album very much aware of the paradox of human relationships – a Bermuda Triangle of emotions where cynicism battles affection, where paranoia goes with trust, and where a soft caress or a carefully placed sweet thing can dissolve a desperate chill in the heart, and where previously accepted socio-political doctrines are queried. Songs like 'Crazy Dreams', 'Busted Loose', the title track and 'Nothing But The Same Old Story' deliver individualistic takes on familiar if ignored stories, with Brady's lyrics (a mix of sardonic and aggressively honest) underpinning granite-solid AOR melodies. The eighties 'sound' of the record might diminish its impact slightly, but Brady's in-built sense of trust and truth endures.

PAUL BRADY

HARD STATION

Released: 1981
Record Label: 21 Records, Polydor
Producer: Paul Brady, Hugh Murphy
Recorded at: Windmill Lane Studios, Dublin;
Keystone Studios, London
Sleeve Design: John Devlin

Tracks:
1 Crazy Dreams **4:56**
2 The Road To The Promised Land **5:39**
3 Busted Loose **4:54**
4 Cold Cold Night **6:07**
5 Hard Station **5:33**

6 Dancer In The Fire **5:36**
7 Night Hunting Time **5:57**
8 Nothing But The Same Old Story **6:03**

THE CAKE SALE

THE CAKE SALE (2006)

BRIAN CROSBY

'There was a really enthusiastic response from everyone who I approached to write songs or perform; everyone involved got the vibe of what I was trying to achieve. There's a really interesting dynamic when people collaborate together and I'm personally very energised by it. Looking back it was a really privileged position to be at the fulcrum of such a group of talented friends and musicians. From a fundraising perspective it achieved above and beyond expectations, and from an artistic point of view it's a piece of work I'm really proud of.'

It is a dream for people who don't take too kindly to the Irish singer-songwriter species: put a bunch of them into a studio under the pretence of making a record for charity, and blow the studio to bits. Thankfully, such an act of irrational musical terrorism never happened, for if it had, this record would never have been released, and we'd be all the poorer for it.

Former member of Bell X1 Brian Crosby formed The Cake Sale collective to raise money for Oxfam Ireland and the Ireland Make Trade Fair campaign. It was initially devised as an Irish-only release, but the number of quality songs and musicians on it upped the profile to the extent that it was released in the UK and America in 2007.

The Cake Sale is unusual in a number of respects: all the publishing royalties raised by the album benefit Oxfam (Oxfam Publishing was specifically established to administer the royalties), and it marks the only recorded/ released occasion where established Irish singer-song-writers pitched together to create what is the best original Irish compilation or 'collection' album. All of the songs were (at the time of the project) previously unreleased and were recorded specifically for it. The roll-call of musicians and songwriters is impressive: say hello and pay your respects to the following: Gary Lightbody, Gemma Hayes, Neil Hannon, Lisa Hannigan, Damien Rice, Glen Hansard, Oliver Cole, The Thrills' Daniel Ryan, and Conor Deasy. Factor in Irish-connected people such as Josh Ritter, Emm Gryner, former Crowded House member Nick Seymour, Tasmanian songwriter Matt Lunson and The Cardigans/A Camp singer Nina Persson, and you already have a formidable bunch. Add in the songs, and it's a softly spoken, all-killer-no-filler enterprise. What really works here, however, is the ensemble approach: the person who wrote the song doesn't necessarily sing it. Expect twists, turns, spins and eye-openers.

And so we have, from Bell X1's Dave Geraghty, the spooky Billie Holiday-referencing 'Last Leaf', sung in suitably solemn 'n' sweet mode by Hannigan; Gryner's 'Black Winged Bird' is cradled in the moisturised hands of Persson; Noonan's aching 'Some Surprise' is the best duet in the hemisphere, courtesy of Lightbody and Hannigan (whose straight-out-of-bed voices float on a cloud of lachrymose country guitars); Hansard's 'All the Way Down' is given true emotional depth by Hayes; Cole's 'Too Many People' is delivered in crooning style by Hansard; and Deasy's sensual, Spector-esque 'Good Intentions Rust' is effectively a Thrills cut (not surprising, given that it features his one-time bandmates Ryan, Kevin Horan and Padraic McMahon).

Whether or not there's a central theme seems redundant; what matters is that the levels of interweaving, cross-cutting and dovetailing work perfectly. The result is a cohesive, exquisite record that happens to be for a charitable cause. You want icing? You got icing.

Released: 2006 (Ireland), 2007 (UK, US)
Record Label: Yep Roc Records
Producer: Brian Crosby
Recorded at: Westland Studios, Dublin
Sleeve Design: Scott Burnett

Tracks:
1 Last Leaf **3:07**
2 Vapour Trail **3:32**
3 Black Winged Bird **4:07**
4 Some Surprise **3:18**

5 All the Way Down **3:21**
6 Too Many People **3:42**
7 Good Intentions Rust **3:01**
8 Needles **4:06**
9 Aliens **6:31**

CANE 141

GARDEN TIGER MOTH (2000)

MIKE SMALLE

'*Garden Tiger Moth* is a perfect document of our early twenties living in Galway: my songs and the songs of Gerard Connolly brought to life using old organs from charity shops, old synths procured from dancehall bands of the seventies, and a letter recorded onto vinyl that I found in a hospital. I worked all night in the post office sorting mail, slept for five hours, and spent all day in the studio with Paul B. laying down the eleven tracks. It was summertime; too hot to sleep in the morning, anyway, so may as well get up and make a record. We went to France and Spain a few times, recorded a John Peel session, and put out an EP with Mark Eitzel and Sean O'Hagan. It was an exciting time, and a good time to be making music way out west.'

The reasons why most people haven't heard of (let along heard the music of) Cane 141 are as follows: no skinny ties, no white-bread guitars, no pale-faced boys or skinny girls with cheekbones like equilateral triangles, no Stooges fixation, no axes to grind, no illusions, delusions, make-up, grandeur or grandstanding.

Instead, the band (who originate from Galway) proffer in their defence (not that they feel they have to) the following: Can, Tim Buckley, Kraftwerk, Sonic Youth, Tortoise, Silver Apples, Cathal Coughlan, Captain Beefheart, Tim Hardin, Père Ubu, John Peel, and tunes. Lots of tunes. In other words, Cane 141 are living proof that experimenting with theremins and other types of 1960s analogue equipment doesn't necessarily have to turn you into Tonto's Expanding Head Band. (Ask your very old uncle.)

Cane 141 also highlight why they are both one of Ireland's best-kept secrets and one of its coolest music acts: they know how to escape from the trappings of mediocrity by matching their love of the past with their ideas for the future. And how exactly do they do this? By keeping a profile that is as low to the ground as a caterpillar's leg.

Formed in 1993 – a weekend garage band that pooled their odd-job money to buy old organs and synthesizers, through which they explored the parameters of the studio rather than the limitations of the live show – the unit's creative lynchpin is Mike Smalle, a former student of music and media technology. He clearly knows his diode valves from his digital codes, and this knowledge (and the intuition contained therein) bursts from *Garden Tiger Moth* like a shower of pollen. Here is a record of ambition and serenity, one that knows its place but also its worth.

Essentially, the album revisits and reshapes territory mapped out by two pioneering 1960s electronic music acts – The United States of America and Silver Apples – and in doing so continues a form of svelte, elegant sonic arrangements along the lines of Stereolab and Brian Eno. Songs such as 'The Grand Lunar', 'In the Sky the Lucky Stars', 'Real Spacemen Never Walk Anywhere', 'Scene from 6 AM' and 'The Look-Out Kid' are unique in Irish rock/pop/alt-whatever, in that they never come across as premeditated. This is music from a faceless, virtually anonymous music entity that is allowed to un- furl without fuss. But not, praise be, without trace.

Cane 141
Garden tiger moth

Released: 2001
Record Label: Decor Records (Setanta)
Producer: Michael Smalle, Paul Brennan
Recorded at: Temptation Studios, Galway;
Sun Street Studios, Tuam, County Galway
Sleeve Design: Cane 141, Mike Sharpe

Tracks:
1 Eager Boy Comics **2:32**
2 The Grand Lunar **3:37**
3 In the Sky the Lucky Stars **2:36**
4 Real Spacemen Never Walk Anywhere
   5:05
5 Photocredit One **1:28**

6 New Day Parade **3:59**
7 The Party **5:31**
8 Photocredit Two **1:17**
9 Scene From 6AM **4:37**
10 Me and Michael **3:31**
11 The Look-Out Kid **4:37**

MARC CARROLL
WORLD ON A WIRE (2005)

MARC CARROLL

'It's quiet, raw, very empty, very naked. It wasn't a guitar record, and that was something different for me – writing on piano, working with strings; most of the songs are one take, and it sounds like that. That was deliberate – we just went in to the studio and banged it out. The worst reviews I ever got were for this record. One reviewer described it as the benchmark for disappointing records in 2005. Offended? No, as I said, it wasn't a guitar record, but rather a very lonely, late-at-night record. Me at my bravest, and riskiest, I think.'

Don't talk to Marc Carroll about buskers, or the inordinate number of Irish singer-songwriters, with their acoustic guitars, their three chords, their own versions of the truth, and their crazy dreams. Marc Carroll just doesn't want to know about them. Anarchist punk-rock groups Conflict, the fondly remembered Surgical Penis Klinic, and Dublin's very own Paranoid Visions? Now you're saying something. In other words, boys and girls: don't you dare place Marc Carroll into a box with the words 'pre-conceived notions' scrawled all over it.

Carroll has been on the receiving end of pre-conceived notions for almost twenty years now. The first instance was when, as a teenager in the early nineties, he and his Dublin-based band Puppy Love Bomb caused something of a storm with their custom-made slogan 'Dublin Is Dead' (a reference to the dearth of good music – among other things – in the capital): back then, most of the city's sour, elder lemons pounced upon Carroll and accused him of being an arrogant young runt. Many years later (following another band, The Hormones, with which fans of *Friends* might be familiar), Carroll released *Ten of Swords*, a stinging guitar record of such strength and beauty that it propelled him, for a while, to the top of the power-pop pile. A compilation album, *All Wrongs Reversed*, followed, making him even more popular with the fanatical, virtually underground power-pop movement in America. Arrogance had little to do with

it: Carroll was a star in the making. On a roll. At the top of his game.

But there was far more to Carroll than a love of bands starting with 'B' – Big Star, The Beach Boys, The Beatles, The Byrds, Badfinger – and a floppy fringe. Standing still? Only statues do that. As if to confuse his growing fanbase even more, *World on a Wire* replaces zinging guitar chords and 'B'-band methodology with a piano-and-strings reflective quality that wouldn't be out of place on a great Neil Young or Leonard Cohen record. Unlike Tom Cruise's character in *A Few Good Men*, Marc Carroll can most definitely handle the truth, as can be gleaned from even a cursory listen to tracks such as 'A Way Back Out of Here' ('Nothing lasts forever; we've just run out of time'), 'No Time At All' ('You can't stop shaking and you can't stop crying'), 'Together We're Strong' ('Everything is an illusion; this whole world is built on lies') and 'God's Wit' ('My mind explodes like thunder and I can't remember my own name').

Those searching for jolly pop songs can move along; there's nothing for you here. Lovers of contemplative, dignified introspection delivered with assured, astute touches will, however, embrace *World on a Wire*'s sombre pleasures with open arms. A Premier League album so good you just have to envy those who have never heard it before.

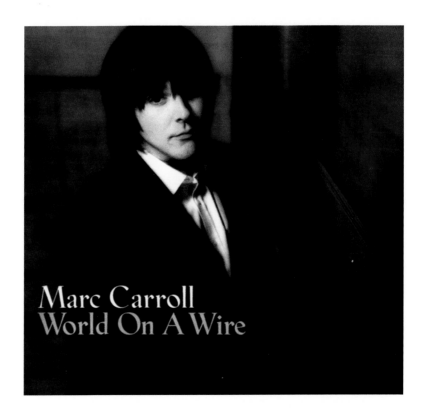

Marc Carroll
World On A Wire

Released: 2005
Record Label: Evangeline Records
Producer: Marc Carroll
Recorded at: Great Linford
Manor Studios, UK
Sleeve Design: Rob at Work, Kevin
Westenberg (photography)

Tracks:
1   A Way Back Out of Here   **4:20**
2   Love Over Gold   **4:47**
3   No Time At All   **4:57**
4   Together We're Strong   **4:21**
5   It Isn't Always Easy   **3:07**
6   And You Are?   **4:15**

7   Talk Again   **3:14**
8   God's Wit   **3:44**
9   Press On   **2:41**
10 In Agreement With Reality   **3:49**
11 Till These Bars Break   **3:35**

CASHIER NO. 9

TO THE DEATH OF FUN (2011)

DANIEL TODD

'I started recording songs around 2006 as Cashier No.9: it was a sort of bedroom/solo project. Then David Holmes got involved, producing some songs that gradually grew into the album . . . It seems to appeal to fans of hooks and melodies, albeit those who like a somewhat darker edge. We set out to make a record that will sound great in twenty years, and we think it will.'

It is a rare thing indeed that a debut album from a reasonably unknown, untried and untested band from Belfast holds such power over an unsuspecting listener. *To the Death of Fun* is an even rarer entity, however, in that it's something of an instant classic – a collection of songs that in lesser hands would have comfortably slotted into the areas known as 'chillwave' and 'shoegazing', but which here leapfrog over such categories by being, simply, terrifically crafted pop songs sublimely enhanced by watertight arrangements. They are, not to put too fine a point on it, so luscious that you want to sink your teeth into them.

Formed in or around 2007 (following on from various coulda/shoulda/nada bands from the murky waters of music-infested Belfast), around the the nucleus of singer/guitarist Danny Todd, bass player Stuart Magowan and guitarist James Smith, Cashier No. 9's story properly started when Todd began to chuck tunes in the general direction of producer, DJ and soundtrack guru David Holmes (see separate entry, page 104), who in 2008 was working on the soundtrack for the Belfast-based movie *Cherry Bomb*. A song called 'Goodbye Friend' found its way into the movie, Todd and Holmes (already on nodding terms from previous session-work collaborations, including Holmes's album, *The Holy Pictures*) clicked even deeper, and before you could bless yourself, Holmes was on board for the band's prospective debut. Not only that, but Holmes put his money where his heart was – recording and producing the tracks at his own expense (sometimes in Los Angeles), but also praising them to any record company boss that happened to be passing.

The album benefits hugely from Holmes's input, and you'd be hard pressed to believe that without him there'd be no way that guests such as Jason Faulkner (Air, Beck) and Tommy Morgan (who played on The Beach Boys' *Pet Sounds*) would have appeared on it. Such guests (nice though it is for they to give of themselves) are small change, though, when it comes to the core content. Throughout the record, influences (from The Byrds and Echo and The Bunnymen to Teenage Fanclub and Phil Spector, from Primal Scream to Joy Zipper) are mopped up and squeezed out. So far, so good – but it gets better.

The band's collective experience (sneer ye not at musicians who have paid their dues) rides sideways through every single track: opening tune 'Goldstar' virtually glistens with giddiness; 'A Promise Wearing Thin' beautifully references classic Tamla Motown-era Supremes and crunching Bunnymen guitars; 'The Lighthouse Will Lead You Out' outshines The Stone Roses; 'Lost at Sea' is a sunglasses-on glance at a simmering type of melancholia; 'Oh Pity' is as yielding and rhythmic as slo-mo sex with Krautrock clicking over in the background. So far, so exceptional.

Familiar yet distinctive, similar yet singular, *To the Death of Fun*, like the best of its type, jogs the memory while at the same time standing its ground. Solid gold or aural velvet? Take your pick: you'll be sorted either way.

CASHIER Nº 9
TO THE DEATH OF FUN

Released: 2011
Record Label: Bella Union
Producer: David Holmes
Recorded at: Drama Studios, Belfast;
Electro Vox & Echo, Los Angeles
Sleeve Design: Glenn Leyburn

Tracks:
1 Goldstar **4:07**
2 Make You Feel Better **4:45**
3 Lost At Sea **4:07**
4 Good Human **3:36**
5 Flick Of The Wrist **3:33**

6 A Promise Wearing Thin **3:45**
7 Oh Pity **4:48**
8 The Lighthouse Will Lead You Out
    5:47
9 Goodbye Friend **5:15**
10 6% **3:32**

CHEQUERBOARD

PENNY BLACK (2008)

JOHN LAMBERT

'I was just following my nose and trying to elaborate on a sound that I was interested in where the claw-hammer style Spanish guitar playing wasn't just fluffy and incidental, but underpinned everything and – along with lots of subliminal signposts – was the primary voice. Essentially, it's a guitar album. I wanted it to be quite dramatic, quite intense – and lean, if you like. I hope it has achieved that. I suppose I'm as happy with the end result as I'll ever be, even though there are always things I'd like to change. I do go over things with a microscope for weeks on end, which I suppose does make me something of an obsessive. I'd be more interested in spending time getting one piece right than doing five pieces that were just okay. I prefer to think of it as quality over quantity.'

It's like a puzzle that, over a period of time – albeit time that moves at an extremely leisurely pace – reveals itself not to be a puzzle at all. It is, rather, an undulating, dissolving sequence of melodies, rhythms, tonal shifts, textural swathes and blatant examples of one person's passion for getting things not just right, but perfect. There is a sense here that in order to get things exactly right, hours become meaningless, provided that the mind is engaged and excited by creativity. You're hanging on to a ledge with the tips of your fingernails, but you know things are going to be OK because you have this melody in your head, and if you just claw your way up and into the studio, then you'll get it from your head into a machine. Job done. Relax. Start all over again.

We read regularly about the state of rock music: where it's at, how bad it is, how terrific it is, how soon it's going to die, how often it will have to regenerate itself in order to continue – yet rarely do we read about a type of music, or an album, that not only doesn't bear the hallmarks of rock, but actively ignores it. One such album is *Penny Black*. One such music act is Chequerboard, a one-man operation/thatched-roof cottage industry overseen by graphic designer/artist John Lambert.

Initially influenced by the likes of Autechre and Aphex Twin, Lambert/Chequerboard's first album, *Gothica*, was released in 2002; this was followed three years later by the mini-album/EP *Dictaphone Showreels*. Each record was released with so little fuss that only those interested in the kind of music loosely termed electronica arose from their slumber and took any notice. The music reflected Lambert's view of how music should interact with the environment, and it seemed as though he was enamoured no so much with the likes of Brian Eno's ambient/interactive soundscapes as with the notion that music must, if it's to have any worth or substance at all, be able to infiltrate, to burrow down deep and stay there.

The latter is certainly true of the fastidiously, almost forensically executed *Penny Black*; taking as its base influences a subtle yet dramatic amalgam of acoustic guitar (a little bit of Spanish, a little bit of Mason Williams's 'Classical Gas'), subversive, swirling, lean melody lines, and more pop nous than he has been given credit for, Lambert has devised the kind of record that sits effortlessly between über-cool, easy-peasy ambient (hello, spa-treatment rooms!) and intricate yet eminently accessible tunesmithery.

Released: 2008
Record Label: Lazybird
Producer: John Lambert
Recorded at: The Modern Arts and Niland
Gallery, Sligo
Sleeve Design: John Lambert

Tracks:
1 Penny Black **3:56**
2 Ornithopter **5:15**
3 Konichiwa **4:06**
4 Quotidian Debris **3:05**
5 The Winter Arcade **3:36**

6 Skating Couple **2:59**
7 20th Century Artillery **2:59**
8 Prince August **4:17**
9 Toy Winds **3:53**

JOE CHESTER

A MURDER OF CROWS (2005)

'As a songwriter, I look back at those songs now and, even though I had been writing songs in various bands for years at that point, I would say I was pretty green. There's a certain naivety about them, I suppose. I'd say I'm a better songwriter now than I was then, or [at least] that I *know* more about songwriting now than I did then. But I'd still say that "Charlie for a Girl" is the best song I've ever written. Sometimes it makes me a little sad, knowing that if I was ever asked to write something like it now, I honestly wouldn't know how.'

Some musicians have to go round the block several, if not many, times before they stumble onto one of two life-changing facts. The first is that they might as well give up – that, for various reasons, things aren't working out for them, and so why waste even more time on something that just isn't going to happen, even though it's passionately hoped for. The second is that, even in their darkest, deepest and most truthful moments, they can make out a glimmer of light that gives them hope.

Joe Chester is not for giving up. This Dublin songwriter and producer might not even be a muted blip on the radar screen for virtually 100 percent of the population, but for years he has burrowed away under the skin of bands such as Sunbear, Tenspeedracer and Future Kings of Spain, as well as being one of the primary go-to guys for better-known musicians if they need some producing or some shape of sonic accompaniment. In short, he's a grafter, a man with some skill. You can sense this without even knowing it, for *A Murder of Crows,* Chester's debut album, is full of graft – and craft. To know that it was recorded in midwinter, solitary, in a ramshackle farmhouse in County Wexford is to go some way towards understanding the album's dual senses of joy and sadness, tension and release.

In a manner akin to a singer-songwriter from the wilds of Borneo, Chester's days consisted of gathering wood, lighting the open fires in the kitchen and the studio, working on his songs until early morning, then climbing the groaning staircase to his bedroom, his mind cross-wired with ideas for the next day's recording. That *A Murder of Crows* didn't turn out to be a collection of songs as desolate and chilly as its surroundings is surprising. Songwriting dynamics is all, though, and by switching creative dispositions, Chester has created something that resembles cutting wire: deceptively light but full of serious intent.

'Like a seaside town in winter', Chester sings on the first (and title) track, 'or that moment when the summer sun gets covered by a cloud'. This pretty much sets the tone: regret and resignation leavened by simplistic, often sumptuous melodies delivered not with egocentric frills but with a modesty that never tips over into lack of confidence. Rarely for an album of such self-effacement, the quality just doesn't dip: 'Charlie for a Girl' is pure heartache wrapped in a melody that refuses to budge, 'A Safe Place to Hide' is a noble duet with Gemma Hayes (see page 98), the elegiac, piano-led 'A Drop of Rain' is imbued with a velvety texture that leaves the listener almost lost for words, and 'I Always Think You're Leaving Me' gets away with such a morose title (snap out of it, man, for God's sake!) by being one hum-dinger of a tune. Chester even covers a Fleetwood Mac/Lindsey Buckingham track ('Bleed to Love Her'); like every other song on this vivid, delicate, perfect-pop record, it touches on the elusiveness of love, but Chester nails it (and the rest) with all the certainty and precision of a shipwright.

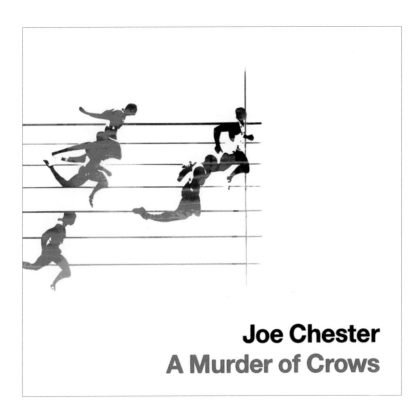

Joe Chester
A Murder of Crows

Released: 2005
Record Label: Barp Ltd
Producer: Joe Chester
Recorded at: Brands Hatch Recording Studios, County Wexford; Apollo Studios, Dublin
Sleeve Design: Simon Roche for Field

Tracks:
1 A Murder Of Crows **4:24**
2 How You Wish, You Feel **5:16**
3 Charlie For A Girl **4:39**
4 A Safe Place To Hide **5:12**
5 The Emptiness Inside **4:13**
6 A Drop of Rain **6:11**
7 Bleed To Love Her **3:45**
8 Pain, Relieve **6:01**
9 I Always Think You're Leaving Me **4:51**
10 Anyway **3:59**

PAUL CLEARY

CROOKED TOWN (2001)

PAUL CLEARY 'The writing process was still the same as when I was in The Blades. And still as painful, without wishing to sound like a luvvie about it. But once you have one or two songs written, I suppose you have to finish it. There is no mystery to it, as such, although some songwriters might like to think there is. I certainly had that feeling of writing songs again, but whether that's a good or bad feeling I'm not sure. My guiding points, lyrically, for this album were not to be too obvious or too vague.'

Paul Cleary – is there any other Irish songwriter/musician that can hold a claim to being one of the country's greatest lost talents? He fronted The Blades (see separate entry, page 28), which were, effortlessly, the best band in Ireland in the late seventies and early eighties. They had superlative pop songs ('Hot For You', 'The Bride Wore White', 'Downmarket', 'Ghost Of A Chance', 'Animation', 'Revelations Of Heartbreak') and a resonating working-class street credibility. The band also had an eloquent front man and ambition to burn. What The Blades didn't have, however, was a front man who was prepared to sacrifice his privacy for success.

And so, gradually, Paul Cleary retreated, initially into other class Irish acts (notably The Partisans), and then into virtually anonymous stints in pub bands. His utter lack of interest in continuing what has been regarded as a potentially glittering career has led some to believe that what he feared most was success. Ironically, such was his sense of professional ambition, what he feared most was failure.

And so almost fifteen years after Cleary effectively took his leave of public life, *Crooked Town* was released. It is a remarkable album for many reasons, some of which might have to do with a songwriter who intuitively knows how to write a pop song. That there are pop songs on *Crooked Town* isn't news; what surprises is that, almost fifteen years after his previous band's studio album (The

Partisans' 1987 album, *Impossible*), the songs are so gloriously good.

Cleary was always one for a socio-realist/romance-rotting scenario neatly tucked into a nugget of a tune, and he doesn't disappoint here. Songs with a knowing, yearning pop flavour that equal master craftsmen such as Elvis Costello, Neil Finn and Squeeze touch on extra-marital affairs ('State Of Confusion': 'Last night I heard the car door slam, low voice, some man'), drug addiction/dealing ('Crooked Town': 'A ray of hope, she's trapped forever in its beam. But for tonight there's only methadone and nightmares . . .'), regret ('The Queen Of Indecision': 'Trouble sleeping in a double bed, dreaming of a troubled past, all the things she should have said'), repentance ('The Ghost Of Christmas Past': 'I remember alcoholic rage, I remember lying to your face') and the gradual disintegration of love ('The Same Face': 'The same face with a bitter smile and a broken heart'). If an artist's indulgence rears its head on the eight-minutes-plus closing track, 'Ecstasy Blues', at least it's of the pop/psych-out variety, which is fine by us.

Amazingly, *Crooked Town* is quite probably the last we'll hear from Paul Cleary – he's the kind of low-maintenance guy who doesn't write, phone, email, text or tweet. Fear of success or fear of failure? The exceptionally talented man who says very little is (as they say in Ireland) saying nothing.

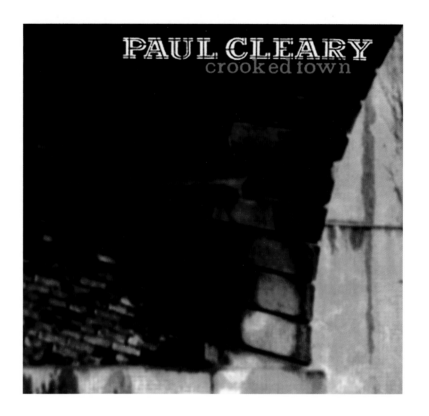

Released: 2001
Record Label: Reekus Records
Producer: Paul Cleary
Recorded at: Sheriff Street, Barrow Street,
Crow Street studios, Dublin
Sleeve Design: Four5One

Tracks:
1 The Queen Of Indecision **3:59**
2 Crooked Town **3:45**
3 A Man Without Love **3:58**
4 The Ghost Of Christmas Past **3:41**
5 When We Had A Future **4:27**
6 State Of Confusion **3:35**
7 Ask Awesome Orson (Rosebud) **4:16**

8 The Same Face **3:56**
9 Liberty Hall **1:48**
10 Lullaby **3:35**
11 Ecstasy Blues **8:19**

OLLIE COLE
WE ALBATRI (2010)

OLIVER COLE

'This was a difficult album for me to make. It was my first solo album and I wanted it to be special. I had just come out of a ten-year relationship, and between that and leaving the band (Turn) I had been in for the last seven years, I was very lost. My confidence had never been lower. I travelled to the Black Forest in Germany, myself and my engineer, Ciaran Bradshaw, and I just tried to make the most honest record I could. I was determined for it not to be a downbeat record, so there is a weird juxtaposition of reflective and personal lyrics with more upbeat and quirky music. It was a very healing record for me. I played everything on the record, too, which was important for me – it was important not to have anyone else's input. The album title is a reference to the albatross bird, particularly the Antarctic albatross, who is a very solitary bird and may never see another albatross as long as it lives. I thought the plural for albatross was albatri. It's not. Oh, well.'

Here's an intriguing proposition for the listener and a nerve-racking challenge for the songwriter: how do you make a worthwhile solo career for yourself following several semi-successful years in a much-admired if low-key rock band? Most artists – unnecessarily, it seems – make the mistake of 'reinventing' themselves to the point where they become virtually unrecognisable; their compulsion to be different at all costs appears to be at odds with who they are and what they, ultimately, want to be.

Not so Ollie Cole. For the uninitiated, Cole used to be lead singer in a band called Turn, a rock act that failed to generate much interest outside their small but fervent Irish fanbase. Turn was a most unusual rock band: even at their hardest, they sounded prissy, almost prim. It was as if, deep down, they knew they weren't cut out for the rough stuff, and so they split up, leaving Cole to embrace a fallow, frustrating period in both his creative and personal life. Eventually, Cole left Ireland, relocating to Freiburg, Germany, with new ideas in his head and new, not always pretty, subjects to write about. The result of his Freiburg sojourn was *We Albatri*, which creatively was not so much a return to form (nor, praise whatever gods you worship, a futile reinvention) as an introduction to virtually a new songwriter.

In brief, *We Albatri* is a stunner. The album's opening track, 'What Will You Do?' initially fuses Cheap Trick with The Beatles but quickly comes across as a whirling, swirling slice of idiosyncratic power pop. 'Oh My Girl', 'Spotlight' and 'Close Your Eyes' channel the spirit of doomed US singer-songwriter Elliott Smith, with the last track, in particular, hitting all the right mellow, melancholic notes.

Other tracks, such as 'Little Bad Dream', 'Drug Song' and 'Spotlight' are, perhaps, indicative of a songwriter drawing from their on-site well of lifestyle and personality screw-ups, yet Cole's innately tuneful melodies (best exemplified by the graceful closing track, 'Moth's Wing') perfectly counterbalance his occasional self-doubt and self-contempt. Also, despite the character flaws expressed in the songs, ultimately he comes across as someone who can look at himself in the mirror each morning and know that, as each day passes he's getting better and better at this thing called living.

Released: 2010
Record Label: EMI Ireland
Producer: Ciaran Bradshaw
Recorded at: Freiburg, Germany; Loft Studios, Exchequer Studios, Ollie's kitchen, Dublin
Sleeve Design: Redman AKA

Tracks:
1 What Will You Do? **3:05**
2 Oh My Girl **3:21**
3 Too Many People **3:33**
4 Close Your Eyes **4:38**
5 We Albatri **3:46**
6 Little Bad Dream **4:24**
7 Drug Song **2:54**
8 Spotlight **2:42**
9 Need You Strong **3:48**
10 Moth's Wing **5:10**

CATHAL COUGHLAN
THE SKY'S AWFUL BLUE (2002)

'I think this is probably my most cohesive solo record, perhaps due to the fact that the songs were mainly written in one group (during 2001–02), and lyrically, I think I managed to encompass the way I felt at that time. The record was made very cheaply, with the aid of the great Richard Preston, on my own dime (for the first time). Everything was recorded, and mainly mixed, in a couple of songwriting rooms in a former pub just off London's Portobello Road. The musicians worked very fast. It was intended to be a dry-sounding "chamber" record, and I think I pulled that off, though the approach may not be for everyone.'

He stands pretty much alone in the pantheon of disgruntled Irish WTF shruggers: saturnine but proud, a cage-rattling mixture of Samuel Beckett, Nick Cave and Scott Walker.

Yet Cathal Coughlan, formerly of Microdisney (see page 128) and Fatima Mansions – two of the best, most disaffected Irish rock bands of the past thirty years – takes his status with a pillar of salt. With his third solo album, Coughlan steers a course between the unfashionable and the unwashed, clocking up the creative brownie points while the world looks his way and waves him off with a contemptuous flick of the hand.

Throughout *The Sky's Awful Blue* (and, yes, there is a wilful duality of intent behind the title), he has the sound of the world-weary in his voice, a notion of regret blending with a particle of optimism. But we're talking about Cathal Coughlan here, so one almost cancels out the other. Like his work with other people, at the core of this album is Coughlan's reliance on structure; this almost traditional work ethic of avoidance of abstraction, and preference for narrative, is the major difference between him and many other artists.

It is what makes *The Sky's Awful Blue*'s reflective noir-folk, neo-torchsong so exceptional. From the life-affirming accessibility of 'Goodbye Sadness' to the spartan introduction of 'And Springtime Followed Summer', from the classic pop of 'The Last of Eternity' to the wobbly dissonance of 'Pawnshop Riches', the album is a supremely melodic slow burner, fusing moral turpitude with a righteous, reasoned sense of rage at the corruption foisted upon us by a highly politicised new world order.

In the blue corner, the record proffers a scenario where people in the industrialised world have been suckered into believing they're living in some kind of smug, trendy utopia that other mortals envy. In the red corner, we have the blue sky of September 11, where vengeful planes came out of the sunshine. The idea surely, posits the record, and Coughlan himself, is that the natural order of things will turn nasty, and then – *quelle surprise!* – turn on us.

So here be songs about death, alcoholism, errant kidneys, decaying lungs, empty graves and, but of course, whores. Cover versions by Westlife? Unlikely.

THE SKY'S AWFUL BLUE

CATHAL COUGHLAN

Released: 2002
Record Label: Beneath Music
Producer: Richard Preston, Cathal Coughlan
Recorded at: Sun Productions, London
Sleeve Design: George Seminara

Tracks:
1 And Springtime Followed Summer 4:03
2 Denial Of The Right To Dream 3:53
3 Three Rusty Reivers 3:44
4 Goodbye Sadness 4:18
5 Toxic Mother 4:14
6 The Last Of Eternity 4:29
7 You Turned Me 4:41
8 Amused As Hell 4:21
9 Pawnshop Riches 4:49
10 White's Academy 4:27
11 A Drunken Hangman 4:53
12 The Female Line 1:42

MARY COUGHLAN
TIRED AND EMOTIONAL (1985)

'Erik and I made the album in a small studio in Galway. It cost about £1,100. I had no ambitions at all for it being heard, because up to the making of it I had never really sung in public. The reaction to it was astonishing, because I'd had a lot of difficulty in getting people to listen to it. It continues to sell more than any of my other records – it isn't so much as lost as one that keeps on giving. Not to me, though – to the fucking record company!'

Has there ever been anyone in Irish music as unique as Mary Coughlan? Don't think so. In fact, know so. Until 1983, the only place, we have been informed, that Mary Coughlan sang was in the bath. Around that time, in her native Galway – a mother of three kids who made ends meet by cleaning toilets and selling hand-knitted woolly hats on the streets – she hooked up with Dutch musician and songwriter Erik Visser, whom she had known for some years. With encouragement from Visser, Coughlan entered a few local talent shows in and around the city.

Back then, social networking was more talking in the pub than typing on the Web, and word quickly spread to Dublin that over in the wild 'wesht' was a flame-haired chanteuse who could singe a man's beard at twenty paces.

In the mid-eighties, there were no Irish female rock stars to speak of, and very few assertive role models for post-pubescent or teenage girls to look to for direction. At twenty-nine, Coughlan was hardly an ingénue (her choice of material veered more towards jazz than pop), but the release of *Tired and Emotional* changed – utterly – the perception of Irish female singers as a batch of sensitive, if skilful, middle-of-the-road performers.

For the first time, here was a woman singing – in a voice of hard intelligence and experience, and in a tone of a person thinking unashamedly dirty thoughts – of sex, domestic violence, social issues, alcohol abuse, and sex. More crucially, perhaps, was Coughlan's stance: she was old enough, pissed-off enough, and unapologetic enough to willingly authenticate her lived-in experiences through old and new songwriting by the likes of Visser and Antoinette Hensey (including 'The Beach' and 'Lady in Green'), Fintan Coughlan ('Double Cross' – written by Mary's ex-husband), Bruce Cockburn ('Mama Just Wants to Barrelhouse'), Steve Allen and Sammy Gallop ('Meet Me Where They Play the Blues') and Gary Tigerman ('Seduced'). The latter song (which Coughlan altered to fit a woman's viewpoint), in particular, would become a signature tune for women nationwide, and the song of choice for their dates.

Released on a small indie label (Mystery Records), *Tired and Emotional* was a huge hit in Ireland, spending more than six months in the Irish charts; inevitably, Coughlan would go on to sign with major record labels, but most of them found it difficult to corral her spirit.

She would go on to battle with the bottle (and win, eventually – thankfully), and to make good, if fitful, albums. None, however, would match the mix of audaciousness and fuck-you (and, occasionally, fuck-me) perspectives of *Tired and Emotional*.

Released: 1985
Record Label: East West Records, a
subsidiary of Warner Music Group (WEA)
Producer: Erik Visser
Recorded at: Greenfields Studios, County
Galway
Sleeve Design: Joe Boske, Frank Miller
(photography)

Tracks:
1 Double Cross **3:49**
2 The Beach **3:21**
3 Meet Me Where They Play The Blues
   4:00
4 Delaney's Gone Back On The Wine
   3:40
5 Sense Of Silence (S.O.S.) **3:23**

6 Nobody's Business **3:45**
7 Mamma Just Wants To Barrelhouse
   3:28
8 Country Fair Dance (The Cowboy
   Song) **3:25**
9 Lady In Green **2:12**
10 Seduced **2:25**

DAVE COUSE

GENES (2003)

DAVE COUSE

'I was alone and afraid; I had lost my band some years earlier, and had been involved in a couple of music ventures that failed to gain a release. Very little made sense around this time. In 2002, my only child was not long born and my father only dead. I was confused and lacking any confidence. I knew very few people in the music business, so I turned to those I did, and asked Edwyn Collins to produce it. After some time figuring and working things through, with a newfound hope in my heart and the enrolment of a new band, we set sail for London and Edwyn's beautiful studio. The rest is a very tiny piece of history, but something I am hugely proud of.'

When Dublin band A House (see page 16) split up in 1997, it seemed for many like the closing of a large private members club. Although the band could never have been termed a commercial success, they nonetheless attracted an Irish fanbase that were as committed and passionate as the band itself – grown men were seen to cry at the band's farewell gig in Dublin's Olympia Theatre on 28 February 1997.

Then, for almost six years, Couse kept a lower-than-low profile; when he wasn't in the studio working on albums that never saw the light of day, he was, well, keeping a lower-than-low profile.

Come 2003, though, *Genes* was released through his own label (Beep-Beep). While the news of its arrival may have initially pleased A House fans starved of new caustic Couse material, when they heard it they reluctantly committed Couse to a slow, solo commercial death. *Genes*, let it be said, is not a happy album; it is, in fact, one of the most introspective and melancholy records you'll ever hear from an Irish songwriter.

No one said that pop music has to be cheerful, of course. Like parents and politicians, pop stars weren't put on this earth to win popularity contests (not all the time, anyway), but *Genes* is so wonderfully morose that the inclusion of a cover of John Cale's hardly cheery 'I Keep a Close Watch' (titled 'Close Watch' here) actually comes as light relief. There was reason enough behind the sombre tenor of the record (the title of which tells its own self-explanatory tale), as it explicitly references life and death – the former of the birth of Couse's daughter, the latter of the death of his father. (Images of both are included in the album sleeve.)

Sandwiched in between and mashed like a boiled spud is Couse himself, conflicted by feelings of intense loss and immense joy, and further confused, perhaps, by the dichotomy of wanting to reconnect with his A House fanbase and knowing that the songs on *Genes* perhaps weren't the best way to go about it.

Yet for all of these issues, *Genes* is a grave, observant album full of distress signals and alarm bells. Songs as obviously salutary as 'Will It Ever Stop Raining?', 'I Almost Touched You', 'Self Obsessed', 'You Don't Know What Love Is' and 'Everybody's Got Their Own Troubles' display someone struggling on the edge of something they'd rather not be anywhere near.

Couse would go on to create albums that garnered a warmer critical reception (2010's *Alonewalk* is as singular and affecting as anything he's done), but none would match *Genes* for its palpable sense of grief.

Released: 2003
Record Label: Beep-Beep Records
Producer: Edwyn Collins
Recorded at: Westheath Studios, London
Sleeve Design: Fergal Bunbury

Tracks:
1 Satisfaction **3:01**
2 At The End Of The Day **3:23**
3 Will It Ever Stop Raining **3:49**
4 Familiar Feeling **2:56**
5 I Almost Touched You **3:30**
6 For Sale **3:14**
7 If This Is Where Love Is **4:10**

8 Self Obsessed **2:33**
9 You Don't Know What Love Is **3:05**
10 Everybody's Got Their Own Troubles **3:06**
11 Intoxicating **2:02**
12 Close Watch **2:24**
13 Peaceful **3:11**

THE CRANBERRIES
'LINGER' (1993)

NOEL HOGAN

'I guess now I look at it as a song that's very close to me, because in many ways it launched everything for us. Musically? If I were to sit down and try to write it now I wouldn't be able to, as the structure is too simple. At the time of writing the song, it was to the limits of my ability of being able to play. Now, it'd be hard to hold myself back and keep it as simple as that . . . It doesn't ask a lot of the listener, I think – that's why the simplicity of it works.'

It started with a rescue operation and continued with a demo tape. The former involved three Irish blokes (Feargal Lawlor, Noel Hogan and Michael Hogan) going around in a circle until the arrival of church organist and choir singer Dolores O'Riordan, who was hired when they heard a prototype version of a song called 'Linger'.

The latter concerned semi-legendary demo tapes (by The Cranberry Saw Us) that were distributed to a number of Irish music journalists in 1990. By early '91, the band name had been changed, the band's music ('Taking The Sundays, The Smiths and 10,000 Maniacs to frame an eccentric, exciting attraction, they're a fine left-field choice', trumpeted a Dublin freesheet) was causing the sort of A&R scrum not seen in Ireland for many years.

By the autumn of '92, the band's debut album, *Everybody Else Is Doing It, So Why Can't We?*, was ready to be released, but it was shelved until the spring of '93. The first single from the album, 'Dreams' (released in September 1992), bombed, as did the second single, 'Linger', released in February '93.

It was with 'Linger' that the band kick-started their career, and as kick-starting songs go, it's one of the best of its type. Written about O'Riordan's first serious romance, it remains one of those lilting, wafting, weaving and gliding pop songs that take hold and simply refuse to let go.

Capturing the likable naivety of an almost Disney-fied love's first kiss ('But I'm in so deep, you know I'm such a fool for you, you got me wrapped around your finger'), touching loyalty ('I swore I would be true, and honey so did you') and heart-crushing deception ('So why were you holding her hand? Is that the way we stand? Were you lying all the time? Was it just a game to you?'), the mixture of orchestral-style strings, acoustic rumblings, a streaming choral background vocal and a beautifully layered dream-pop melody is beyond irresistible. Add in O'Riordan's distinctly Irish, occasionally slurred pronunciation of certain words and lines (notably through 'If you could get by trying not to lie, things wouldn't be so confused and I wouldn't feel so used, but you always really knew I just wanna be with you'), and a woozy, weepy guitar solo, and you have a shoe-gazing, finger-lacing, starry-eyed pop song that hitches a one-way lift to heaven.

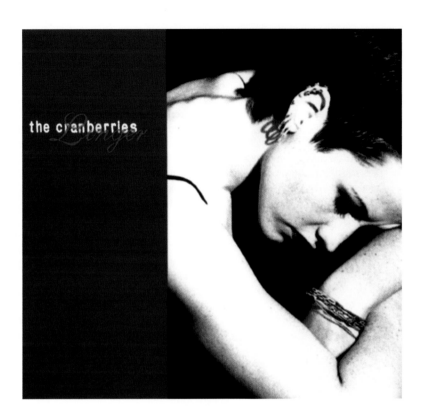

Released: 1993
Record Label: Island Records
Producer: Stephen Street
Recorded at: Windmill Studios, Dublin;
Surrey Sound
Sleeve Design: Martin (Cally) Callomon
(art director, Island Records)
Duration: **4:34**

ADRIAN CROWLEY
LONG DISTANCE SWIMMER (2007)

ADRIAN CROWLEY

'The recording process was idyllic. We had the use of a big, old empty house in County Dublin for a week, and, with producer Steve Shannon, set up a recording station in the front room. We had cables running everywhere. One funny thing was that in order to keep visual contact with the drummer while doing a live take, I had to stand outside the sitting-room window with my electric guitar and an umbrella gaffer-taped to the mike stand. It worked, but the occasional passerby would be stopped in their tracks. There was something about *Long Distance Swimmer* that was a new step for me: the songs were different, somehow. Maybe I had found a new clarity . . . Since its release, quite a few singers/artists have done cover versions of songs from the album. That would never have happened before.'

Rolling Stone magazine, 2005. American maverick Ryan Adams is asked who is the best songwriter that no one has ever heard of. His answer: 'Adrian Crowley.' It is, say those who know about such things, the quiet ones you have to watch out for . . . the ones who utilise the tortoise-and-the-hare approach.

From Galway via Malta, Crowley's demeanour befits his music. Outwardly serious, innately reflective, with a sharp intellect and wit just waiting to be sparked, he is the calm one who has been making bigger and bigger noises as the years have passed. With an academic background in architecture and a creative background in illustration, Crowley doesn't seem to have any notions whatsoever above and beyond writing songs and performing them in front of a small but highly appreciative audience.

Meticulous about his recorded output, Crowley isn't the most prolific of songwriters; he writes quickly but then has a tendency to mull over the resulting work carefully. It has happened that if the record he's working on doesn't actually turn out to be what he had envisaged, then it could – without too much thought – be cast aside. The past few years have seen Crowley loosen up in this regard; as his songwriting process has developed, he has become even more vigilant in deciding what to discard and what to retain.

Say hello, then, to Crowley's fourth album, the subtle, elegiac *Long Distance Swimmer*. Alone of Irish singer-songwriters, here the outsider takes a tentative step inside. There has always been an acute sense that Crowley rarely – if ever – belonged to whatever singer-songwriter club Ireland as a country was swaying along to. His music is far removed from the banal and the guttural; it occupies instead a space closer to the high-intensity, every-word-counts, lo-fi recordings of Red House Painters' Mark Kozelek, Smog's Bill Callahan, Will Oldham and American Music Club's Mark Eitzel.

Assisted by unobtrusive drumming, a benign baritone, piano frills and subtle augmentation of strings, songs such as 'Brother at Sea', 'Electric Eels', 'Star of the Harbour', 'Walk On Part', 'These Icy Waters' and 'Harmony Row' evoke a druggy ambience that gets increasingly insidious with each listen. Ultimately, *Long Distance Swimmer* is the sound of someone who has turned his back on convention yet has an eye – and an ear – for an odd pop melody.

It is, if truth be told, a record made under the assumption that its music would fall on the right ears. Eventually.

Adrian Crowley

Long Distance
Swimmer

Released: 2007, 2008 (US)
Record Label: Tin Angel Records
Producer: Adrian Crowley,
Stephen Shannon
Recorded at: Various, including
Experimental Audio, Dublin
Sleeve Design: Iker Spozio (illustration and
artwork), Amelia Stein (photography)

Tracks:
1 Bless Our Tiny Hearts   **2:47**
2 These Icy Waters   **4:14**
3 Star of the Harbour   **2:50**
4 Temporary Residence   **3:52**
5 Walk on Part   **3:30**
6 Victoria   **2:48**
7 Harmony Row   **3:53**
8 Theft by Starlight **1:35**
9 Electric Eels   **3:33**
10 Leaving the Party   **4:18**
11 Brother at Sea   **3:42**
12 Long Distance Swimmer   **5:09**

CATHY DAVEY
TALES OF SILVERSLEEVE (2007)

'After recording *Something Ilk* it was apparent that it held little emotional substance to keep me engaged for very long, and one thing I wanted from this album was for it to still move me when I had finished making it. While I was writing . . . *Silversleeve* my life was a jumble of events that I deemed too private for commercial exploitation. What emerged was my attempt to marry uplifting music with abstracted versions of quite painful experiences. I also had bouts of insomnia, so I began creating characters to deal with some of the less palatable voices one tends to hear when sleep-deprived; putting them to joyful music seemed to remove any threat they may have posed . . . "Reuben" and "The Collector" were born out of this, and I reckon for me that's the best thing about songwriting: you can dress up your fears in colourful clothing and they can't frighten you any more.'

Cathy Davey? She is something of a puzzle. Not the Rubik's Cube sort, where applied strategic twists and turns can create the finished product. Rather, she is more of a conundrum hidden in a jewellery box placed in a time-locked freezer. Cathy Davey? She is an adept, deft purveyor of songs that hang in the balance between pitch night and misty day. It would come as no surprise whatsoever if we were told that her favourite colour is grey.

She surfaced in 2004 with her debut album, *Something Ilk*, a likeable collection of songs in the reasonably identikit singer-songwriter mould. With her family background gaining an initial flurry of interest – her father is composer Shaun Davey – Cathy quickly retreated from the spotlight through a mixture of nervousness and unfamiliarity with the machinations of the music industry.

While her litany of childhood and teenage travails tells a story of sorts, with their blend of dyslexia, disconnectedness, stress and hyperactivity, the era of *Something Ilk* was hardly more edifying, with a list of overlooked opportunities, worried parents, skipped gigs, fretting management, missed television shows and frustrated industry personnel. Throwing up became a

virtual by-product of gigging; sleepless nights the norm, nervous exhaustion an enemy.

Tales of Silversleeve, however, highlights the talents of a different person. There's hardly a wrong move here – from the opener 'Sing For Your Supper' to the final track, 'All of You', Davey has it sussed via highly accomplished pop music, insinuating rhythms and vocal performances that hint at cheek without actually displaying it.

Let's put it this way: *Something Ilk*'s output comes across as the work of a student, whereas *Tales of Silversleeve*'s is that of a teacher.

Put the changes down to a self-editing process that is almost cruel, and a swift realisation that writing and singing songs she didn't believe in was actually making her queasy. (Davey has described her early material as 'shite, introspective, self-gratifying, teenage'.) Minor chords and their associative feelings of sadness were the primary problems – which is possibly why this album is so skittish it could book itself into a cattery and play with balls of wool for days.

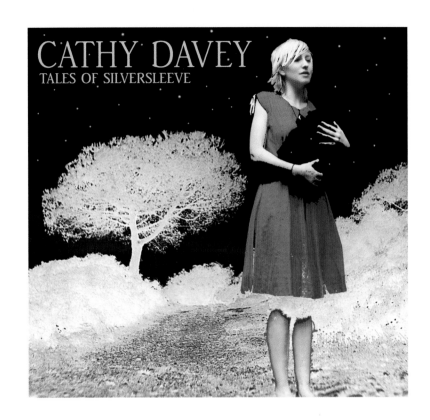

CATHY DAVEY
TALES OF SILVERSLEEVE

Released: 2007
Record Label: EMI, Regal
Producer: Cathy Davey, Liam Howe,
Stephen Street
Recorded at: Various locations in Dublin,
Wicklow, London
Sleeve Design: Alex Hutchinson, Pauline
Rowan (photography)

Tracks:
1   Sing For Your Supper   3:44
2   Reuben   4:10
3   The Collector   2:51
4   Moving   3:44
5   Mr Kill   4:28
6   Overblown Love Song   4:17
7   No Heart Today   3:41

8   Harmony   2:48
9   Can't Help It   4:08
10   Rubbish Ocean   4:17
11   All Of You   3:39

DIVINE COMEDY

LIBERATION (1993)

NEIL HANNON

'By '91 my early D.C. comrades had jumped ship and I was back in my parents' attic, lost in a world of Walker and Nyman, Forster and Fitzgerald . . . I did nothing but read wonderful books, watch foreign films, walk the family hounds and write reams upon reams of music and lyrics. Eventually Keith Cullen of Setanta got me "a week" in a glorified demo place attached to Dave Stewart's Church Studios in Crouch End. Of course, being a well brought-up young man with an idiotic protestant work ethic, I didn't say "that's impossible"! If a week was what I had, a week is how long I would take . . . I decided upon the title Liberation before I'd entered the studio, I think. I knew this was a whole new beginning. The implosion of my first band had meant a joyous release from the constraints of indie rock. I'm just glad I wrote *Liberation* when I did; unfettered by rock and roll tradition, unbound by public expectations. The harpsichord sounds may have been provided by a Yamaha PS-10, the constant references to books and films may be a tad cringe-worthy, the voice may be a bit screechy and un-developed, but I think it's as accurate a look into the heart of a shy and bookish twenty-two-year-old as you're ever likely to find.'

Brilliant baroque pop music? Musical instruments that include harpsichord, violin, viola, cello and French horn? Songs that reference the writings of F. Scott Fitzgerald, E. M. Forster, Anton Chekov and William Wordsworth? Yes, please, to all of these, if you don't mind.

A semblance of balance, maestro, if you please: Divine Comedy's 1990 debut album, *Fanfare for the Comic Muse*, is rubbish. In fact, around this time the band were dreadful (particularly live): an ordinary Irish rock group with pretentions way above their station. Yet clearly something was bubbling up from under the morass of their debut: shortly after the album was released, the band's cast-iron linchpin and sophisticated mouthpiece, Neil Hannon, streamlined operations (that is, chucked everyone out) and set about writing songs that would act as the real foundation for what has turned out to be an impressive career.

Not that it matters anymore (although there was a time when it did), but *Liberation* doesn't sound the least bit 'Irish'. Instead, an archness of style that Hannon, the son of a Church of Ireland bishop, described some years ago as 'accidentally, quintessentially English' runs through the album. We can thank his background and upbringing for the kind of songwriting that informs this and subsequent albums (see separate entry for Divine Comedy's *Bang Goes the Knighthood*, page 66), but there is a danger lurking (in the woodshed, perhaps?) that threatens to smother everything with mounds of tweeness, cleverness and calculation.

As it turned out, cleverness and calculation – with, thankfully, diminishing levels of whimsy, waggishness and the type of *oh I say!* wit that fused Frankie Howard with *Howard's End* – are Hannon's stock-in-trade. Sensitivity, poignancy and pristine items of pop songwriting would arrive later (one perfect example, of many, is 'A Lady of a Certain Age' on 2006's *Victory for the Comic Muse*). For this early display of Hannon's work, however (which he regards, correctly, as the first Divine Comedy album proper), suffice it to say that he gets away with creating such a highly stylised record by being the most swellegant, elegant party guy in town.

THE DIVINE COMEDY LIBERATION

Released: 1993
Record Label: Setanta Records
Producer: Neil Hannon, Darren Allison
Recorded at: Fundamental, London
Sleeve Design: Brian Robbins

Tracks:
1 Festive Road **1:55**
2 Death of a Supernaturalist **3:19**
3 Bernice Bobs Her Hair **4:00**
4 I Was Born Yesterday **3:31**
5 Your Daddy's Car **3:55**
6 Europop **4:31**
7 Timewatching **3:53**

8 The Pop Singer's Fear of the Pollen Count **4:19**
9 Queen of the South **4:27**
10 Victoria Falls **4:11**
11 Three Sisters **4:42**
12 Europe by Train **4:28**
13 Lucy **4:38**

DIVINE COMEDY
BANG GOES THE KNIGHTHOOD (2010)

NEIL HANNON

'There are a couple of over-arching lines of enquiry on *Bang Goes The Knighthood*: what goes on in the minds of those in positions of political and/or financial power, and what goes on the mind of a newly single Irishman on the verge of forty . . . No one can tell you what you can and can't write a song about. The scenarios I like to investigate – a young woman eking out an existence in post-war Naples, an underground cell dedicated to the spreading of pro-conversation propaganda – seem to jar with received wisdom on the subject . . . For a few years I tried too hard to surprise and confuse those who would try to put me in a generic box and throw away the key. Now, I couldn't give a toss. My music is what it has always been - a mélange of '20s/'30s songbook, 'sixties easy-listening, British new wave '78–'83, a spot of be-bop jazz, a dash of early twentieth-century classical, and God knows what else. All I'm really ever after is an interesting idea married to a memorable tune.'

If you have a spare few minutes, let's just ponder on the state of Irish pop music around about now. On the one hand there are the talent-free mini-celebrity types – people that have been picked out of obscurity by a team of 'experts' and thrust into the limelight for their fifteen minutes of national fame, only to wonder what happens next when the flash from the paparazzi camera fades to black. On the other hand, you have established acts that know their place within the pop music firmament: they may experiment occasionally, deviate from the expected norm, but by and large they deliver the goods in neatly wrapped packages. Sometimes, if we're lucky, the packages are finished off with a pretty little bow.

Which is where – stage left, wearing a bowler hat, pretending to smoke a pipe – Neil Hannon enters with *Bang Goes the Knighthood*. The compact, concise Irishman, under the umbrella title of Divine Comedy, has been releasing albums since 1990 – an average of one every two years. Most of these albums have been stylised affairs, individual yet referencing influences, and always imbued with a level of intelligence and wit missing from what generally passes for pop music. From 1993's *Liberation* (see page 64), Hannon created

a yardstick for others to measure up to, and with *Bang Goes the Knighthood* he sets the benchmark even higher.

On record as in person, Hannon is literate and smart, yet despite his image as a suave, cavalier aristo, he's actually a doubter: a deep, often profound thinker. This album's 'When a Man Cries' is a case in point: in the wrong, whining hands, it's a topic that could implode on the writer. Yet Hannon treads assuredly, blending realism and poignancy with hints of deceit. It isn't all sorrow, of course. If there is a jauntier pop song than 'Assume the Perpendicular', a more warmly nostalgic view of teenage romance than 'At the Indie Disco', or a more evocative view of an island made for two than 'Island Life', we have yet to hear them.

What Hannon excels at here, however (and it's a measure of how much he has developed as a songwriter over the years), is the creation of the corner-of-the-canvas vignettes that tell a far more informed story than the large-scale picture. As for being a songwriter who uses words such as 'architraves', 'Thracians', 'transubstantiation' and 'buttresses', and cleverly depict blow-jobs in graveyards ('Neapolitan Girl') as well as S&M in Westminster ('Bang Goes the Knighthood') – well, frankly, Mr Hannon, we salute you.

THE DIVINE COMEDY **BANG** goes the **Knighthood**

Released: 2010
Record Label: Divine Comedy Records
Producer: Neil Hannon
Recorded at: Exechequer Street Studios, Westland Studios, Dublin
Sleeve Design: Emagine Media, Pauline Rowan (photography)

Tracks:
1 Down in the Street Below **5:08**
2 The Complete Banker **3:43**
3 Neapolitan Girl **2:49**
4 Bang Goes the Knighthood **2:48**
5 At the Indie Disco **3:18**
6 Have You Ever Been in Love **3:10**

7 Assume the Perpendicular **4:06**
8 The Lost Art of Conversation **4:01**
9 Island Life **4:36**
10 When a Man Cries **3:54**
11 Can You Stand Upon One Leg **3:32**
12 I Like **3:48**

DOCTOR MILLAR
THE DEAL (1998)

DOCTOR MILLAR

'*The Deal* was recorded in January 1997 at Margeurite Studios in Dublin. I had just become a father for the first time, and my life, although very happy, was going into a tailspin. I had zero money. It was also my first time to produce my own work, the first time I got to come up with the arrangements, etc. *The Deal* was co-produced by Joe Chester (see page 46) and was, I think, one of his first big jobs. We are both extremely proud of it. Our templates were Planxty, Velvet Underground and the Rolling Stones; we would listen to Planxty every day before we mixed the songs. You can kind of hear this best on "Dead Man's Hand". Despite excellent reviews, it was my least commercially successful record — and that is saying something! But it has, like each of my albums, die-hard fans all over the world, and I think it's my best.'

We have a recollection of Sean Millar in his guise as nominal leader of Doctor Millar and The Cute Hoors: arrogant, assertive, a string-thin performer wearing a brown mac and holding in his hand a book by Albert Camus. *The Outsider*, perhaps?

Back in the late eighties, Millar – who spent time in London scaring the natives – was a narky dude, seemingly angry at the world and howling at the moon. The Cute Hoors disbanded in 1992, leaving Millar to prowl around and scavenge like the penurious Irish singer-songwriter he was. Nineteen ninety-five saw the release of his debut solo album, *The Bitter Lie*, an album so good that he was, improbably and very much against type, cast as the singer-songwriter *du jour* in award ceremonies that had him lining up with the likes of Van Morrison, Gavin Friday and Paul Brady (see respective entries, pages 130-133, 84 and 34). Sean Millar and awards? Oh, how we gasped.

Come 1998, however, *The Deal* - was released. Put together on a frayed-shoestring budget, it's the kind of album that makes you wonder how and why so many other singer-songwriters (and not necessarily Irish, either) manage to get away with putting out the drivel they do. Millar, then, is something of a cult item, an acquired taste (the backhanded payback for being brutally honest and against-the-grain), and a vastly underrated songwriter. He is also (as per his aforementioned liking of European literature) distanced in terms of support afforded him by the music industry.

Millar's outlook on life may be bleak, but it is offset by shards of humour, a keen observational streak, and some of the best, most scabrous lyrics an Irish singer-songwriter has given us. The prose song 'Billy Meany' focuses on sibling incest, with Millar injecting equal amounts of fascination, nostalgic reverie and dread into the subject. The sexually explicit 'Finally OK' reverberates to the lyrical battering ram of what Millar terms 'life's purest embrace' ('In a jacks in Paris, fucking, moaning with a woman who says she can't help it, she's coming, she's coming. You could have sworn that the door was locked but apparently it wasn't'), while simultaneously daring radio programmers not to playlist his material.

The songs throughout form a sparse sound that is complemented by shimmers of violins and backing vocals. The main ingredient at work here, however, is Millar. He is a singer in the non-technical sense, lo-fi to the core, and a very fine storyteller to boot, his voice a perfect companion to the songs' many attributes. These include no star trips, no ego massaging, no music-business strategies. Just the facts: pure, simple, raw and hard.

Released: 1998
Record Label: Self Possessed Records
Producer: Sean Miller, Joe Chester
Recorded at: Marguerite Studios, Dublin
Sleeve Design: Jeff and the Mickster

Tracks:
1 Dying For The Light **3.14**
2 Sympathy for David Icke **3.17**
3 Finally OK **3.34**
4 Billy Meany **4.42**
5 Donna Quixote **2.49**

6 Dead Man's Hand **3.54**
7 Wild Girl **3.23**
8 The Little Cross **3.54**
9 Every Soldier Knows **3.29**
10 The Deal **4.07**

JOHNNY DUHAN

THE BURNING WORD (2010)

'To make any song work, for me, there has to be real lived experience behind it. Dreams, moments of enlightenment found in contemplation, rituals looked at in a new light – I used all sorts of devices to get below the surface. Melody is always the starting point for me. Melodies haunt me till I find the right words to put flesh on the musical bones. While I was writing the title song, the line "pure as a lily flower closed in its petal tower, you opened to the power of love" took me by surprise and then led me into the wonder of the dissonance of one of the most unusual choruses I've ever written. Radio stations have shunned the album, but I've had some wonderful responses to the collection from people all over the world. My audience remains small, but maybe that's a good thing.'

Some artists can be around for so long they become almost indistinguishable from fog – you can make out vague shapes and indistinct sounds, but try to focus on them in any way and they're gone. Whether that's by accident or some sort of cunning, strategic planning is something perhaps best left unexplored.

Johnny Duhan is one such artist. He's been on the scene since the 1960s, first as a young lad in a Limerick band called Granny's Intentions, a smart (and hotly tipped, let it be said) act of their time who wanted to save holy Ireland from the onslaught of showbands, but who – after an apparently very enjoyable stint swaying like a pendulum in Swinging London – gradually deflated, punctured by the fame game and expectations of the music industry. The band returned home to Ireland, defeated for a period of time.

Since those pop-star days, Duhan has created an existence of sorts as a singular if virtually reclusive singer-songwriter. Long-since based in the west of Ireland, he has quietly continued to release albums to, mostly, much acclaim, yet none has made him a sizeable financial nest egg on which to retire. All his records mark him out, however, as a distinctive and special kind of songwriter – reflective, egoless, emotionally and often painfully expressive.

That Duhan has gone largely unnoticed by even the Irish public at large is no great mystery: while his output is of undeniable quality, it is clearly just not snappy or snazzy enough for the kind of celeb-fed audience that lap up faux sincerity without breaking into a sweat, guilty or otherwise.

With *The Burning Word*, Duhan continues to ply his trade in a typically under-the-radar (off the radar screen, even) fashion. There is a unique undertow of spiritual rumination running through the record, a questioning, discerning observance, as evidenced by the singer's brief note on the inside of the sleeve, wherein he confesses to digging 'below the surface of my faith for these songs'.

With sparse but occasionally joyous instrumentation (the application of cello may be maudlin but equally it's as blithe as a selfish teenager), songs such as the title track, 'The Coat', 'The Flame Is Lit', 'Song of the Bird', 'Part Of A Tribe' and 'Old Story' branch out like veins beneath translucent skin and intersect at the heart. A strong sense of loss is also threaded through the album, as is love, tenderness, friendship; the album is imbued with taut and contemplative disclosures for which other songwriters, irrespective of age, level of creativity or financial circumstances, would trade in their rhyming dictionaries.

The Burning Word

Johnny Duhan

Released: 2010
Record Label: Bell Records
Producer: Johnny Duhan
Recorded at: Studios of Eugene Kelly &
Tony Maher
Sleeve Design: Johnny Duhan

Tracks:
1 The Coat **2.21**
2 The Flame Is Lit **2.23**
3 This World Is Not Conclusion **3.54**
4 Wonders **2.36**
5 Surrender **2.58**

6 The Burning Wood **2.33**
7 Song of the Bird **3.17**
8 The Storm **2.49**
9 Sure Amen **3.08**
10 Part of a Tribe **3.50**
11 Old Story **2.28**

DUKE SPECIAL
I NEVER THOUGHT THIS DAY WOULD COME (2008)

'Inspiration for the album came from a number of places: the book *Man Walks into a Room*, by Nicole Krauss; the story of a young girl who wakes up after many years of being in a coma following an ice-skating accident; an illustration a friend drew of a ghost dancing in an old ballroom with a sleepwalker; and from my own experiences at the time of writing. I wanted where I recorded the album to come to bear on the sound of it, so we began sessions at Pogo Studios in Champagne, Illinois. Pogo is an incredible place full of fun and vintage instruments and gear, and many unusual musicians from the area appear on the record, thereby adding unique flavours and textures.'

All hail to the family tradition of playing the piano in the drawing room. If it weren't for this honourable passing down of heritage, we would never have songwriters of the calibre of Duke Special (aka Peter Wilson). Having passed through the usual rites-of-passage apprenticeships in Northern Ireland, Wilson went solo in the early 2000s, took on the name 'Duke Special', released three EPs – which were filleted for his 2005 debut album, *Adventures in Gramophone* – and set about establishing himself, his dreadlocks and his 'guy-liner'.

Special's second album, *Songs from the Deep Forest*, went on to become a multi-platinum-selling record, but it's his third, *I Never Thought This Day Would Come*, that really resonates, with equal amounts of musical cajoling (think Tom Waits and Magnetic Fields) and lyrical honesty (think Aimee Mann and Elliott Smith). The mood throughout is sombre; if you need proof, just check out the song titles: 'Mockingbird, Wish Me Luck', 'Those Proverbs We Made in the Winter Must End', 'Why Does Anybody Love?', 'By the Skin of My Teeth', 'Nothing Comes Easy', 'Nothin' You Can Do Can Bring Me Around'.

Still, the music is several steps above even Special's fastidious methodology. Not even the ska-driven jauntiness of 'Diggin' an Early Grave' can take away from the overall sense of hopelessness and foreboding ('why is everything I want always something I can't have?') – which, curiously, never threatens to spoil the listening pleasure. This could be because Special has, in his first three albums, engineered the knack of mixing dispiriting topics with a sure-footed musical approach that never undermines the content.

Some people don't get him at all. They are blindsided by his appearance, which resembles shape-shifting images of Catweazle, a rat-tailed busker and the child-catcher from *Chitty Chitty Bang Bang*. People are also confused by the music, which owes as much to pop as it does to burlesque and music hall. (Percussive sounds arrive courtesy of a cheese grater and an egg whisk; other self-made instruments include a stumpf fiddle, which consists of a tin lid, springs and a bicycle bell.) Those who fail to see beyond these superficialities, however, miss out on the most important aspect of Special's work: his forensic attention to detail.

So forget the gender-skewing dreadlocks, the kohl eyeliner and the amateur-hour instrumentation. With 'I Never Thought This Day Would Come', Duke Special matches the lost art of the popular song with the found sound of swirling pop/rock and symphony orchestras. With a bit of Bridie Gallagher and Ruby Murray thrown in for good Irish measure. (That'll be the title track, then.)

Released: 2008

Record Label: Universal Music Ireland, V2

Producer: Paul Pilot, Bernard Butler

Recorded at: Various including Wapping and Westheath Studios, London; Pogo, Champaign, IL; Culleybackey, Northern Ireland

Sleeve Design: Tim Millen, Sparks

Tracks:

1 Mockingbird, Wish Me Luck **3:43**
2 Sweet Sweet Kisses **3:03**
3 Those Proverbs We Made in the Winter Must End **2:59**
4 Diggin' An Early Grave **3:17**
5 I Never Thought This Day Would Come (But Now It Won't Go Away) **3:22**
6 Why Does Anybody Love? **4:02**
7 Flesh & Blood Dance **3:29**
8 If I Don't Feel It **4:47**
9 Let Me Go (Please Please Please) **3:32**
10 By the Skin of My Teeth **3:43**
11 Nothing Comes Easy **3:40**
12 Nothin' You Could Do Can Bring Me Round **3:53**

ENGINE ALLEY

A SONIC HOLIDAY (1992)

CANICE KENEALY

'*A Sonic Holiday* was a blend of the prog tendencies we had gleaned from *The War of the Worlds* and our post-punk year-zero whippersnapper stance. This is why I used to describe it as psychedelic pop – we dressed in satin as a reaction to the prevailing ordinariness of stage presentation (baggy, shoegazing, grunge, and so on). It was primarily constructed as a vinyl album: side one was more pop, side two more prog, and instrumentals closed each side, while a lot of the songs are linked together by audio devices to give a continuous effect. It was named after one of our demos. We had spent eighteen months prior to the album gigging and making demos, which were produced by our guru, Pete Holidai, and recorded at Sonic Studios, hence the album title. We had a great experience making it and have extremely fond memories of the process and the sound of the record. It was released in October 1992 in Ireland, but was reconstructed for UK and USA release (UK, October 1993; USA, October 1994), blandly retitled and shortened – key tracks were replaced by newer material – which was the result of a corporate employee's half-asleep vision of the album. And you can quote me on that.'

The vast majority of debut albums fall into a self-defeating category: a four-year encapsulation of the act's very personal and intimate blood, sweat and tears, recorded and released for the world to either accept or dismiss. In some cases, however, there comes along a debut album that doesn't much care about being worthy, or being an emotive diary/travelogue about the life and times of the people who wrote the songs. Other than an abiding passion for the nature of time, space, girls and fame, *A Sonic Holiday* isn't obviously revealing about its creators. So far, so peculiar.

At the point of its release, the album was something of an event: the Kilkenny band had signed to Dublin-based Mother Records, which was owned by U2. The album was produced by Steve Lillywhite; their photographs were snapped by Amelia Stein; graphic designer Steve Averill was in charge of the style; and the album was recorded in Windmill Lane Studios. There was, you might well say, no expense spared. (Look at the band members on the cover, and ask yourself exactly how much money was spent on slap and satin?) Of course, what happened next wasn't

particularly surprising: the band released a classic glam/sci-fi/psychedelic pop album that bombed. What's that sound? Engine Alley being dropped from a height.

Did we mention that part of the album focuses on women? It does, yes, but not in an overtly sexual or typically rock 'n' roll way. The females mentioned here (Mrs Winder, Crazy Jane, Diamond Jill, Telescope Girl, Roller Girl) aren't one-dimensional 'chicks' but fully rounded characters in a series of spooky nursery rhymes. The characters may or may not directly interface with other characters, which in turn may or may not symbolise the rise and fall and rise of psychedelic pop. Frankly, we're not sure.

Whatever the ambiguities involved, one thing is certain: the album is full of psycho-killer pop, crunchy riffs and spine-tingling guitar solos, as if Pink Floyd (*c.* 1966) and David Bowie (*c.* 1973) were being chased through the streets by The Clash (*c.* 1977) and given a good kicking. Rarely has such rouge-faced cheek and downright panache been so roundly ignored by so many people.

Released: 1992
Record Label: Mother Records
Producer: Steve Lillywhite, Aidan Foley
Recorded at: Sonic Studios, Dublin
Sleeve Design: Works Associates, Amelia Stein (photography)

Tracks:
1 Mrs Winder **3:07**
2 Summertime is Over **2:40**
3 Infamy **2:59**
4 Song For Someone **3:46**
5 Insignificance **4:29**
6 Diamond Jill and Crazy Jane **2:41**
7 Spare Me **3:27**
8 Ballad of the Sinking Star **4:19**
9 Photo Lens **3:18**
10 Beautiful **5:03**
11 Telescope Girl **2:33**
12 Rollergirl **3:51**
13 The Flowers **3:57**
14 Lame Dog Lament **4:09**

JULIE FEENEY

PAGES (2009)

'A feeling or aura enveloped me just before I made *pages* – it was an overwhelming feeling of comfort. I felt compelled to share that through the album, and I knew that that's what the essence was going to be before I made it. I also had a strong desire to communicate and share with people, whereas on my first album, *13 Songs*, I was just expressing whatever I wanted to express. I also wanted with *pages* to make a pop album with my own songs using an orchestra, and not with any electronic or MIDI instruments whatsoever. I couldn't find an album that had been made like that before – I had no reference point or anyone to ask – so I just listened to the resources within myself.'

Orchestra conducted by Julie Feeney; singing in all octaves by Julie Feeney; all words and music by Julie Feeney; sessions edited by Julie Feeney. Part-time lecturing? Julie Feeney. Occasional modelling? Julie Feeney. Undertaking a masters in psychoanalysis? Julie Feeney. Studying composition and sonology at the Hague's Royal Conservatory? Julie Feeney. Wearer of hats so incredibly silly that it makes the collected works of Phillip Treacy look like a leftover bunch of beanies? Julie Feeney. Ever get the feeling, dear readers, that your life just isn't busy enough?

Artists of the calibre of Feeney are few and far between – probably because she is so much outside the supposed norm of what a singer-songwriter should sound like. Certainly, come 2006 she arrived pretty much out of nowhere with music that had no obvious connections with stock-in-trade formats.

She stands alone, and so far beyond her contemporaries that she would be in danger of achieving diminished returns were it not for the fact that her songs blend weird and wired with wonderful and why-ever-not. In 2006, Feeney won the inaugural Choice Music Prize with her debut album, *13 Songs* – a fine record, not least because its innate strangeness and charm dare you to strip it bare.

But then, almost three years later, came *pages*, a lower-case testament to Feeney's skill and innovation that fuses fully formed pop songs with instinctive, empathetic and seamless orchestration. It isn't an exaggeration to say that you will not hear anything like it. Songs such as 'Love Is a Tricky Thing', 'Impossibly Beautiful', 'Mr Roving Eye Guy', 'Stay' and 'Nothing to Declare' started out as poems and were eventually married to melodies; the primary intention, we can safely say, was to include the listener by avoiding indulgence and embracing accessibility, while simultaneously sounding just a little bit odd.

In this, Feeney has succeeded brilliantly. The biggest surprise about *pages*, however, is its warmth, joy and light-headedness. Whenever we hear of a pop or rock artist fiddling about with an orchestra in order to enhance their music, we can also detect – trailing not too far behind – the clang of alarm bells. But Feeney has done the often-justifiably-derided fusion a huge service by seamlessly integrating one form with the other. Instead of tacking on an orchestra, or using it as a crutch, she utilises it in tandem. The curviest curve ball thrown by an Irish female songwriter/musician? So far, yes.

pages

Julie Feeney

Released: 2009
Record Label: mittens
Producer: Julie Feeney **Recorded at:**
Irish Chamber Orchestra Studio, Limerick;
Julie Feeney's studio **Sleeve Design:** Julie
Feeney (design and concept), Rob Murphy
(photography), Sharon Costello Desmond
(tree house design)

Tracks:
1 Love Is a Tricky Thing **3:14**
2 Impossibly Beautiful **2:53**
3 Grace **2:57**
4 Valentine's Song **2:42**
5 One More Tune **2:49**
6 Myth **3:03**
7 Mr Roving Eye Guy **3:33**
8 Stay **4:11**
9 Life's Nudge **3:04**
10 Monster **2:02**
11 Nothing to Declare **2:20**
12 Knock Knock **2:45**

FIGHT LIKE APES

FIGHT LIKE APES AND THE MYSTERY OF THE GOLDEN MEDALLION (2008)

JAMIE FOX, AKA POCKETS

'We always thought of our first album as a collection of the best songs we had at the time as opposed to a complete piece . . . My main thought? It probably had a careless sense of abandon – sure, we'll fuck it out there and see if it bites. The only thing I remember having to consider was clearing samples. That was a pain in the arse . . . Obnoxious pop music was always the idea, to try and distract as much as we could from the core of the song, which was always incredibly simple, and create chaos around it, making the song itself slightly obsolete. I've always found that the best melodies are the ones you have to search for. That said, I'd love to rewrite some of the melodies now, because if I have to hear, never mind play "Lend Me Your Face" one more time I might face-plant myself into a spiky gate.'

EPs called *How Am I Supposed to Kill You if You Have All The Guns?* and *David Carradine Is a Bounty Hunter Whose Robotic Arm Hates Your Crotch*. Album tracks such as 'Lend Me Your Face', 'Digifucker', 'Snore Bore Whore', 'I'm Beginning to Think You Prefer Beverly Hills 90210 to Me'. Are we sensing a theme here? If there's one thing worse than the band with a sense of humour it's the band that morphs into a novelty act. And yet there are such high hopes for Fight Like Apes that sometimes we feel like we're Frank Sinatra singing that very same song in the movie it first appeared in: *Hole in the Head* (which, come to think of it, could very easily be extended into a Fight Like Apes song title).

Formed at the fag-end of 2006, and fronted by one-time cherub-cheeked choir singer Mary-Kate Geraghty (aka MayKay), Fight Like Apes divided opinion from the very start. Within a year of forming, they had released the aforementioned EPs, and had caused much debate among the media/blogging community as to whether the band were a) the most exciting Irish rock act in recent memory, or b) the worst example of gimmickry to have paraded on a stage in years.

The truth, of course, is whatever you want it to be. Yet the landing of the band's debut album in the autumn of 2008 informed champions and detractors alike of one immutable fact: there was no Irish band, past or present, that even remotely resembled Fight Like Apes. It takes more than a minute before MayKay gets her vocal mojo revved up on opening track 'Something Global', but even before the song is half over, you're in the zone with lyrics like 'Hooks are for wimps, choruses for gays . . . You're running like a preacher's hand caressing, feeling up, all the cleavage in town'. And so it continues: songs that make a racket, lyrics that make you laugh (you *do* remember jokes, don't you?), songs that make you want to jump up and down ('Tie Me Up with Jackets', 'Lend Me Your Face'), lyrics that would surely make Prince flinch ('Digifucker': 'And did you fuck her? And did you stick things up her? And did she love it?'), music that surprises (the *Hawaii Five-O* intro to 'Do You Karate?'), backing vocals that make no apparent sense ('Suplex, suplex, suplex backbreaker', 'I'm Beginning to Think You Prefer Beverly Hills 90210 to Me'), and an overall musical sensibility that matches the unpredictable with unbridled energy.

Gimmick? Nuts to you, mate: *Fight Like Apes and the Mystery of the Golden Medallion* is a pretention-free, graffiti-art playground of a record; equal parts abrasive, emotive, vulgar, enlightening, demented, light-headed, heavy-hearted and (always an opinion-divider) funny. You'll love it. You'll hate it. You'll argue the toss.

Released: 2008
Record Label: Strangeways Records
Producer: John Goodmanson
Recorded at: Two-Sticks Audio, Seattle
Sleeve Design: Loreana Rushe,
gazjonesdesign.com

Tracks:
1 Something Global **3:50**
2 Jake Summers **3:44**
3 Tie Me Up with Jackets **2:35**
4 Digifucker **3:25**
5 Lend Me Your Face **1:49**
6 Battlestations **3:33**

7 Do You Karate? **2:21**
8 Megameanie **0:08**
9 I'm Beginning to Think You Prefer
   Beverly Hills 90210 to Me **3:23**
10 Lumpy Dough **3:20**
11 Recyclable Ass **2:30**
12 Snore Bore Whore **5:20**

THE 4 OF US

CLASSIFIED PERSONAL (1999)

'The lyrics came easily. I had plenty to write about. I was single again, having ended a lengthy relationship, and Declan and myself had left the North in 1997. We both loved Belfast, but it was still a dangerous place to live in the years before the Good Friday Agreement. We knew the album was very different from what we'd done before, and we were nervous but excited at the prospect of doing it on our own. The songs on the album are about letting go of the past and starting again, both in music and in our personal life. I decided to record the songs simply, the way they were written: we wanted the album to sound honest and emotional.'

There are many hundreds of pop/rock acts that have burned brightly and quickly, their once sizeable profile receding to a dot in the rear-view mirror.

In the case of The 4 of Us (in effect, brothers Brendan and Declan Murphy), their initial flurry of fame in the late eighties petered out in the early nineties when, dropped by Sony (despite the commercial achievements of their 1989 debut, *Songs For The Tempted*, and the critical success of their superb second album, *Man Alive*, released in 1992), they took some time before they again featured in the public consciousness.

For a while, they were also (unjustifiably so) regarded as one of the many hyped Irish rock bands that floundered in the wake of their association with a major label. The 4 of Us have long since taken stock of their post-Sony career and come up with business (including becoming one of the first successful Irish music acts to operate their own record company, and a savvy online presence) and creative mission statements that have seen them operating at the top of their game and, crucially, on their own terms.

While *Man Alive* remains an early and exhilarating career highlight, it is *Classified Personal* that cautiously transformed them from a nifty pop/rock act to something altogether weightier and more mature – they have released several others albums since, of course, but none has achieved the level of forlornness that emanates from this emotionally bereft collection.

Hushed, beautifully melancholic and often so crestfallen you feel like wanting to assume the foetal position and hide under a duvet with a hot water bottle, Murphy's voice is as intimate as it is needy; the acoustic-driven, late-night ambience songs might not have been as bravado-fuelled a return to the fray as their mainstream fans would have hoped for, but it was nevertheless the record that saved their career.

Songs such as 'One More Shot' ('Maybe I sometimes lied, but my crimes are small . . .'), 'Time To Turn Around' ('Class reunion day and I can't think of a word to say'), 'Wasted' ('I only hurt you once, but you never lost the shame; I find myself a hole and climb in') and 'Let's Face It' ('It was only sex that kept us hanging on') display a tenuous hold on emotional issues. Talk about hanging by a thread . . .

It seemed on its release that the tenor of *Classified Personal* came out of a place at which no one wanted to look, and a mindset that no one wanted to admit was in any way similar to their own. Because of this, it remains one of Irish rock's most personal, honest, fragile and unsentimental albums – treasured by few, lost to thousands.

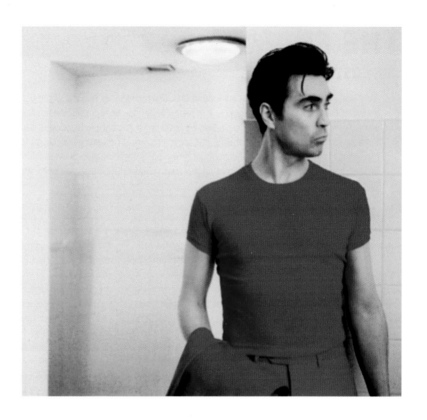

Released: 1999
Record Label: Future Inc Records
Producer: Pat O'Donnell, The 4 of Us
Recorded at: Sandymount, Dublin
Sleeve Design: Chevie at Boyle Design
Group, Redmond Cabot, Suki Stuart
(photography)

Tracks:
1 Pure Release **3:44**
2 Volatile **4:11**
3 Time to Turn Around **3:42**
4 Wasted **3:51**
5 Come Alive **2:33**
6 Maybe It's You **3:51**
7 Change **3:45**

8 Love Keeps You Waiting **2:50**
9 Sweetheart **2:50**
10 One More Shot **4:15**
11 Uptight **3:46**
12 Fingerprints **1:04**
13 Let's Face It **3:38**
14 Long Before I Make That Call **3:37**

THE FRAMES
THE COST (2006)

GLEN HANSARD

'This was a record that marked some kind of end. Not necessarily the end of the band, but the end of a period of doing things in an old way. In a breaking of habits, we recorded these songs in straight takes; all instruments, including vocals, were live; we recorded it in a barn in France and had a great time doing it, living together, sharing the cooking, and cleaning. A great memory – although when I look back on the songs I feel it was a record of despair, of giving up. Something was showing up in the songs that felt angry, or even hopeless . . . The Frames have always followed the music as a band. At this time, however, the songs were leading me elsewhere, and I was compelled to follow. '

It's no small irony that, on occasion, major success comes to those who would rather whittle wood and talk to themselves in ramshackle sheds miles away anywhere. Take, for example, Glen Hansard (see separate entry, with Markéta Irglová, page 96), the lead singer of The Frames, unquestionably one of the most influential Irish bands of the past twenty years in terms of establishing a blueprint of self-help and independence.

The Frames quickly rose to the top of the pyramid, in the process becoming standard-bearers for an anti-commercial attitude that didn't define success in terms of record sales and/or securing a major-label record deal, and didn't wish to be mercenary about such matters. Hansard also cared little for the celebrity tag (a blasphemous attitude in a music industry tripping over itself to promote acts that have the creative depth of a puddle).

Yet Hansard's craft has been allowed to mature slowly. Through a series of archetypal record deals, The Frames' career has spluttered and started a few times – a sequence of events viewed by some as little more than a case of working with the wrong people. Hansard himself has said on more than one occasion that success for him is a stage, a guitar, some songs, and a bunch of people at the gig. The old adage (so regularly a cliché) of three chords and the truth hits the spot here, and the fact that he has never seemed to wear a mask and simply refuses to play the media/music industry game cements such honesty. *The Cost* is full of similar heart-on-sleeve approaches. The Frames' sixth studio album criss-crosses with Hansard's work on *The Swell Season* and the *Once* original soundtrack by featuring different, somewhat harsher, but no less aching versions of 'Falling Slowly' and 'When Your Mind's Made Up'.

As usual, The Frames play as if their lives (and not their bank balances) depend on it, but special beyond-the-call-of-duty mentions must go to violinist Colm Mac Con Iomaire (whose playing throughout forms a fortified bridge between temporal and spiritual, scratching and soothing, each style ecstatic) and guitarist Rob Bochnik (whose work, plain and simple, pillages and pleasures in equal measure). Such tactics inform tracks as authentic as 'Song for Someone', 'People Get Ready', 'Rise', the title track, 'The Side You Never Get to See' and 'Bad Bone'. The key is that you never really know where the songs are heading. Yes, there are pointers, and here and there you can almost guess the destination, but Bochnik and Mac Con Iomaire's swerves and turns (as much as Hansard's lyrics, which reveal secrets in every song) have you looking every which way. If *The Cost*'s work ethic is epic, and the sound is slow-build anthemic, then the result is quiet-loud-quiet grandeur (and grace) of the highest order.

Released: 2007

Record Label: Plateau Records (Ireland), Anti Records (US)

Producer: David Odlum, Stephen Fitzmaurice

Recorded at: Black Box Studios, France

Sleeve Design: Banjo, Glen Hansard (photography)

Tracks:
1 Song for Someone **5:36**
2 Falling Slowly **4:35**
3 People Get Ready **5:28**
4 Rise **3:26**
5 When Your Mind's Made Up **3:44**
6 Sad Songs **3:09**
7 The Cost **4:20**
8 True **5:14**
9 The Side You Never Get to See **3:40**
10 Bad Bone **4:42**

GAVIN FRIDAY

CATHOLIC (2011)

'Too much music today feels co-ordinated, manufactured and blocked. You listen to bands and you know they've read the right books, because they're just making albums by the numbers. When you're doing certain songs, you should be following a scent, a trail that you don't know where it's going to bring you. I'm doing it my way, which is something I've always done, even in the days of The Virgin Prunes. I think you have to be as excited, as vulnerable, as driven as you were when you were eighteen. The thing I miss about being that age is that you didn't think too much, but now knowledge and wisdom kicks in, and you go, "oh, that's going to cost a fortune, and the audience will walk out halfway". Back in the day you didn't care if the audience walked out. The truth is, I won't change my ways just to suit.'

Gavin Friday has never really bothered with being in kilter with the rest of the world; in tune, yes, but regarding the day-to-day, run-of-the-mill things, he'd be the kind of person who would run a country mile. He is, you might like to know, the same Gavin Friday who, as a co-founding member of Ireland's prime anarcho-art rock band, the Virgin Prunes (see separate entry, page 212), was wrist-deep in muck and blood: his head was full of conflict, and his raison d'être was to agitate and confront.

Released sixteen years after his previous album, *Shag Tobacco*, *catholic* is the culmination of several years of personal upheaval, invasive surgery, and the death of his father. Things change, of course, because that's just the way life is, but the album (which features, perhaps typically, Friday on his deathbed dressed in an Irish soldier's uniform, draped with a tricolour; then again, maybe he's just sleeping after a hard day's night at a fancy-dress party) is as subversive in its own way as The Virgin Prunes were in their prime.

Friday says he wanted to go back to basics with *catholic* – to, as he has said, 'make a record like you had just signed to Rough Trade in 1979'. Befitting his solo status (no wife, no father, no creative collaborations as such), the album is Friday in middle-aged, reflective mode. Sonically, the results are superlative: svelte, subtle and idiosyncratic juxtapositions of Friday's internal soap operas with luminous touchstones such as David Bowie, Scott Walker and Leonard Cohen.

Like those artists, the songs here are slow burners and stealthy buggers, substantial and beautiful. Like Friday, the songs are against the grain, but in keeping with his solo work, running through everything is a trademark sense of melody that is distinctly cinematic and sexual, particularly in 'Lord I'm Coming' (and, yes, there is quite likely a double meaning here), 'Where'd Ya Go? Gone', 'Able' and 'The Sun & The Moon & The Stars'.

A serious album? No. In fact, it's *deadly* serious, as nocturnal as a vampire, as vulnerable as a kitten, and as wise a coming-of-age record as any you'll ever hear.

Released: 2011
Record Label: Rubyworks
Producer: Ken Thomas
Recorded at: Chairworks Studios, West
Yorkshire, High Bank, Hampshire (UK);
Curlews, Dublin; Exchequer Studios, Dublin;
Toy Town Studios, Cork
Sleeve Design: Redman AKA, Perry Ogden
(photography)

Tracks:
1 Able **4:46**
2 Land On The Moon **5:06**
3 A Song That Hurts **5:32**
4 The Only One **4:16**
5 Blame **4:53**
6 The Sun & The Moon & The Stars **4:16**
7 It's All Ahead of You **4:34**
8 Perfume **3:34**

 9 Epilogue **3:09**
10 Where'd Ya Go? Gone **4:40**
11 Lord I'm Coming **6:51**

RORY GALLAGHER

RORY GALLAGHER (1971)

DONAL GALLAGHER

'Rory had to go through a fairly cruel three-month farewell tour with Taste, a tour that had been booked by the record company, which he had to do because he was flat broke. And following the demise of Taste, a sort of depression had set in . . . Things got better, though, due to a management connection with Peter Grant, and so Rory went into the studio for this album with much more confidence, and a lot of baggage left behind. There's a sense of innocence in the songs, a sense of optimism. The album is by a person who had the shackles taken off.'

In 1969, shortly after he performed arguably his most famous gig (at Woodstock), Jimi Hendrix was asked by a magazine interviewer: 'So, Jimi, what's it like to be the best guitarist in the world?' Hendrix replied, 'I dunno, ask Rory Gallagher.'

Everyone loves a hero (clean-cut, invulnerable, always there when you need them), but it's the flawed anti-hero (the type who bucks against the system time and time again yet who never gives in, who battles against inner demons that threaten to bring them down, and eventually wins – but always at a cost) that gets the public vote. Rory Gallagher – whose death by liver failure in June 1995 marked the passing of a more innocent, less mercenary time in Irish rock – was that anti-hero.

Born in Ballyshannon, County Donegal, in 1949 (the family moved to Cork in 1956), Gallagher picked up a guitar at the age of nine, and joined The Fontana Showband (later to become The Impact Showband) at fifteen. It was an eye-opening entry for the young Gallagher into the world of show business: The Impact supported visiting UK bands such as The Kinks and The Who, and exposure to them prompted Gallagher, in 1965, to leave the showband and their facsimiles of Top 20 hits, and form his own group, Taste (see page 190).

When Taste split up in 1971, Gallagher, spurred on by what he recognised as an opportunity to flex his creative muscles, flung himself into recording his self-titled debut.

You can get a glimpse of the music itself from the cover, which features the guitarist in sheepish mode; similarly, the album is more restrained than either his previous work with Taste or his future output. Yes, there are the excellent trademark rockers, such as 'Laundromat', 'Hands Up' and 'Sinner Boy', and the jazz-influenced (via his regard for the likes of John Coltrane and Eric Dolphy) 'Can't Believe It's True'. If you're looking for featherlite, fleet-fingered solos from a technically astute and pinpoint-perfect guitarist of the rock/blues/roots persuasion, then you'll find them in 'For the Last Time'.

The true flavour of the album, and the nature of the man, however, can be found on the quieter tracks: 'Just the Smile', 'I'm Not Surprised' and 'Wave Myself Goodbye'. Each of these tracks unite Gallagher's signature solitariness with intuitive melodies and Delta blues sensibilities.

Gallagher's legacy remains one of triumphs and failures – a jumble of fond memories, great guitar work and terrific gigs. On later records, he'd be louder, brasher and more commercial (this said, Gallagher was a musician of his time: he cared little about the business end of his work), but here there is a raw beauty that he would rarely capture on one album again. Had he lived, one can only imagine how he would have thrived in a music scene which raises an eyebrow that Kurt Cobain should know Leadbelly White Stripes' stripped-down blues.

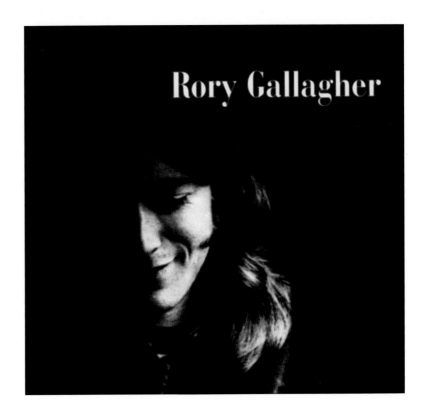

Released: 1971
Record Label: Polydor
Producer: Rory Gallagher, Donald Gallagher
(executive producer)
Recorded at: Advision Studios, London
Sleeve Design: Mick Rock (front cover
photography)

Tracks:
1 Laundromat 4:38
2 Just the Smile 3:41
3 I Fall Apart 5:12
4 Wave Myself Goodbye 3:30
5 Hands Up 5:25
6 Sinner Boy 5:04

7 For the Last Time 6:35
8 It's You 2:38
9 I'm Not Surprised 3:37
10 Can't Believe It's True 7:16

THE GOLDEN HORDE

THE GOLDEN HORDE (1991)

SIMON CARMODY

'We certainly wanted American, in fact, New York producers, and to feel the magic energy of the city sound that inspired us. Rolling home in a taxi from Jersey as the dawn broke when we were mixing the album; getting into bed with the windows looking out onto Gramercy Park and listening to The Chieftains to chill. Wonderful . . . If freedom is something to do with self-expression, then I felt free. We were high-energy guys with a mystical streak, a broken heart, a hard-on and a hangover . . . Overall? My memory is of making my dream, our dreams, come true. Everybody focused on making the music we loved, expressing themselves, digging it. We were young and doing that glorious, damned rock 'n' roll. It was beautiful, baby. What could be better?'

It's a crazy, mixed-up, psychedelic, Ramones-centric world, that's for sure, and for a time, throughout the eighties and into the early nineties, The Golden Horde were right in the centre of it, swirling around in the vortex without vomiting, with lead singer, main songwriter and all-round frontman Simon Carmody giving it the peace sign, the two-fingers sign, the single middle-digit sign.

The Golden Horde started life as an unwieldy prospect, but chaos can only welcome so many ricocheting sparks, and so they morphed into a coherent five-piece that – after original band members had left or been replaced – definitively consisted of Carmody, Des O'Byrne (guitar), Sammy Steiger (guitar), John Connor (bass) and Peter O'Kennedy (drums).

Founded on the guiding principles of obscure garage rock, personal freedom, punk rock, individual expression, surf rock, rock 'n' roll trivia, girl groups and other such hare-brained notions (such as having a laugh and putting fun back into an otherwise depressingly serious U2-dominated Irish music scene), the band released several records, and the occasional cassette. Everything, pretty much, was festooned with go-go-girl garish, hey-ho day-glo, and a certain B-movie aesthetic. Their stage shows, however, quickly established The Golden Horde as a supremely nifty proposition that you'd have been foolish to have ignored. Carmody, in particular, was growing into his role as frontman *in excelsis* (he was, back in the day, one of the very few Irish rock singers that you could easily have imagined charming the pants off arena audiences), while his band members stepped up to the mark as the coolest cohorts of any Irish rock act before or since.

As the late eighties approached, you could sense the band transforming from a couldn't-give-a-fuck unit (in thrall to the Johnny Thunders school of gaiety) into an utterly effective rock act. The songs, too, started to match the demeanor, and before you knew what had happened they had signed to Mother Records and released their debut major-label album.

For all its psychedelic notions, the album is a brilliant, seriously streamlined collection of punk/pop tunes that easily transcend their influences. From the lyrics ('There's a hundred boys who'd say, Simon please come out to play, we're sorry that you lost your mind, and we trust it all works out okay', '100 Boys'; 'our love was worth its weight in candyfloss', 'Endless Weekend') to the music (the hardcore US bubblegum of '100 Boys', 'She's a Weirdo' and 'Paula' via classy softer tunes 'Friends in Time', 'Hell' and 'Over Here'), the album is a diary of one man's descent into the pleasures of girldom, the dangers of self-gratification, and one hell of an ecstatic journey back.

Released: 1991
Record Label: Mother Records, Island
Producer: Andy Shernoff, Daniel Rey
Recorded at: STS, Dublin
Sleeve Design: Sam Steiger, Charlie
Whisker (paintbox), Works Associates
(artwork)

Tracks:
1 Endless Weekend **3:44**
2 Lisa **3:39**
3 100 Boys **3:21**
4 Hell **4:17**
5 She's a Weirdo **2:07**
6 Friends In Time **5:25**

7 Have a Scene **3:37**
8 I Never Came Down **3:06**
9 Now I'm Gone **2:56**
10 Rorschach **3:20**
11 Over Here **5:32**
12 House of Girls **3:51**
13 Paula **3:03**

EMM GRYNER
SONGS OF LOVE AND DEATH (2005)

EMM GRYNER

'My manager Michael Murphy put the idea in my head to pay tribute to my small but important Irish heritage and make an all-Irish covers album. In 2004, I met with Myles Dungan and Fachtna O'Ceallaigh, both of whom were great fountains of knowledge on what music I should look into. From Myles' suggestion of "Shining Light" to Michael introducing me to Something Happens, I ended up choosing songs that I could relate to lyrically, even if they had nothing in common with each other. I was mesmerised by the diversity of Irish pop music that I had never heard before. While the album may not have sold much, it was a great introduction to Ireland's music scene.'

On the face of it, Canadian singer-songwriter Emm Gryner shouldn't be in this book; the fact that her grandmother is from County Monaghan also shouldn't have any bearing on her inclusion. Well, forget about that: out goes the rulebook, in comes the granny clause. And while you're at it, why don't you stick *Songs of Love and Death* on the iPod?

On paper, at best it's a recipe for disaster: take ten Irish rock songs, burrow underneath their skin, snag at the tissue, and twist it ever so slightly out of shape. By covering songs from the likes of Thin Lizzy ('Running Back'), The Undertones ('Julie Ocean'), The Thrills ('Deckchairs and Cigarettes'), Horslips ('Dearg Doom'), Ash ('Shining Light'), Gilbert O'Sullivan ('Nothing Rhymed'), Something Happens ('Forget Georgia') and Therapy? ('Nowhere'), Gryner has, if nothing else, set the proverbial cat among those pesky proverbial pigeons. Oh, and just for the fun of it, she also tackles The Virgin Prunes ('Bau-Dachong') and The Corrs ('Breathless').

Gryner has engaged with testosterone before in a previous covers album (2001's *Girl Versions*, where she pummelled into feminine shape material from the likes of Ozzy Osbourne, Nick Cave, Def Leppard and The Clash).

Here, she engages with the material (all male-written songs, with the exception of 'Breathless') in a similar manner. The result is not so much a work of muscular deconstruction as a renovation overseen by a fragrant interior designer.

Where to start? Therapy?'s 'Nowhere' comes across as a singer-songwriter country tune; Ash's 'Shining Light' is hymn-like, virtually a piece of classical music. The two most curious tracks on this most curious of records are 'Bau-Dachong' and 'Breathless'. Surely no one has ventured close to reinterpreting the notoriously unclassifiable Virgin Prunes? And the smothering blandness of The Corrs? Yet 'Bau-Dachong', with its 'If I die, I die' refrain, is presented as an exercise in solace; 'Breathless', meanwhile, is transformed from a needy pop song into a meditation on loss.

Made in a bubble, with modest ambitions, *Songs of Love and Death* avoids easy options and obvious targets: it is a simple idea put across with a minimum of fuss and a lot of intuitive talent. Gryner has gone beyond the call of duty and done us all a service with an album that remains a touchstone in how to sieve through rubble for gems.

Released: 2005
Record Label: Dead Daisy Records
Producer: Emm Gryner
Recorded at: Sous-Royale, Montreal; other locations
Sleeve Design: Sean Odell

Tracks:
1 Forget Georgia   3:39
2 Running Back   3:17
3 Deckchairs and Cigarettes   2:44
4 Breathless   3:25
5 Dearg Doom   3:18

6 Shining Light   4:49
7 Nothing Rhymed   2:06
8 Bau-Dachong   3:52
9 Julie Ocean   2:58
10 Nowhere   2:47
11 The Moorlough Shore   4:41

HAM SANDWICH
WHITE FOX (2010)

PODGE MCNAMEE

'*White Fox* was dedicated to our manager Derek Nally, who died in July 2010, for massive, massive reasons, as it always felt like we did the album for him – he was our rock throughout our career. Where many great bands, and bands that had more success than us, called it a day, his belief in us kept us going when times got hard or things weren't happening for us. He was like a proud father to us and I think *White Fox* would have been right up his street. We can only wish he could be around for what's to come.'

Back in the mid-Noughties, this ostensibly ramshackle band came into existence, and, well, let's be honest and harsh, we laughed at their name as if it had been the first great joke we had ever heard. We laughed so hard, in fact, that for a time we almost forgot about the music.

The band's 2008 debut album, *Carry The Meek*, was fit to bursting with ideas and notions that ably transcended their initial shortcomings, yet it seemed as if Ham Sandwich were the kind of band that didn't know the difference between the 'standby', 'reset' and 'off' buttons: one week they'd play the kind of blinder that made you rub your eyes, the next they'd be so off their collective face you just didn't know where to look. That was when we stopped laughing and just dismissed them as a hard-working novelty act that might not amount to much. Two years later, however, came *White Fox*, and the advancement in arranging, songwriting and general sense of achievement in it is staggering.

At 33.33 minutes (the timing is a precisely pitched retro joke that anyone under the age of twenty might need to ask their older relatives about), the album certainly doesn't outstay its welcome, yet it's good enough to yearn, as it ends, for an extra few songs.

Whatever about these concerns, the album's brevity is respectably matched by quality; tracks such as the title track, 'The Naturist', 'Models', 'Fog', 'Ants', 'In December', and 'Animals' (and, equally worth a mention, the remaining three – 'Floors', 'OH-OH', and 'Long Distance') are structured in a way that leaves little to the imagination yet at the same time makes you certain you've never heard them before. Is it fair to pick out specific tracks? Probably not, but who said life was fair? Just fall in love with the 'The Naturist's intro of acoustic guitar picking and its lyric of 'I liked you better with your homemade haircut, and then she goes and cuts your favourite t-shirt . . .'; ask to marry into 'Ants's heartfelt, too-true sensibilities ('wish I could carry you like an army of ants . . .'); and live until you're old, hairless and toothless with 'Long Distance's languid, palpitating sense of regret and lost love ('you used to spend the night in my arms . . .').

Because of the indie pop nous involved, because of the lean, nugget-shaped songs, because of the superlative pop vocals of Niamh Farrell (in immaculate harmony with deep-throated Podge McNamee) and because every chord, instrument and lyric dovetails one into the other, *White Fox* ends up being one of those extremely rare records that you can listen to all the way through without being tempted to skip a track. In pop/rock music terms, brothers and sisters, that is some achievement.

Released: 2010
Record Label: Route 109A Records
Producer: Karl Odlum
Recorded at: Sun Studios, Temple Bar,
Dublin; May Lodge, County Meath
Sleeve Design: Leon Butler, Kevin Breen,
Enda Casey (photography)

Tracks:
1 The Naturist **3:23**
2 White Fox **3:49**
3 Ants **3:59**
4 Oh-Oh **3:26**
5 Models **3:05**
6 The Fog **3:00**

7 Long Distance **3:08**
8 In December **3:03**
9 Animals **3:43**
10 Floors **2:44**

LISA HANNIGAN
SEA SEW (2008)

'*Sea Sew* was recorded quickly: two weeks in a basement studio in Dublin. The previous year had been spent writing, arranging and rehearsing the songs, and it was really a matter of figuring it out as I went along. Although I had been involved in making records before, the steering, fuelling and navigating of the ship had never been my responsibility, and that year followed a steep but enjoyable learning curve. Looking back, I think the record is as much about that process as the stories told by the individual songs.'

Any preconceptions there may be about Lisa Hannigan (let's see . . . how about that she's a willowy, whispery Damien Rice acolyte floating around and twittering on about birds, bees and how best to offset your carbon footprint) will be well and truly upended by *Sea Sew*, her debut album.

That's not to say, of course, that Hannigan shatters certain assumptions by coming across as, for example, a mixture of a potty-mouthed Alanis Morissette and a raw, randy confessional Liz Phair. In fact, what Hannigan is here is something else altogether. Indeed, she avoids the pitfalls of your archetypal female singer-songwriter by sidestepping the blatantly obvious and instead follows a sporadically cracked yet less-travelled path.

Simply put, the song arrangements on *Sea Sew* are brilliant. As mentioned, Hannigan avoids the traditional approach, the like of which can instantly date even the best songsmiths. Rather, she filters the melodies as if through a prism; these highly defined tunes are as tough as granite and as durable as a Japanese car engine.

By avoiding the tried and tested (while at the same time browsing through the back catalogue of artists like Joanna Newsom), Hannigan has, at the very least, raised the bar for her peers and contemporaries and set a new benchmark for aspiring creative singer-songwriter types.

Hannigan's lyrics here are also grade A: she subtly gets to the nub of matters emotional and romantic in a manner that is both fanciful and truthful. Lines such as 'I spoon you into my coffee cup, spin you through a delicate wash, and wear you all day' ('An Ocean and a Rock') and 'I don't know if you write letters or if you panic on the phone – I'd like to call you all the same. If you want to, I am game' ('I Don't Know') highlight a frisky yet intuitive mind at work, rest and play. It is this blend of playfulness and stealth that makes *Sea Sew* such a startling achievement.

As for Hannigan herself? There are too many singer-songwriters around these days that are ten-a-cent and often quite dull. With this album, in all its calm, hippy-ish glory, Hannigan is the full Euro, and as exciting as a creative proposition can be.

Released: 2008
Record Label: Hoop Recordings
Producer: Jason Boshoff
Recorded at: The Cauldron Studios, Dublin
Sleeve Design: Lisa and Frances Hannigan
(knitwork), Conor & David (paper surround)

Tracks:
1 Ocean and a Rock **4:21**
2 Venn Diagram **4:20**
3 Sea Song **3:23**
4 Splishy Splashy **3:16**
5 I Don't Know **4:56**

6 Keep It All **4:11**
7 Courting Blues **4:06**
8 Pistachio **3:25**
9 Teeth **3:08**
10 Lille **4:06**

GLEN HANSARD & MARKÉTA IRGLOVÁ
THE SWELL SEASON (2006)

GLEN HANSARD

'This record is made up of the first fruits from my collaboration and friendship with Markéta Irglová, and it meant a lot to us for a few reasons. John Carney had asked me to write some songs for his film, *Busker*, which later became *Once*... But it was also my first step away from The Frames, and an exciting detour which stripped the songs bare and let them breathe with their own life, piano, guitar, voices and some strings. It felt fresh and alive and was recorded fast, within five days. It was also the cheapest record I'd made and was recorded in Prague; the sensibility of the recording technique and language barrier with the engineer meant that the whole session was very intuitive. The artwork is simply photos I took of Markéta and photos she took of me. It was a deeply personal and introspective time, and I'm proud of that record.'

It's the name of the album, it's the name of the band, and it's the name of Josef Skvorecky's 1975 novel. But it's also a love story, and one that was subsequently referenced in the 2007 Oscar-winning movie *Once*. In that low-budget film, Glen Hansard (lead singer with The Frames, see page 82) played a struggling Dublin musician who fell tenderly, shyly in love with an eastern European immigrant flower-seller (Markéta Irglová). Their advancing relationship was played out to a backdrop of writing and recording songs that you soon realised weren't really going to go places, yet this didn't take away from the fact that the music was impossibly romantic: a love affair unsure of itself but willing to explore whatever possibilities came its way.

And so the album *The Swell Season* became the name of the band, and the guy and girl characters in *Once* (which, along with earlier albums by The Frames, features songs from this album) became real-life lovers. If you're looking for happy endings, read a Barbara Cartland novel or watch a Disney movie. If, however, you're searching for a record (and never mind if the album cover looks like it has been ripped from *The Book of Worst Album Covers of All Time*) that mixes elements of real love and real life with music that, yes, swells with the swift rise of a lump to the throat, then pull up a chair, pour yourself two

fingers of Jack, and wallow.

'We made a plan that was subject to change, so whatever way it works out we both get the blame', sings Hansard on the opening track 'This Low', a song so gorgeously mellow you feel ripe by the end of it. It's followed by 'Sleeping', wherein Hansard distills a level of regret about an episode of lost temper and questions a supposedly unshakeable relationship that ends because of it. Like most tracks on this record, the pace and delivery are understated, the musicianship assured and elegantly displayed (including Marja Tuhkanen on violin and Bertrand Galen on cello), the themes coherent, the sentiment trustworthy.

The centrepiece for many is the Academy Award-winning 'Falling Slowly', where, in harmony, Hansard and Irglová's voices epitomise the faltering steps of being sucked into a relationship from which there seems no way out. Yet songs such as 'Lies', 'When Your Mind's Made Up', the piano/strings instrumental title track, and Irglová's noble end-of-the-day 'Alone Apart' match 'Falling Slowly's endgame drama note for note. An authentic love song is difficult to dislike; two fistfuls of them makes it impossible to do so. Resistance is futile: submit, then, without shame or guilt.

GLEN HANSARD and MARKETA IRGLOVA
THE SWELL SEASON
with MARJA TUHKANEN and BERTRAND GALEN

Released: 2006
Record Label: Overcoat Recordings
Producer: Glen Hansard, Markéta Irglová
Recorded at: Sono Studio, Prague
Sleeve Design: Banjo

Tracks:
1 This Low **4:55**
2 Sleeping **3:38**
3 Falling Slowly **4:51**
4 Drown Out **5:38**
5 Lies **3:58**
6 When Your Mind's Made Up **3:59**
7 The Swell Season **2:56**
8 Leave **3:20**
9 The Moon **4:43**
10 Alone Apart **4:49**

GEMMA HAYES
THE ROADS DON'T LOVE YOU (2005)

'The title of the album is taken from a Magnetic Fields song called "Long Vermont Road". I felt quite displaced around this time. I was travelling from Dublin to France to the US a lot and never really settling anywhere. I heard this song and had to steal that line (well, I asked eventually . . .). *The Roads Don't Love You* took me three years to write! Funnily enough, it was released for only three weeks before I was dropped, and the album was shelved. I begged to get it back, as I had worked so hard on it, but it didn't happen. For that reason, though, the record still seems fresh to me. I never got the chance to exhaust it every night at gigs. Sadly, I don't own a copy anymore. I keep meaning to track one down, as it's an album I'm very proud of. I feel I can stand beside every song.'

There has always been a touch of class about Gemma Hayes. From her 2002 debut, *Night On My Side*, to this subtle yet innately exciting record, she has shown what needs to be done to ensure that melancholia is given a renewed lease of life and sense of purpose.

So, yes, she rocks the glee/glum equation with ease (and, yes, there actually is a song called 'Happy Sad' here), but also with a level of style and quality that will always easily mark her out as one of Ireland's best songwriters. That she has never gained the kind of commercial success that is bestowed on lesser songwriters and performers is down to her self-confessed weird side. And it's true: just when you think a song of hers will go down the middle of the road, along comes an errant guiding hand on the steering wheel to drag it into the ditch. It's quite remarkable, then, that even in the ditch the songs survive.

Ironically, *The Roads Don't Love You* was almost killed at birth. Following the success of *Night On My Side* (which, among other plaudits, nabbed a Mercury Prize nomination), Hayes experienced a bout of creative tiredness so debilitating that she regarded her guitar as no longer a comfort but a leech. There was, it would become all too apparent to her, more noise in her world than she could cope with, and so she retreated to a rented house in rural Ireland, went for walks, read books, watched television, picked up the guitar tentatively, and effectively started all over again.

The Roads Don't Love You, then, was created out of a cleansing period in Hayes's life, and while it comes across face-scrubbed and fresh, you can't delete personality or creative DNA. So songs such as 'Another for the Darkness', 'Easy on the Eye', 'Undercover', 'Something In My Way' and 'Horses' (to mention just five) achieve the intent of their creator by being effortlessly melodic (there's a waft of Joni Mitchell here and there) while simultaneously being just that little bit dissonant.

Other, far more famous songwriters have tried to blend smooth with stubble but have ended up sounding false and facile – as well as looking decidedly frazzled. Gemma Hayes does all of this without putting a hair on her head out of place. She is, without question, the real deal, a class act, and one of the very few songwriters around who can assure people that – despite the traceable scars of connective tissue – there is a world of difference between misery (her incorrectly perceived default setting) and melancholia.

GEMMA HAYES
THE ROADS DON'T
LOVE
YOU

Released: 2005
Record Label: Source Records (Virgin/EMI)
Producer: Gary Oldham, Gemma Hayes,
Joey Waronker
Recorded at: Blackbox Studios, France;
Westland Studios, Dublin
Sleeve Design: Max Dodson (photography)

Tracks:
1 Two Step **4:04**
2 Another for the Darkness **3:48**
3 Happy Sad **4:19**
4 Easy on the Eye **3:55**
5 Keep Me Here **4:12**
6 Undercover **4:09**

7 Nothing Can **4:49**
8 Helen **3:29**
9 Something In My Way **4:05**
10 Horses **4:08**
11 Tomorrow **2:44**

Gemma Hayes – © Nathalie Marquez Courtney.

MARTIN HAYES & DENIS CAHILL
LIVE IN SEATTLE (1999)

MARTIN HAYES

'This recording was made in response to requests from fans who felt that our live performances were very different from the studio recordings. In the studio we don't perform a recording from beginning to end; we stop, we may make another attempt, we examine and we look back. The music we play in concert is different because it's shaped by the acoustics and the atmosphere of the venue, the musical dialogue with the audience, and the gathering energy of a performance. Our response to the new situation each night creates a different energy and produces different music. Though this recording is more than a few years old I think it still gives a good sense of how we play in concert.'

Irish traditional music played in formal surroundings is something of a contradiction in, well, if not terms, then certainly in context. This is music, remember, that luxuriates, teases, and then sprints in the intimate surroundings of a pub, where in winter the fire is sparking, and where whistles are played and whetted.

So how, then, do Martin Hayes and Dennis Cahill manage the apparently insurmountable task of making a performance in a small theatre space (the Tractor Tavern) in Seattle sound like they're playing a gig in the back room of a cosy bar in County Clare? Probably because, as Hayes writes in the sleeve notes, 'our primary wish is that the musical experience be one that lifts our spirits and those of the audience'.

Hayes knows about such things. His background in Feakle, east County Clare, and the knowledge of traditional music handed down to him by his father (the late P. Joe Hayes, founding member of the highly influential Tulla Céilí Band) instilled in him a love and knowledge of the genre that seeps from every one of his fiddle-playing fingertips. Hayes took this experience to America in the eighties, where he experimented with other musics (contemporary classical, jazz, scores) while still retaining unbreakable links with the music of his native county. *Live in Seattle* plays to these enduring strengths while simultaneously never undermining them.

The most brilliant aspect of the playing here is that both Hayes and Chicago guitarist Cahill ably resist the temptation to magnify their creative impulses. So while Hayes, in particular, effortlessly steals the show with a tremendous, tactful fluidity, there is nothing boastful about his performance. The opening track, Martin Rochford's 'Green Gowned Lass', is a sweet-natured template of things to come. Lock the doors and switch off the lights, then, for the eleven-titled, interweaving second track. At almost thirty minutes, this is regarded as the majestic centrepiece of the album, and rightly so: this suite of reels, dances and slow tunes includes the delicate 'Kilnamona Barndance' and 'P. Joe's Pecurious Pachelbel Special' – Hayes's rakish take on Pachelbel's 'Canon in D Minor'.

For a 'live' album, this is especially respectful to both musicians and audience: there is no easy rehashing of old material, and if you didn't hear occasional whoops from the latter, you'd swear it was a studio recording. But it's more than that: here is an album fashioned by experts who are empathetic to each other's rhythmic ways and moods, and who each understand that soul, heart and vision are as much pivotal elements of the listening experience as the music itself.

martin **HAYES**
dennis **CAHILL**
LIVE in seattle

Released: 1999
Record Label: Green Linnet Records
Producer: Martin Hayes, Dennis Cahill,
Helen Bommarito (assistant producer)
Recorded at: The Tractor Tavern, Seattle
Sleeve Design: Greenberg Kingsley, Giorgia
Bertazzi (photography)

Tracks:

1 Martin Rochford's/Green Gowned Lass
   3:54
2 Port na bPucai/Kilnamona Barndance/
   Ship In Full Sail/jer The Rigger/The
   Old Blackthorn/Exile of Erin/Humours
   of Tulla/Fitzgerald's Hornpipe/Rakish
   Paddy/Finbarr Dwyer's Reel No. 1/P

Joe's Pecurious Pachelbel Special
27:39
3 Carraroe/Out on the Ocean **4:47**
4 Mary McMahon of Ballinahinch/Miss
   Lyon's **4:25**
5 Dowd's No 9/Come West Along the
   Road **5:53**

DAVID HOLMES

THE HOLY PICTURES (2008)

DAVID HOLMES

'In theory, this album really started when I lost my mum . . . My mum was so supportive of everything I did. She used to stay up till two in the morning listening to my mixes on Pete Tong and tell me how great they were. She would go to visit family in Chicago and bring boxes of hard-core dance music back for me: soul, rhythm and blues. Suddenly you realise that you've taken your parents for granted your whole life . . . I was in the studio six weeks after my father died and I thought, right, I'm going to try to encapsulate these emotions and put them into the music . . . In a way, I wanted to create a document that immortalised my parents, that I could keep forever.' *Belfast Telegraph*, September 2008

Question: when does a producer turn around perceptions about what they do (in non-musician language, this essentially means tinkering with sound, twiddling recording studio knobs, pushing/pulling fader switches, and suggesting to musicians young and old that it might be better to approach their songs in ways that they're not used to) and make people view them in a completely different light? Answer: when you're David Holmes. Of course, Holmes – who once worked as a barber and a chef – is also a remixer/DJ, which means that when he isn't reworking music by the likes of U2, Primal Scream, Manic Street Preachers and Doves, he is judiciously dropping tracks in one nightclub or another around the world. With *The Holy Pictures*, however (his second proper solo album, following 2000's *Bow Down to the Exit Sign*), Holmes added something else altogether to his impressive list of achievements: he proved he was a genuine songwriter.

We know him to be someone to whom filmmakers entrust their soundtracks (Holmes has soundtracked the likes of *Out Of Sight*, *Ocean's Eleven*, *Twelve* and *Thirteen*, *Hunger*, and *Code 46*), so he's well versed in how to synchronise the visual with the aural. In *The Holy Pictures*, however, he utilises a heretofore-hidden sense of remarkably streamlined melodies and a heartfelt, personal and distinctly visual lyricism ('All songs painted and produced by David Holmes', it says on the back of the album sleeve) that he had never previously been thought capable of. In short, it's an album less about Holmes's exemplary record collection, and more about Holmes and home, about the significance of memory and the importance of upbringing, of background and family. (It's dedicated to the memory of his mother, Sarah, who died in 1996, just prior to his international career taking off, and his father, Jack, who died in 2007.)

Utilising a smart mixture of pop, rock, ambient, stoned-psychedelia and Krautrock, the album starts off brilliantly with 'I Heard Wonders' (co-written by Suicide's Martin Rev, and featuring Holmes singing for the first time, in a breathy, underplayed manner) and goes on to mesh guitars and synthesizers, ambience, collages and drones that bring to mind a Falls Road cocktail of Stereolab, Can, Jesus & Mary Chain, Brian Eno, Spiritualized, Stone Roses and My Bloody Valentine.

Textured throughout with Holmes's unerring sense of instrumentation, tracks such as 'Love Reign Over Me', 'Holy Pictures', 'Kill Her with Kindness', 'Hey Maggy', 'Birth' and 'The Ballad of Sarah & Jack' usher in a new form of beauty: a dusky collection as emotive as it is conceptually cohesive. Life, death, parents, children, and coming to terms with them all. A soundtrack to the soul – it doesn't get more personal than that, does it?

Released: 2008

Record Label: Go! Beat, Mercury, Canderblinks

Producer: David Holmes

Recorded at: Drama Studios, Belfast; Echo Records, Los Angeles

Sleeve Design: Andy Votel, Keith Connolly, David Holmes

Tracks:
1 I Heard Wonders **5:35**
2 The Story of the Ink **5:22**
3 Love Reign Over Me **3:47**
4 Theme / I.M.C. **3:55**
5 Holy Pictures **5:19**
6 Kill Her with Kindness **4:03**
7 Melanie **3:59**
8 Hey Maggy **4:58**
9 Birth **1:07**
10 The Ballad of Sarah and Jack **4:29**

THE HORMONES
WHERE OLD GHOSTS MEET (1999)

MARC CARROLL

'Listening to the songs, I hear the voice of a confused, sometimes angry but always sincere young man. If anything, I am sincere when it comes to music and my approach to it. In some way I think back and wonder if I even knew what I was doing, whether I knew how to write a song – but, of course, that's just in hindsight. Experience changes everything. I'm listening to me at a time of uncertainty, fear, insecurity, sadness, sorrow – desperate, directionless – looking for approval, but from whom I don't know.'

Elsewhere in this book we'll meet Marc Carroll (see page 40), but The Hormones is the band he was in before he embarked on a superb solo career. The band – the name referenced Manchester's Buzzcocks' indie record label, New Hormones – was formed in the mid-nineties, following the demise of Carroll's first (Dublin-based) group, Puppy Love Bomb.

Finding himself in London, somewhat adrift but eager for a new start, Carroll set about honing a collection of songs that he had wholly written and part-demo'd in Dublin. If there's a certain naive us-against-them stance about the songs, then put it down to Carroll's teenage outlook and the often stultifying attitudes of an essentially parochial Dublin music scene. And yet it's impossible to deny what might turn out to be your most important memories (upbringing, close friends, school, family, lost girlfriends), and so rather than reference his new life in London, Carroll instead focused on Dublin. The results are quite possibly the richest and most resonant songs about growing up, reaching out and going away you'll ever hear.

Despite a professed dislike of dredging up recollections ('Memory you are a curse, you bring hell upon my life' sings Carroll in 'A House by the Hill'), he eloquently evokes less problematic times of him and his mates raising merry hell and knowing it all ('All We Thought': 'Meet at the disco and get in if allowed, and then kicked out again because of a row. Walking home discussing our teachers, we had a head-on conclusion that they were the jokers'), of self-alienation and self-belief ('Feel Alright': 'You see, I like it on the outside, never in with all the rest, because the words of many wise men say, winners shine through best') and of hero worship ('Mr Wilson': 'I love you and I thank you, Mr Wilson, Mr Cool').

Thematically, then, it's a reverie of remembrance, regret and pure emotions. Musically, it's a declaration of ringing guitars that, while touching on obvious reference points such as The Byrds and Teenage Fanclub, remains true and distinct. But there is also a potent folk-ballad influence ('Dig Like Merry Hell', which mentions Brendan Behan, 'drunken madmen' and church bells, was structured by Carroll as if The Ramones jammed with The Dubliners for a few hours) that displays Carroll's cultural, natural skill for a well-written narrative song.

What next? Despite signing to V2, and a potential career-changing appearance on television romcom show *Friends* (The Hormones were the wedding band at the nuptials of Ross's wedding), music industry politics scuppered *Where Old Ghosts Meet*. The day after the album was released, it was promptly deleted, and The Hormones dropped. Which is where we came in . . .

the hormones
WHERE OLD GHOSTS MEET

Released: 1999
Record Label: V2 Music
Producer: Steve Power
Recorded at: Great Linford Manor; Mayfair & Battery Studios, London
Sleeve Design: Rob Crane at Satellite, Dorothea Lange (photography front and back cover)

Tracks:
1 Stay Ahead 3:44
2 Don't Let Them Get You Down 3:59
3 This Is The Sound 3:45
4 Radio Stars 4:14
5 Mr Wilson 3:35
6 A House By The Hill 3:59
7 All We Thought 3:44
8 Dig Like Merry Hell 4:40
9 Someplace Somewhere 3:32
10 The Kisser 3:18
11 Feel Alright 3:35
12 Where Old Ghosts Meet 3:33

HORSLIPS

THE BOOK OF INVASIONS: A CELTIC SYMPHONY (1976)

BARRY DEVLIN

'*The Book of Invasions* as a title had been lurking for a while . . . Someone (it may even have been me) suggested a symphonic thing – a Celtic symphony – and Eamon mooted doing it in the three Celtic movements: *geantraí, goltraí, suantraí.* So we had a notion of scale, scope, a modus operandi, but no subject yet – until Eamon's special-interest subject reared its head again: the arrival of the first peoples on these islands . . . When Johnny Fean and Jim Lockhart noodled what was to become "Trouble with a Capital 'T'" before a gig, we were on our way . . . We recorded it, and that autumn were back on the road in, well, jig time? I'll get my coat . . .'

Formed in 1970, Horslips (Charles O'Connor, Jim Lockhart, Eamon Carr, Barry Devlin and Declan Sinnott – the latter was subsequently replaced by Johnny Fean) turned professional on St Patrick's Day, 1972, simultaneously releasing their debut single, 'Johnny's Wedding'.

The idea of Horslips (the name a play on words on the Four Horsemen of the Apocalypse) came about more through happenstance than anything else. They didn't have a master plan to bring a rock sensibility to Irish traditional music, yet neither was the band's existence accidental. (The backgrounds of at least three of the band's members – Charles O'Connor, Jim Lockhart and Declan Sinnott – were rooted in Irish music from Seamus Ennis to Seán Ó Riada, the latter a notable influence – see page 142; Eamon Carr was immersed in Irish history and folklore.)

Having rebuffed offers of interest from major record companies such as Transatlantic and Chrysalis, the band released their debut album, *Happy To Meet . . . Sorry To Part* on their own label, Oats, in 1973. Combining authentic traditional music with electric instrumentation, Horslips can justifiably lay claim to having invented Celtic rock. They also gave Ireland's then city slickers and country cousins an identity in terms of an indigenous music they could actually relate to. In short, the band was an antidote to a peculiarly Irish malaise in the early seventies – a youth culture stifled by the twin forces of conservatism and tradition. Also, unlike other Irish bands of the era (notably Thin Lizzy), Horslips decided to crack the national market before attempting the UK and beyond. It was this that warranted their acceptance as a 'people's band': they were genuine travelling folk/rock heroes, bringing their amped-up jigs, reels, riffs, lights, smoke bombs, satin suits (curtain and sofa material from a Dublin homeware store, remodelled/refashioned by Jim Lockhart's wife!) and shamrock-shaped guitars from Bantry to Bundoran, from Clifden to Clogherhead.

Come 1976, the band began to devise a conceptual collection of songs that would comprise their most ambitious, original and successful album. In a nutshell, *The Book of Invasions* – the title is taken from a twelfth-century manuscript that documented (or mythologised?) the birth of Celtic consciousness in Ireland – triumphantly merged such information with an urbane stream of Celtic rock. Constantly overreaching itself, the album was an audacious undertaking that worked on many levels. Split into three movements, in essence the music constitutes a nigh-on perfect integration of prog rock, folk, rock 'n' roll and traditional music – in the latter area, certainly, the level of use of whistle, fiddle, flute, concertina and mandolin was unprecedented for the time. The defining band of Celtic rock. The defining album, too.

Released: 1976
Record Label: Horslips Records (Ireland), DJM Records (Worldwide)
Producer: Alan O'Duffy, Horslips
Recorded at: Lombard Sound Studios, Dublin; Miracle Studios
Sleeve Design: Charles O'Connor, Eric G. Bannister (original artwork)

Tracks:
1 Daybreak **2:30**
2 March Into Trouble **0:51**
3 Trouble (With a Capital T) **3:24**
4 The Power and the Glory **3:56**
5 The Rocks Remain **2:49**
6 Dusk **0:37**
7 Sword of Light **4:55**

8 Dark **1:37**
9 Warm Sweet Breath of Love **3:26**
10 Fantasia (My Lagan Love) **2:55**
11 King of Morning, Queen of Day **4:32**
12 Sideways to the Sun **4:47**
13 Drive the Cold Winter Away **2:35**
14 Ride to Hell **4:07**

NINA HYNES

STAROS (2002)

NINA HYNES

'*Staros* was a coming of age and a breaking point for me. Everything around it led to a breakdown of sorts, and my feelings are complicated for this record. They are tied up with my ex-manager/label and a sour relationship that developed very soon after the release. I don't own a copy, and I don't earn a cent from it. I still love the record, though, and the artwork is really special. *Staros* meant everything to me, but it kind of feels like someone stole my lover and tied him up in a room, blindfolded and gagged, and locked the door. Maybe I'll find the key again someday.'

You'll be very pleased to know that Nina Hynes isn't just another identikit singer-songwriter. Oh no. There are (excuse me) at least fifty-seven varieties of this particular Hynes, each one wrapped up in a song that has spread across her debut (mini) album, 1999's *Creation*, and *Staros*, her second.

An interesting, petite figure with a bustling, busking background, Hynes is the youngest of ten; her parents once ran O'Donoghue's pub (in Dublin's Merrion Row), once the famous breeding ground for The Dubliners and other Irish folk talents, so you could safely say that from an early age she wasn't unaware of musical instruments.

Busking in Paris, spending quiet time in Donegal, where she stayed mostly indoors writing songs and painting – if you're getting an impression of Hynes as a focused figure with an individual streak, then you're on the right track. Her early material was ungainly, sombre, a tad gloomy.

So where does *Staros* come from? Where do wonderful, light-headed but serious songs such as 'The Other Side of Now', 'Last Song of the 20th Century', 'Time Flies', 'Universal', 'Swallow', 'Mono Prix', 'Zhivago Blue' and the title track come from?

The brilliance of *Staros*, and these songs, is that they naturalistically blend observations of real, everyday life with something a tad more abstract. The album teems with lengthy café eavesdropping on other people's conversations, personal relationships, reading newspapers, listening to the news and – plain and simple, and mundane, but true – just watching the world go by. Are there occasionally too many ideas in the same song fighting for their life? Yes ('Tenderness', for example), but better that, surely, than too few scrapping for supremacy.

Musically, it's inventive, melodic, mellow, trippy indie pop/folk (The Frames (see separate entry, page 82) assist throughout; like quite a number of Irish albums in the noughties, *Staros* is produced by former Frames member David Odlum) that mixes strings and samples with horn arrangements, electro bleeps and a beating heart so full of emotion it almost bursts.

It's all a bit rough and ready – the overt pop tunes, for example, have a crunchy garage sensibility – but the overall and ultimate mood-altering feeling you get here is that Hynes has scored a direct hit to the head with heavy hints of idealism and firm touches of a truthful person trying to make sense of a crazy world.

Released: 2002
Record Label: Reverb Records
Producer: David Odlum, Nina Hynes, Steve
Osbourne (additional production)
Recorded at: Black Box Studios, France
Sleeve Design: Pete Reddy, Redman AKA

Tracks:
1 Time Flies **3:39**
2 Mono Prix **3:37**
3 Universal **3:49**
4 The Other Side of Now **3:10**
5 The Last Song of the 20th Century
   3:08

6 Tenderness **5:52**
7 Shine **2:56**
8 Swallow **2:33**
9 Dive **4:35**
10 Zhivago Blue **4:23**
11 Now **4:45**
12 Staros **4:24**

JAPE

COSMOSPHERE (2003)

RICHIE EGAN

'At the time of making *Cosmosphere* I had just started to play solo gigs, and had no idea about how I wanted to sound. The gigs would sometimes be hilariously ramshackle, and I tended to think every crazy idea that came into my head was worth pursuing. This quixotic spontaneity is reflected in the album: it's very much the sound of somebody trying to find their feet when they don't even know where their legs are.'

We all have lofty ambitions, before life comes along to either kick us in the teeth or help us on our way. When Richie Egan started playing a musical instrument in the early nineties, as into Nirvana and Black Flag as any teenager was back then, he wanted to be a big star – even though he admits that he was writing the worst of songs on a four-track, and creating lyrics about topics as illuminating as collecting dead flies.

Over time, though, as any good musician knows, the focus changes to why you play music. Possibly after a period of ups, downs and in-betweens, music turns into a crutch that you need. Gradually, the realisation lands, like a partner telling you across a crystal-clear phone line that you're dumped: you actually can't live without them. The tipping point for a musician comes when you do it because you need to do it, have to do it, rather than just want to do it. Richie Egan knows all about having to, needing to – the must instead of the should.

Cosmosphere is Egan's first album under the guise of Jape (which has advanced from being a one-time side project to something far more long-lasting, having gradually replaced his role in Dublin band The Redneck Manifesto (see separate entry, page 162). Where Redneck Manifesto can be vaguely defined as a post-rock outfit, Egan's solo work is somewhat more classically educated in the art of pop/rock – a little bit alt-folk, a little bit odd singer-songwriter, a little bit smooth laptop, a little bit jittery electronica.

Throughout its brief but mesmerising thirty-three minutes, *Cosmosphere* shows Egan's experimental side and sense of purpose with swooshing, stoner folk ('Into Lines', 'Wishful Thinking'), groovy-spooky workouts ('Haunt Me'), pulsating 8-bit electronics ('Nilsson'), wonky vocoder/guitar solo freakouts ('I Don't Know' – think robots dropping the hand on Peter Frampton), proper weird introspection ('All My Friends': 'my head is still foolishly twisted towards a world I don't fully believe in', Egan sings mournfully) and funny-bone tunes ('When You've Lost All Your Looks'). The title track, meanwhile, unhurriedly travels the distance from slow walk to gentle stroll, and is one of the loveliest slices of electronica you'll hear.

Among the album's many other pleasures, you will also detect bits and pieces of Stereolab, Kraftwerk and Yo La Tengo. If you have any sense (and we know you have), you'll recognise *Cosmosphere* for what it is: the first, most naive (perhaps) yet most charming opening salvo from one of the best Irish songwriters of recent times.

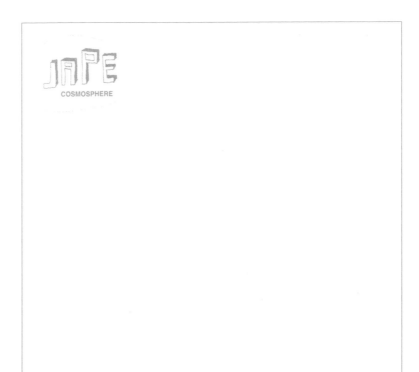

Released: 2003
Record Label: Volta Sounds
Producer: Karl Odlum, Aidan Foley
Recorded at: Niall B's house, Avoca,
Wicklow
Sleeve Design: My Brain Design

Tracks:
1 Cosmosphere **5:33**
2 Into Lines **5:09**
3 Wishful Thinking **3:28**
4 Haunt Me **3:22**
5 Nilsson **3:51**

6 I Don't Know **4:24**
7 All Your Friends **4:18**
8 When You've Lost All Your Looks
   3:00

JUNO FALLS

WEIGHTLESS (2007)

MYLES O'REILLY

'Weightless was the culmination of many years finding my feet creatively. I put everything I had into it. So much so that I had nothing left, and very little steam, to keep going after some pretty hard-grind promotion. The record started as a major-label project with a decent budget and international release prospects, but ended with just my manager and me trying our very hardest to keep sales alive from behind the merch desk at gigs. From a bang to a whimper.'

Imagine a songwriter being told by their mother that she knew more about them from their lyrics than she ever did from them on a one-to-one basis. Imagine being signed to a major label – the same label your favourite band, Elbow, is on – and being told by them in a small hotel bar in, of all places, Dingle, that the label was on its way to ruination? From caring, disappointed if enlightened mothers to pragmatic, beer-drinking harbingers of doom – for Juno Falls it has been a long, strange, frustrating trip.

If there are a few genuinely lost gems in this book, then *Weightless* by Juno Falls (aka Myles O'Reilly) is unquestionably one of them. O'Reilly first came to notice in 2004 with an album called *Starlight Drive*. It was a pretty if austere affair that attracted interest and proposals from major labels, one of whom (V2) he eventually signed to. There was a misconception about Juno Falls, however, that initially proved hard to shake: they were lumped in with a batch of acoustic artists who in part (and not wholly of their own making) formed what was known as the New Acoustic Movement. In other words, these artists made attractive, gentle music that wouldn't scare either horses or children.

Weightless falls into this category, but its back-story is fascinating, as well as being harsh-but-true. O'Reilly's record label, in their wisdom, had him working with producers in London and Nashville, all to no avail. He ended up – after a spate of 'words' from V2's A&R office

– in Wicklow, in the house of the album's engineer and producer, Ken McHugh. Here, for three months, crazed by attention to detail and consumed by each and every note, *Weightless* came together.

In keeping with the title, the songs have an airiness about them that belies their substance. 'Atom Bomb' muses on the human race's uncanny ability to regularly push the self-destruct button ('If God wants a storm he'll get it in a flash'); 'Slowly Fizzy' takes its inspiration from Crowded House's adultery tune, 'Into Temptation', with O'Reilly's cheating heart fully on display ('Shame burning me down to sorry, sorry ashes'); 'The Boy Whose Skin Fell Off' is biography-cum-tragedy ('I wasn't made like anybody else, production line faltered this once'); 'This Song Is Your Own', meanwhile, is a perfect example of how truly significant pop songs can often carry the most simple messages. Every song is transported by exceptionally harmonic music, which is itself enhanced by some of the best-ever strings for a pop song (sometimes deliriously dissonant, sometimes straight-up delightful) by classical musician Corus Venus Lunny.

The result is substantial, layered pop/folk that, by rights, should have been a multi-million seller. Alas, it wasn't to be, and Elbow were right: just as *Weightless* was released, V2 underwent a major refit, and the album, as if cursed, disappeared from view.

Released: 2007
Record Label: V2 Music Ireland
Producer: Ken McHugh
Recorded at: My Sanctuary Studios, Wicklow
Sleeve Design: Myles O'Reilly

Tracks:
1 This Song Is Your Own **3:55**
2 The Opposite Of Everything **3:33**
3 Atom Bomb **3:58**
4 A Melody Ten Years Long **3:43**
5 Slowly Fizzy **4:29**
6 The Boy Whose Skin Fell Off **3:59**
7 Waxworks **3:21**
8 Nova Scotia **4:36**
9 Dapper Dan **3:38**
10 Double The Part Of One **4:06**

LUKE KELLY

THE DEFINITIVE COLLECTION (2010)

'When he sang at his best, he was like a combination of Dickens and Joyce – and all that's best about Ireland . . . He was soft, warm and personable in his singing . . . And when Luke was singing a good song, you could feel the hair rise on the back of your neck.' Quoted in *Luke Kelly: A Memoir* by Des Geraghty

Artistic honesty is a rare commodity; we see around us every day a peacock's display of nominal pop and rock stars who sell themselves for a piece of the action. Luke Kelly, just as well known for his solo work as for being a member of The Dubliners, began his career in a different era, of course, but the song (as the saying goes) remains the same: he could have sweetened his life by responding to probing questions with feeble answers, but instead he opted for the truth.

He was born in Dublin in 1940, and left school at thirteen; in 1958 he went to England, where he worked with his brother on a building site in Wolverhampton. Within two years he had travelled around the north of England, visiting folk clubs in Newcastle-upon-Tyne and Leeds, feeding into the folk revival that was under way. His interest in folk music was kindled by his involvement in left-wing politics, which in turn inspired songwriters such as Ewan MacColl and Peggy Seeger to write insightful, politically motivated material.

All of these influences were fermenting in Kelly's mind in and around 1960-62; the development of his political leanings, however, proved to be his strongest cultural ally, as his increasing commitment to left-wing ideologies gave his material a sharpness and confidence that would have neutered less capable performers. He returned to Dublin from London in 1962, and joined The Dubliners; he left that band – and Ireland – in 1964 to return to London, where he became involved in MacColl's so-called Critics Collective, which grew out of MacColl

and Seeger's famous Singers' Club, and was formed specifically to develop songwriting and singing potential. It was here that Kelly – who considered MacColl to be the greatest single influence in his musical evolution – came into his own as an interpretative singer.

Kelly never released a bona fide solo album (although he released a solo single, a fine version of The Kinks' 'Days', included here), so all that remains in album form are compilations. Some are shoddy and lack integrity, but this is the best, most representative and well packaged we've come across. Depending on your tolerance for folk music, and songs that start with the words 'As I roved out', you'll either engage with or retreat from the form, but it's a very foolhardy person indeed that will not warm to the likes of The Dubliners trad/arr tracks 'Maids When You're Young Never Wed an Old Man', 'Paddy on the Railway' and 'The Black Velvet Band'.

These aside (and boisterously enjoyable though they are), the heart and soul of Kelly surely resides in the likes of the peerless 'Raglan Road', 'Scorn Not His Simplicity', 'The Town I Loved So Well', 'Dirty Old Town' and – quite likely his finest moment – 'The Springhill Mining Disaster'. Written by the likes of Seeger, MacColl, Phil Coulter and (in the case of the poem 'Raglan Road') Patrick Kavanagh, these songs dwell in Kelly as much as he dwells in them. He remains a crucial cultural treasure whose legacy never devalued the importance of a political song.

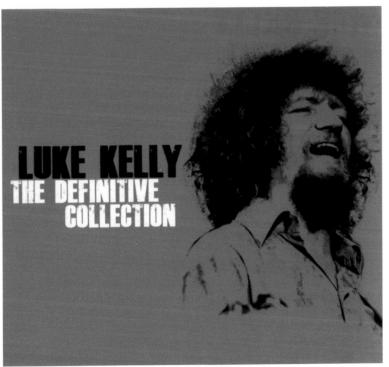

Released: 2010 **Record Label:** Celtic Airs
Producer: Various **Recorded by:** Various
Sleeve Design: Philip Melly (design), Brian
Shuel (photography)

Tracks: Disc 1:
1 Thank You For the Days **2:39**
2 Farewell To Carlingford **2:59**
3 Murshin Durkin **2:31**
4 Scorn Not His Simplicity **3:39**
5 The Gartan Mother's Lullaby **2:43**
6 Peggy Gordon **3:28**
7 The Maid of the Sweet Brown Knowe
   2:06
8 Kelly the Boy From Killane **2:49**
9 The Travelling People **3:54**
10 Go To Sea No More **4:11**
11 The Net Hauling Song **2:15**

12 The Sun is Burning **3:34**
13 Alabama **3:00**
14 The Auld Triangle **2:57**
15 For What Died the Sons of Róisín **2:09**
16 Whiskey In the Jar **2:45**
17 The Black Velvet Band **4:31**
18 The Town I Loved So Well **6:24**
19 Joe Hill **2:50**
20 A Song For Ireland **4:43**

Disc 2:
1 Maids When You're Young Never Wed
   an Old Man **3:31**
2 The Rocky Road To Dublin **2:30**
3 The Shoals of Herring **4:55**
4 Paddy On the Railway **2:52**
5 Raglan Road **4:17**

6 Schooldays Over **3:02**
7 The Dundee Weaver **1:27**
8 The Thirty Foot Trailer **3:42**
9 The Banks of the Sweet Primroses
   2:53
10 I Know My Love **2:51**
11 Dirty Old Town **2:53**
12 I'm a Rover **4:54**
13 Tramps and Hawkers **3:01**
14 The Rising of the Moon **2:51**
15 The Galway Races **3:22**
16 The Peat Bog Soldiers **2:33**
17 The Lifeboat Mona **4:07**
18 The Springhill Mining Disaster **4:06**
19 The Night Visiting Song **3:30**
20 The Wild Rover **3:04**

NICK KELLY

BETWEEN TRAPEZES (1997)

NICK KELLY

'When I split The Fat Lady Sings at the start of 1994, my guitars were all sold. I'd become so frustrated and unhappy with the stresses of being in a band that I honestly didn't think I'd ever make music again. I moved back to Dublin from London . . . I wrote a poem every day for a year, and gradually the notion of making another record came up on me very gradually. Much of the writing took place in Luxembourg. I'd just started courting the woman to whom I'm now married when she was posted to the European Court for two years. Hence many long visits to the most boring place in Europe . . . The recording process for *Between Trapezes* could not have been more different to how I'd been used to working with a major-label band. It was recorded over several short sessions, in various tiny studios, spread over nearly two years. I worked with different combinations of musicians and producers whom I hardly knew. I'm still quite astonished that such a ramshackle process produced such a coherent record – but maybe if it had been less hand-to-mouth, it wouldn't have become what I now see as a real opening out and growth in the way in which I write and record.'

One of the many Irish rock contenders in the early 1990s was a band called The Fat Lady Sings. They went through the usual hoops that hundreds before and after them went through: plucked from an independent label, they signed to a major record company – which subsequently ripped out their collective heart and soul in the (vain) search for a hit single.

Frazzled to a crisp by the end of (among other things) yet another energy-sapping meeting about what colour the T-shirts should be (does pink *really* reflect the demographic of their fanbase?), the band's lead singer and main songwriter, Nick Kelly, retired, hermit-like, in 1994. He didn't entirely give up the ghost, however, as his debut solo album proves. (Incidentally, the recording was paid for by more than 300 avid fans, who purchased it months before it was released, thereby funding the costs of pressing the CD). From an independent label to a major record company, and back to a penurious state?

The lack of record company involvement doesn't appear to have had a deleterious effect on *Between Trapezes*; indeed, as has happened more often than not over the years, the sense of liberation for the artist is so intense that the creative juices flow easier and stronger. So it is with Kelly and this often exquisite singer-songwriter album.

In person, and on form, Nick Kelly can talk the legs off a centipede, yet he writes lyrics that are concise and expressively poetic. 'Faint Heart' is a perfect example of Kelly's eloquent, prose-like approach; they will fair make you wonder at the depth of feeling in them: 'There are toys lost in my attic; there is damp in my cellar; my walls don't feel as strong as they should; my windows let in the windy weather; and in its rocking chair, alone, my faint heart waits on the telephone, and you're the only one it's ever wished to give that number to.'

Such remarkable insights are filtered throughout. Other songs, such as 'Republic', 'The Night Cesare Lombroso Met the Elephant Man' and 'Grey and Blue' (one of the best songs you'll ever hear about a relationship turning from sweet to sour) lay true claim to being the most assured, tender and vivid in Irish songwriting.

Released: 1997
Record Label: Self Possessed Records
Producer: Neil MacColl, Mike Roarty, Step
Murray, Nick Kelly
Recorded at: Cannibal Studios, Dublin
Sleeve Design: Adrian Fitz-Simon, Clare
Langan (photography)

Tracks:
1 Faint Heart **5.53**
2 Starving Seed **5.50**
3 Republic **4.31**
4 Lover's Easy to Say **3.24**
5 Crawl **5.21**
6 The Night Cesare Lombroso Met the
   Elephant Man **3.37**
7 Steal **3.44**
8 Tiburon Prayer **5.50**
9 Grey and Blue **4.30**
10 Walking Back to My Heart **5.12**

DAVID KITT

THE BIG ROMANCE (2001)

DAVID KITT

'*The Big Romance* was an extension of *Small Moments*, and most of the songs for this album would have been written almost around the same time. I wanted to keep the feel and sense of what were essentially home recordings, but with a bit of an upgrade. There was a quality, an intimacy, to those home recordings, of one person working alone, that I wanted to maintain . . . A few things about the record have bugged me over the years, but in general I'm surprised at how simple it sounds, and that is where I succeeded, I reckon. I also wanted to maintain the painterly aspects, musically, of *Small Moments*, and I think I did that here.'

Some people just stray from the beaten track – not because they feel they have to in order to satisfy a latent tendency to be on-trend, but just because it best suits their personality. It takes a while to know this, of course – which is why David Kitt was first pitched, or started out, as your average sensitive singer-songwriter. He was nothing of the sort, however, as he (and we) soon found out (despite having to endure audience heckles to 'Cheer up!' while playing support).

It probably helps if you have an academic grounding in music technology. Because that will enable you to record and mix your debut album in your bedroom – which is exactly what Kitt did with his 2000 entry into the fray, *Small Moments*. It was, as the title suggests, full of delicate acoustic folk songs that relied more on evocative, patchouli-soaked communiqués from 1971 than on dramatic, hard-earned statements. Such a languid approach has served him well, but he struck the motherlode with *The Big Romance*, which (as the title once again signposts) references matters of the heart.

The album came at the point in Kitt's career where he leapt from being the Irish indie scene's great white hope to (in the interim period, having signed with a major-ish label) reasonably big-budget could-be. In most cases, acts that graduate from indie to major label go out with guns blazing. Kitt, however, in keeping with his inconspicuous attitude, keeps his powder dry and delivers a collection of naturalistic, almost elemental songs ('Step Outside in the Morning Light', 'Pale Blue Light', 'Strange Light in the Evening', 'Into the Breeze') that come across like a tender and reflective travelogue. The theme of falling in love weaves its way throughout, and it's executed in such a droopy-eyed way. Whether by design or default, though, this is intimate in all the right ways. Opening tracks 'Song from Hope St. (Brooklyn NY)' and 'You Know What I Want To Know' set the scene (beats, melodies, unhurried delivery), but its subsequent tracks raise the pleasure principles.

'Pale Blue Light' is skittish (Kittish, even), with bits of Brian Eno and Henry Cow crossed with John Martyn; the album's centrepiece, 'What I Ask', mes-merises with a lyrical mantra (co-sung by Kitt and Nina Hynes (see page 110)) that bobs on waves of softly sung harmonies. Midway, it changes to chirrupy guitar lines and further lyric-repeats until it fades out, leaving you wondering whether you've just heard Mogwai, Cocteau Twins and Joy Division sharing their vision of the future. It gets better: 'Strange Light in the Evening' segues into 'Whispers Return the Sun, Rest the Moon'; it is in the melding of these two songs that the core of the record lays. With faint trumpet and a ping-ping coda, the mood is hopelessly romantic while remaining handsomely downbeat. A (very quiet) triumph from a man who follows his heart.

Released: 2001
Record Label: Blanco Y Negro
Producer: David Kitt, Ken McHugh
Recorded at: Area 51 Studios, Dublin
Sleeve Design: Robert Parkinson (cover
art), Kittser, Salvador

Tracks:
1 Song from Hope St (Brooklyn NY)
   5:20
2 You Know What I Want to Know **3:51**
3 Step Outside in the Morning Light
   5:28
4 Private Dance **2:35**

5 Pale Blue Light **5:33**
6 What I Ask **7:54**
7 Strange Light in the Evening **5:54**
8 Whispers Return the Sun, Rest the
   Moon 6:11
9 You and the City **6:43**
10 Into the Breeze **5:39**

PHIL LYNOTT
'OLD TOWN' (1982)

JIM FITZPATRICK

'The first time Philip played it for me we were walking along the beach close to where I live . . . I thought there and then it was amazing. It was really the demo of what would later become the definitive version. The song would later take on a mythical sense, and I'd attribute that largely to the video . . . It captured Philip as he really was. They got him on a day off, almost, for "Old Town" . . .'

Phil Lynott was thirty-six when he died in 1986; he left behind a wife, children, a mother, a rock band, a myth, a legacy, a public image. His solo debut, *Solo in Soho* (1980), reached the UK Top 30 albums chart, and yielded a moderate haul of three UK hit singles: 'Dear Miss Lonely Hearts', 'King's Call' and 'Yellow Pearl' (which was chosen as the theme tune to *Top of the Pops*). His 1982 follow-up, *The Phillip Lynott Album*, failed to chart, yet amid the detritus were two gems: 'Ode to Liberty', featuring nicely atmospheric work by Dire Straits guitarist Mark Knopfler, and 'Old Town' (co-written by Rainbow's Jimmy Bain).

'Old Town' didn't set any charts ablaze, but if the song didn't kill you, then (and particularly if you lived in Ireland around the time of the song's release) the video for it did. In the promo film, directed by Gerry Gregg and produced by Dave Heffernan, we see Lynott walking along Grafton Street, hailing well-wishers, kissing fans, strolling over the Ha'Penny Bridge, drinking in the Long Hall pub, messing about on the bandstand at Herbert Park, stretching his long, thin legs at South Bull Wall, and generally just being Phil Lynott, the dashing black Irish man (of which there weren't too many to be seen in the Ireland of the early eighties).

So, yes, the cut of his jib is neatly tailored and pressed, and, yes, it's occasionally a little bit too celebratory for its own good, but there's something else at play here: Lynott the returning hero, the much-loved rock-star rapscallion imbued with ineffable cool, improbable style and romance, ambling among his people, his tribe, on his home turf. Other Irish rock stars of the era (Van Morrison and Rory Gallagher, latterly The Boomtown Rats' Bob Geldof and U2's Bono) just couldn't match him. But then at this point, Dublin and Lynott had history, and 'Old Town' (both the song and the video) perfectly slotted into a coming of age for Irish rock and a creeping awareness that the old guard was soon to be toppled.

You could argue that Gregg's video did more to raise the song's profile and to generate emotional warmth for the singer than any amount of radio play at the time; certainly, the film added extra depths of romanticism. As for the song itself? Well, despite the Cockney intro ('The old Covent Garden? I remember only too well . . .'), the rest is guaranteed Irish, with Lynott's worryingly nasal-heavy voice raking through the ashes of a broken relationship. It remains a consummate pop song with resolutely Dublin overtones, with everything kicking in harmoniously: the string arrangement by Fiachra Trench, the retrospectively poignant lyrics ('this boy is cracking up, this boy has broken down'), the pom-pom drums, the tinkling piano rivulet (played by Darren Wharton) followed by Lynott's 'Ola!', and then, as if to cap it all, the piccolo trumpet solo (played by John Wilbraham, at the time the principal trumpet with the BBC Symphony Orchestra).

From Thin Lizzy swagger to Phil Lynott swoon: it's all here in a pop song masterpiece that lasts three minutes and twenty seconds. Within a year, Thin Lizzy had split up; within four, Lynott had suffered an ignominious death. The old song is right: the good, indeed, die young.

Phil Lynott – © Denis O'Regan/Corbis.

Released: 1982
Record Label: Virgin Records (Ireland),
Vertigo (UK)
Producer: Philip Lynott, Kit Woolven
Recorded at: Windmill Studios, Dublin;
Good Earth Studio, London
Duration: 3:27

Thin Lizzy – © Fin Costello/Redferns.

BARRY McCORMACK

LAST NIGHT AS I WAS WANDERING (2006)

'I recorded the album in my flat on Capel Street in 2004 . . . It was appropriate that it was made on Capel Street, as this was once the heart of Dublin's trad scene, and I was going through a serious trad phase at the time – Planxty's *Cold Blow and the Rainy Night* and obscure Dubliners albums were on constant rotation. By the time I was finished it was a bit of a sprawling mess; there's no shortage of chutzpah on the record, but it has a charm despite the obvious flaws on show.'

Barry McCormack is one of Ireland's most resourceful singer-songwriters. A former member of the band Jubilee Allstars, such is the lack of commercial demand for McCormack's work that if he chose to write songs and sing them for a living, you'd find him huddled in some corner in Dublin, begging for food and waiting for the hostels to open for the evening. Like most people operating in the lower commercial levels of the music industry, he has a day job. Outside official working hours, though, McCormack will toil for hours on end, writing songs that few people hear yet which resonate with experience soaked in observational detail and love of folklore. If he could afford not to work? He'd probably be the most satisfied, budget-conscious singer-songwriter in the world, slowly sipping coffee in a Dublin coffee house, staring out the window, checking out this character, clocking that person, and wondering what kinds of lives they're living.

At the core of McCormack's work is the kind of no-fanfare, sparse balladry that has its roots in the collected works of Luke Kelly, Christy Moore and Ewan MacColl. After Jubilee Allstars split up (an inevitability considering it comprised three highly opinionated brothers), he released his debut solo album, *We Drank Our Tears*, in 2003. Three years later, the follow-up, *Last Night as I Was Wandering*, slipped out. If the debut hinted at a formidable songwriting talent, then this album not only openly embraces Irish folk balladry but actively enhances

it, by doing what folk music is supposed to do: placing social history into context, and connecting slippery threads between the commonplace and the macabre, love, murder, romance, sex, humour, life and death. All of these and more are filtered and concentrated throughout *Last Night as I Was Wandering*.

There is an entry in this book on The Hormones album *Where Old Ghosts Meet* (see page 106). Well, in *Last Night as I Was Wandering*, you'll discover where old ghosts drink to excess, throw up, cheat and lie and soil themselves, pay for sex, and not give a tinker's curse about the complications the morning after. There is, of course, more than this. Characters in the songs read 'dark books' ('As I Went Up to Redmond's Hill'), philosophise ('choose your ideals carefully, for one day you must prove them true', 'Only Jesus Knows'), dispense words of wisdom ('never live with someone who was born in a bar, it'll only end in tears', 'In the Watches of the Night') and steal for booze ('I took a fifty from her purse', 'I Fell into Old Ways').

There are some obvious reference points here, but McCormack's winning shots include his awareness of place, sense of description, application of humour, and dutiful loyalty to a diehard tradition. He once described – offhandedly, one hopes – his early work (like this album) as having been written by a songwriter merely trying to learn his craft. He needn't have been so self-dismissive: this is as assured, confident and beautifully unadorned a record as you'll ever hear.

Released: 2006
Record Label: Hag's Head Records
Producer: Barry McCormack
Recorded at: Enforcer Mobile, Dublin
Sleeve Design: Niall McCormack, Adam Pomeroy (cover art)

Tracks:
1 Only Jesus Knows 2:41
2 As I Went Up to Redmond's Hill 3:50
3 Come All You Young Sinners 5:09
4 Do Not Revel In Your Woe 2:50
5 In the Watches of the Night 1:28
6 Scaldbrothers Ghost 3:03
7 The Night They Drank the River 1:52

8 Ballad of Booze and Bedragglement 4:39
9 Waiting for Joe 3:05
10 The Debtors Jail 3:41
11 I Fell Into Old Ways 1:58
12 Broombridge Incident 0:42
13 Lament for Black Head 3:53
14 Goodnight to You One and All 4:01

MICRODISNEY

CROOKED MILE (1987)

'This was Microdisney's first totally painstaking and scrutinised record. Sadly, I think we made the wrong record. I learned a lot about putting songs across, though mainly for future reference. Sean's guitar playing at that time was really great – even though the record doesn't document the best of it. I don't care for the lyrics. I was ill at ease with being out of poverty for a while, and – infuriatingly, with hindsight – not able to find a way to stretch myself. Lenny Kaye came from the US to produce, and illuminated our future creative lives with his enthusiasm and sophistication, although the songs remained static.'

An awful lot of time spent messing about is how Cathal Coughlan (see page 52) once described Microdisney's creative sojourn in London in the mid-eighties. Hindsight is a wonderful thing, of course, but as far as Coughlan is concerned, for Microdisney, 'nothing ever really gelled sufficiently to make it seem as if it was worth our while being governed by that work ethic.'

It was far from the music industry work ethic that Microdisney was raised; back in the late seventies and early eighties, the duo of Coughlan and Sean O'Hagan belonged to that select bunch of Cork post-punk bands which showed how to grasp the nettles of distinction and merit. Like most other dissonant Cork-based bands of that era (typically Nun Attax and, associatively, Five Go Down to the Sea), Microdisney were nutters on the lam. 'Mutant funk', they called it back then.

In lead singer and lyricist Coughlan, they had a fiercely intelligent and embittered front man of exceptional energy. Microdisney also had O'Hagan, who was the scented handwash to Coughlan's gardener's scrub: while Coughlan dished out the bile, O'Hagan drifted quietly in the background, executing swirls of interesting melodies. A move to London in the mid-eighties, the band having signed to Virgin Records, proved disastrous (the band-sanctioned 'Microdisney Are Shit' T-shirts probably didn't help), yet they nonetheless released two albums

(1985's *The Clock Comes Down the Stairs* and 1987's *Crooked Mile*) that often vie for the title of their best.

Despite what Coughlan says about *Crooked Mile* (see the quote above), it remains a sterling piece of work, full of finger-picked guitars, little waltzing organs and a sense of the strange. Innately odd, songs such as 'And He Descended Into Hell', 'Our Children', 'Give Me All Of Your Clothes', 'Angels', 'Mrs Simpson', 'Armadillo Man', 'Rack', 'Town to Town', and 'People Just Want to Dream' come across as wonderful blends of Scott Walker and Willie Nelson, John Cale and Gram Parsons, and yet kowtow to none of them. It is acerbic, aching pop music with avant-garde fringes, Americana stylings and (thanks to Coughlan) a lyrical, visual awareness, occasionally documenting the imprint of his Cork background, which regularly hits home. It's also an album fuelled (thanks to O'Hagan) by a kind of disciplined musicianship that tackles genre specifics while being simultaneously very much its own boss.

It's a bit like the waspish singer of an anti-pop band paying a visit to Blackpool in order to sing an anti-nuclear song (say, for example, 'Town to Town') on the *Tom O'Connor Roadshow* while wearing a bright yellow cardigan and a blazing smirk. But that's another story altogether.

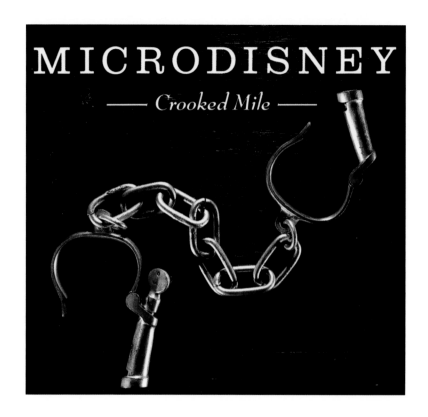

Released: 1987
Record Label: Virgin Records
Producer: Lenny Kaye
Recorded at: JAM, London
Sleeve Design: Keith Breeden

Tracks:
1 Town to Town **3:21**
2 Angels **3:44**
3 Our Children **4:33**
4 Mrs Simpson **3:54**
5 Hey Hey Sam **4:21**
6 Give Me All Of Your Clothes **4:03**

7 Armadillo Man **3:05**
8 Bullwhip Road **3:39**
9 And He Descended Into Hell **3:45**
10 Rack **4:30**
11 Big Sleeping House **3:04**
12 People Just Want To Dream **5:20**

VAN MORRISON
ASTRAL WEEKS (1968)

GREIL MARCUS

'It was forty-six minutes in which possibilities of the medium – of rock 'n' roll, of pop music, of what you might call music that could be played on the radio as if it were both timeless and news – were realised, when you went out to the limits of what this form could do . . . You showed everybody else that the limits they had accepted on invention, expression, honesty, daring, were false. You said it to musicians and you said it to people who weren't musicians: there's more to life than you thought.'

Martin Scorsese based the first fifteen minutes of *Taxi Driver* on *Astral Weeks*. Not many people know that. Indeed, there are an awful lot of people that don't know anything about *Astral Weeks*, other than that it speaks to them in ways that very few albums do. Frankly, it has baffled and eluded people (this writer included) for decades, yet it has frequently been cited as one of the best, most important, most original recordings in the rock-music canon. On initial release, it sold in the region of 20,000 copies.

Recorded shortly after his twenty-third birthday, following his release from a creatively restrictive recording contract with Bang Records, Van Morrison informed his new management team of Lewis Merenstein and Robert Schwaid that for his debut solo album on a major label he wanted to explore jazzier elements. Which is how he found himself at Century Sound Studios, New York City, on 25 September 1968, with a group of high-calibre jazz session musicians he hardly knew.

Morrison never really got to know them, either, as the album's eight tracks were recorded between that September session and a further one on 15 October. In keeping with the jazz aesthetic, Morrison gave the musicians minimal guidance (he sang in an enclosed glass booth), allowing them to improvise within very wide parameters.

Morrison himself, who rarely talks about the album's themes, once described *Astral Weeks* as 'an imagined opera, a song-cycle of poetry and mythical daydreams', and you can see what he's talking about as he riffs on memories of Belfast ('Cyprus Avenue'), of distinct characters ('Madame George'), and of love ('Sweet Thing'). Are the songs – on the face of it, not the work of a twenty-three-year-old –even semi-autobiographical? Not according to Morrison, but ultimately, who knows?

Musically, the songs benefit from a free-flowing, often warm and tender atmosphere, and it is here that the album either scores or misses. For some reason that is difficult to specify (insofar as it can be pinned down – although that hasn't stopped many from vainly trying), the album has an uncanny ability to generate powerful emotional responses in the listener.

What matters above all else, though, is the album's anti-rock singularity, its sense of audacious purpose and lack of compromise. Many musicians have tried to emulate its wisps, vapour trails and curlicues over the decades, but they have failed. For better or worse, there is really nothing quite like *Astral Weeks*. Inevitably, Morrison would come nowhere close to recapturing its many indefinable moments.

Released: 1968
Record Label: Warner Bros.
Producer: Lewis Merenstein
Recorded at: Century Sound Studios,
New York City
Sleeve Design: Joel Brodsky, Ed Thrasher

Tracks:
1 Astral Weeks **7:06**
2 Beside You **5:16**
3 Sweet Thing **4:25**
4 Cyprus Avenue **7:00**
5 The Way Young Lovers Do **3:18**

6 Madame George **9:45**
7 Ballerina **7:03**
8 Slim Slow Slider **3:17**

VAN MORRISON

MOONDANCE (1970)

'Astral Weeks was a success musically, and at the same time I was starving. Practically not eating. So for the next album I realised I was going to have to do something [that sounded] like rock, or starve . . . So I tried to forget about the artistic thing because it didn't make sense on a practical level. One has to live.'

Van Morrison's debut major-label album, *Astral Weeks*, initially bemused people with its jazz inflections and curious range of lyrics. He had, remember, signed to Warner Brothers on the back of his 1967 chart hit, 'Brown Eyed Girl', and when *Astral Weeks* was delivered, an initial air of disenchantment floated around the corridors of the record company. Where, you could almost hear them ask, was 'Brown Eyed Girl'? Where was Van Morrison? Well, 'Brown Eyed Girl' had gone indoors, and Morrison was on a path to somewhere that his record company didn't necessarily want him to go.

That path led to a village close to Woodstock in upstate New York, which is where Morrison and his wife Janet moved after the recording of *Astral Weeks*. With a bunch of musicians recruited from close by, Morrison once again allowed them to riff on their instincts, urging them to capture the moment on a batch of songs that, while retaining the free-flow mood of his previous album, were far more accessible in commercial terms.

Released when people were still coming to terms with (or more than likely had plain forgot) *Astral Weeks*, *Moondance* provided Morrison with much-needed hit songs. In truth, the reason behind the much-diminished anti-rock stance was the songwriter's own need for money: *Astral Weeks* may have been something of a musical triumph, but it didn't pay the bills.

That Morrison felt the need to write a batch of radio-friendly songs says as much about his pragmatism as his skill set (one of the songs cast aside as being unsuited to *Moondance*'s all-encompassing pop/R&B sensibility was 'Listen to the Lion', which two years later would find its way onto *St Dominic's Preview*). He hit paydirt, too, with extensive FM radio play for at least half of *Moondance*'s songs, generating revenues he wasn't yet getting from recording or publishing companies.

From the opening track, 'And It Stoned Me', *Moondance* simply shimmers through inventive, confident, inherently true songwriting. While the title track has since become a standard easy-listening/lounge-music tune (which has caused it to suffer greatly – at least when taken out of the album's context), songs such as 'Crazy Love', 'Caravan', 'Into the Mystic', 'Come Running', 'These Dreams of You', 'Brand New Day', and 'Everyone' mixed an assured lightness of touch with vivid, old-school R&B. The result would not only open out Morrison's world, but would also make the world open out to him.

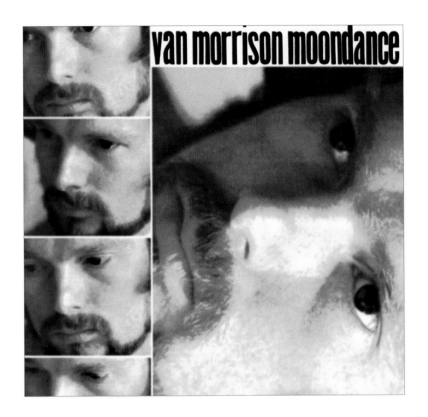

Released: 1970
Record Label: Warner Bros.
Producer: Van Morrison, Lewis Merenstein
Recorded at: A & R Studios, New York City
Sleeve Design: Bob Cato, Elliot Landy
(photography)

Tracks:
1 And It Stoned Me **4:30**
2 Moondance **4:35**
3 Crazy Love **2:34**
4 Caravan **4:57**
5 Into the Mystic **3:25**
6 Come Running **2:30**
7 These Dreams of You **3:50**
8 Brand New Day **5:09**
9 Everyone **3:31**
10 Glad Tidings **3:13**

MOVING HEARTS

MOVING HEARTS (1981)

CHRISTY MOORE

'I remember it as being a vital time. Urgency and obsession. Hard, fast music reflecting the mood of the time. [*Hot Press* writer] Bill Graham on the bus for three days. Special Branch at the gigs. Moustaches everywhere. But we were tight: tight in the music, and tight in the playing. We gave it everything we had . . . For me, this [album] was Moving Hearts at its best.

By the turn of 1981, the traditional Irish group Planxty (see separate entry, page 150) had come to a point of, if not full stop, then certainly creative uneasiness. Two members of the band, specifically, had reached a point where being in it was more of a burden than a blessing. Both Dónal Lunny and Christy Moore had been down this road before when Planxty had split up in 1975, but had managed to balance their artistic differences by developing individual projects. Planxty reunited in 1978, yet by 1980 matters once again came to a head: Moore became increasingly eager to sing and write songs that appealed to his strong political concerns, while Lunny became progressively interested in travelling down musical roads that simply wouldn't suit Planxty – notably the integration of bass, drums and keyboards.

The major problem for Lunny, as the effective musical director of the group, was how to utilise these instruments without crossing over into rock music. The key was for different genres to intermesh and, hopefully, to explore, and then find common ground. In a musical approximation of the Magnificent Seven, other like-minded musicians were brought into the fold: Declan Sinnott (guitar), Eoghan O'Neill (bass), Davy Spillane (uileann pipes and low whistle), Keith Donald (soprano and tenor sax) and Brian Calnan (drums). The ensemble rock/folk/blues/jazz/trad band quick-stepped it into the fray, recording their debut self-titled album during the summer of '81, and releasing it that autumn.

To say that the album caused something of an upset is an understatement: here was a political record that spoke directly and with no small levels of protest in its attempts to discover, and connect, the relationship between Ireland's past and present 'situations'. Songs such as Jim Page's 'Hiroshima Nagasaki Russian Roulette', Phil Chevron's 'Faithful Departed', John Gibbs's 'Irish Ways and Irish Laws' and Jackson Browne's 'Before the Deluge' satisfied Moore's keen political edge, while instrumentals 'McBrides' and 'Lake of Shadows' showcased the deftness and dexterity of the musicians.

For many thousands of Irish people, the album soundtracked mass emigration, high employment and contentious political issues. In the latter area, for example, Jack Warshaw's 'No Time for Love' is viewed as either grossly naive or a fine, righteous contemporary rebel song. However one views that particular song (or, indeed, Moving Hearts' staunch support of the H-Block protests; one certainly couldn't accuse them of being like so many other Irish bands of the era – apolitical), after two albums, Moore left, for reasons connected with the band's often-criticised 'muso' one-upmanship approach, and (much to Lunny's increasing frustration) Moving Hearts mutated into what he once tersely described as 'a rock band with traces of Irish music'.

Such tailspins happen, of course, even when a beady eye is hovering, but all involved on this startling (and, some would argue, unique) debut can take satisfaction in the knowledge that a new hybrid had been created.

Released: 1981
Record Label: Warner Music Group (WEA)
Producer: Dónal Lunny
Recorded at: Keystone Studios, Windmill Lane Studios, Dublin
Sleeve Design: Bel Air Studios

Tracks:
1 Hiroshima Nagasaki Russian Roulette 4:25
2 Irish Ways and Irish Laws 3:54
3 McBride's 5:40
4 Before the Deluge 5:42
5 Landlord 2:36
6 Category 2:58
7 Faithful Departed 4:46
8 Lake of Shadows 4:48
9 No Time for Love 7:25

MY BLOODY VALENTINE

LOVELESS (1991)

BILINDA BUTCHER

'I think it's a good thing we never released anything more. It would just have been a charade. There were songs that Kevin worked on but they never materialised. It just ended. I think Kevin also thinks that everything about *Loveless* is exaggerated. He did do things that hadn't been done before with the guitar, and he deserves credit for that – the album is a milestone. But all the reaction to it paralysed his way of creating music. He felt he had to come up with something as ground-breaking as *Loveless*.'
Totally Dublin, September 2008

There are stories about My Bloody Valentine's Kevin Shields we'd rather not believe. How about the one when, during a recording session, Shields had to discard the work because of a ringing phone – a quarter of a mile away? Or what about this one: at four years of age, living in Queen's, New York, Shields would hear his sister humming a note, imitate her, and then shift his note ever so slightly out of tune until he discovered the precise modulation of it that would drive his family demented.

The parallels are obvious, of course, with the recorded output of My Bloody Valentine, but particularly with *Loveless* – Shields has clearly been on a mission to drive us all insane.

You'd never have guessed it back in the early eighties, when the band left Dublin for Holland and then Germany, adrift in their admiration for Jesus and Mary Chain as well as other (lesser) bands that knelt in supplication at the altar of indie pop. At this point, ordinariness was My Bloody Valentine's USP, but something was afoot: come 1988, just as matters could have ground to a halt due to lack of funds, Alan McGee signed them to his Creation label.

By the end of the year, their debut album, *Isn't Anything*, was released; but its slow-mo, multi-layered textures – praised to the hilt – was nothing compared to *Loveless*, which was delivered two exasperating years later, leaving behind a trail of nineteen unsatisfactory recording studios, eighteen exhausted studio engineers, and a tidy £250,000 (a figure likely exaggerated).

It's easy to look beyond the album for its back-story (how it almost bankrupted Creation; how it temporarily caused breakdowns of varying shapes and sizes; how the band's drummer Colm Ó Cíosóig became seriously ill and homeless during recording; or how the relationship between Shields and vocalist Bilinda Butcher was fragmenting – not for nothing was the album so titled), but the real meat is the music itself.

Butcher's on-the-spot, ineffably mournful lyrics and dreamy, just-about-there vocals (due in part to lack of sleep; the other 'parts' you can probably guess) were sonically melted into Shields's use of guitar effects as well as ear-candy orgasms like distortion, reverb and Shields's signature technique of causing the guitar strings to bend slightly in and out of tune. Some have called it 'sonic rapture', and they're not far off; 'Soon', 'Blown a Wish', 'When You Sleep', 'Sometimes', 'Touched' and 'To Here Knows When' are a mixture of simplistic, vague, forward-looking, virtually spiritually charged tunes.

After *Loveless*? Lots of talk, but nothing concrete. A legacy but no follow-up. There is, after all, only so many records you can create that make the familiar at once extremely disturbing and very beautiful.

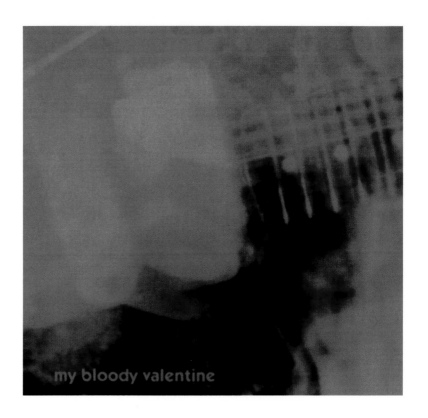

Released: 1991
Record Label: Creation
Producer: Kevin Shields, Colm Ó Cíosóig
Recorded at: Blackwing Studios,
Southwark, London
Sleeve Design: My Bloody Valentine,
Designland

Tracks:
1 Only Shallow **4:17**
2 Loomer **2:38**
3 Touched **0:56**
4 To Here Knows When **5:31**
5 When You Sleep **4:11**
6 I Only Said **5:34**

7 Come in Alone **3:58**
8 Sometimes **5:19**
9 Blown a Wish **3:36**
10 What You Want **5:33**
11 Soon **6:58**

SINÉAD O'CONNOR
UNIVERSAL MOTHER (1994)

'*Universal Mother* to me represents the point at which I began, as a singer and an artist . . . to be me. It was the first time I wasn't masking anything, vocally or emotionally. Emotionally speaking, it is the first record, also, where I began to grapple with, and acknowledge, an indescribably painful set of feelings I was carrying as a result of the extremely severe violence and abuse I had experienced as a child, from my mother. And also a terrible pain I was carrying about the fact she died in a car crash when I was seventeen. On my first album I covered my heart with anger. My second album, too, but *Universal Mother* was where I admitted I was broken. I lay down and almost died. It was a controversial album in some people's minds in the Ireland of the time, where so much child abuse had happened under people's noses and we never said anything. Up until that point anyone talking about abuse was shadowed out. *Universal Mother* was in your face, the first artistic expression of some of the well of grief that was so blocked up inside us, and is only beginning to loosen. So it was an uncomfortable album for some people. It was a *very* sad record. A diary of a very great sadness. You can't recover from something you don't acknowledge exists . . . In short, it was a very *Irish* record.'

Universal Mother was Sinéad O'Connor's first album of original material since her 1990 breakthrough second album, *I Do Not Want What I Haven't Got*. That second album, of course, with its worldwide hit single, Prince's 'Nothing Compares 2 U', thrust O'Connor into a spotlight so hot and glaring that she melted often and in public.

If there was one primary perception of O'Connor in the early nineties it was that she was too controversial for her own good. Against the grain, O'Connor tackled the taboo subjects (child abuse, Papal fallibility, Catholicism) and undertook public confessionals via television appearances and full-page poems/letters in national newspapers.

With 1990-94 as a backdrop to her personal issues, along came *Universal Mother*, a starkly confessional album layered in hymnal hues that range from the overtly spiritual to the insidiously hypnotic. It is the work of a courageous songwriter and one of the best singers of this or any other generation. Lyrically, it is a direct descendent of John Lennon's 1970 *Plastic Ono Band* album, the Dr Arthur Janov/Primal Scream therapy-inspired record that expressed childhood and adolescent bitterness. Like Lennon, O'Connor finds solace of a sort in sparse, melodic songs laced with a frightening rage that is equally disturbing, exciting and voyeuristic. The balance between tension and tenderness, however, is extremely well executed, which means that what could have been, in lesser hands, shrill and beseeching is actually calm, lucid, focused and, therefore, even more unsettling.

For a performer that once held the world captive with her beauty and voice, *Universal Mother* contains enough on it to make the cynically minded regard O'Connor as someone still desperately searching for a lost plot. None of this will change certain people's opinions of O'Connor, yet there is here an overwhelming sense that her art has helped her to survive, to make her stronger. Is *Universal Mother* too personal? Good God, yes, but that's why it works – whatever voyeuristic elements there are here are blinded by an expressive directness so honest it often chills the bones.

Released: 1994

Record Label: Ensign Records, Chrysalis

Producer: Sinéad O'Connor, John Reynolds, Tim Simenon, Phil Coulter

Recorded at: Westland Studios, Dublin

Sleeve Design: Sinéad O'Connor

Tracks:

1 Germaine **0:38**
2 Fire on Babylon **5:11**
3 John I Love You **5:31**
4 My Darling Child **3:09**
5 Am I A Human? **0:24**
6 Red Football **2:48**
7 All Apologies **2:37**
8 A Perfect Indian **4:22**
9 Scorn Not His Simplicity **4:26**
10 All Babies **4:29**
11 In This Heart **3:11**
12 Tiny Grief Song **1:56**
13 Famine **4:56**
14 Thank You for Hearing Me **6:25**

IARLA Ó LIONÁIRD

INVISIBLE FIELDS (2006)

'Childhood, its magic and power are at the heart of *Invisible Fields*. That time in life when imagination is the vital energy at the centre of our experience . . . I wanted to reach back to that time, experience the ecstasy and joy of the child mind. It was also a time for me to play with the toys of the studio. It was my first time doing it to this intensity and level of dedication, playing with sound worlds, finding and making events and stories for the ear to experience. It was also my first engagement with parenthood in my work, the still beauty and wonder of it.'

If Iarla Ó Lionáird were a politician, he would be a radical conservative. Or maybe a conservative radical. Life is like that for the Cork *sean nós* singer. He has one of middle-class Ireland's most traditional backgrounds: born in 1964, he grew up in a rural village, attended the school where his father was headmaster, and sang in the local church choir.

It started with his choirmaster. Coir Cúil Aodha, which Ó Lionáird joined at the age of five, was founded by Seán Ó Riada (see page 142), who was instrumental in reviving interest in traditional Irish music through his score for the 1956 film *Mise Éire*, and his founding of the group Ceoltóiri Chualann. In 1964, in order to be closer to the source of the musical traditions he was so passionate about, Ó Riada moved to the west Cork Gaeltacht, to the village of Cúil Aodha, the graveyard of which is littered with tombstones engraved with the words 'singer' and 'poet'.

Ó Lionáird was still a teenager in the seventies and early eighties, and he would often hitch a ride into Cork city to buy the latest album by Neil Young, Bob Dylan, Talking Heads or, perhaps more crucially, Brian Eno. In the same way that Eno worked fluidly across genres, from his influential ambient music to more mainstream work (producing David Bowie, Coldplay and U2), so Ó Lionáird moves, like a ghost, it seems, through boundaries. He does it so effectively that, rather than sound like two traditions randomly or sloppily thrown together, the result is a genuine, seamless fusion of modern chill-out and medieval plainsong.

Invisible Fields differs from his work with Afro Celt Sound System (see page 18), however, by virtue of several important elements: its purity of vision, its individuality, and its mesmerising, minimalist sophistication. Utilising his gift as a *sean nós* singer, but merging his love of what can only be termed symphonic folk, Ó Lionáird pours water over turf fires and puts the smelly dog in the shed. Songs such as 'A Nest of Stars', 'Cu-cu-ín', 'Taimse Im' Chodladh', 'I'm Weary of Lying Alone', 'The Day That You Were Born', 'Oisin's Dream', 'Tuirim Mhic Fhinin Dhuibh' and 'Aurora' authentically explore and continue an inherited tradition that uniquely transmits something you'd be wary of putting into words.

Whatever it is he does, Ó Lionáird couches it in music of sublime proportions. Here be traditional Irish music for people who profess to hate it: just when you think it might veer into overly familiar territory, out comes delicate use of piano, synthesizers, harmonium, cello and dulcimer. Before you can resist, you're sucked into a dream world where music is rightly regarded as an ancestral memory source, and where Ó Lionáird deftly balances economy of style and monastic reflection with a soundtrack that, no two ways about it, floats in space.

Iarla Ó Lionáird | Invisible Fields

Released: 2006
Record Label: Real World Records
Producer: Iarla Ó Lionáird, Kieran Lynch
Recorded at: Kilkenny, Ireland; Real World
Studios, UK
Sleeve Design: Marc Bessant
(Real World Design)

Tracks:
1   A Nest of Stars **6:28**
2   Cu-Cu-Ín **4:43**
3   Taimse Im' Chodladh **6:35**
4   I'm Weary of Lying Alone **5:20**
5   The Day That You Were Born **4:53**
6   An Buachaillín Ban **5:20**

7   Oisin's Dream **5:31**
8   Tuirimh Mhic Fhinin Dhuibh **6:40**
9   Aurora **5:35**
10 Scathán Na Beatha **3:25**

SEÁN Ó RIADA

MISE ÉIRE (1959)

PEADAR Ó RIADA

'The Irish nation loves a green island, generosity, a belief in the spiritual, the resurrection in the underdog and the power of the creative. The film *Mise Éire* and, in particular, the soundtrack, seemed to me to personify all of these rolled together when it was released into our consciousness. The music is a sonic key that unlocks the recognition of our love for these values. It has echoes of love, of loneliness, of pride and of empathy with our past. I never cease to be amazed at the strength of these feelings in myself and of observing it in others as they experience the music again.'

Seán Ó Riada was born John Reidy in Cork city in 1931 (and died in 1971), the son of a fiddle-playing garda sergeant father and a concertina- and melodeon-playing mother. By the time John was ten, he was fairly proficient at playing the violin and piano. At the age of seventeen, he had won a scholarship to University College Cork, taking Arts with music, whereupon, under the tutelage of Professor Aloys Fleischmann, he went head-to-head with French culture, the Greek classics, and – sweet Jesus, Mary and Joseph! –started listening to (and playing) jazz and European avant-garde music.

In a cultural context, the mid-1950s were not kind to Irish traditional music, confined as it was to rural regions of the country, Irish-language revivalist groups and rural-born, city-based musicians. By 1955, meanwhile, Ó Riada had married, moved to Dublin, resigned from a noteworthy position as Assistant Director of Music in Ireland's national broadcaster, RTÉ, and high-tailed it to Paris. Such a decision now seems a pivotal one, as composition and piano recitals of his work were very much a part of his day-to-day life. Yet Paris was also where he experienced a cultural epiphany of sorts, in that he began to embrace his heritage (hence the Gaelic variant of his name) and to formulate ways of fusing this with his classically trained, yet casually imparted, knowledge of European art music. In the same way that classical art music was employed by, among other composers, Edvard

Grieg (Norway), Jean Sibelius (Finland) and Ralph Vaughan Williams (England) as a declaration of national culture, so too would Ó Riada. The idea to present traditional Irish music outside the context of the come-all-ye céilí-band format (which Ó Riada derided) mutated into something akin to what he termed a folk orchestra – or Ceoltóirí Chualann.

The scored fusion of classical instrumentation with Irish dance music, airs and compositions revolutionised the way in which Irish music was listened to (particularly among the middle classes). The key example of this was *Mise Éire (I Am Ireland)*, a film by George Morrison (inspired by the 1912 Irish-language poem by republican revolutionary Padraig Pearse) concerning the founding of the Republic of Ireland. Configuring Irish folk music in a manner that pays due diligence to the likes of Mozart, Mahler and Sibelius – playing the right notes at precisely the right points, using textures without over-layering – Ó Riada created a virtually futuristic form of beauty, giving countless traditional Irish musicians and musicians-to-be (as Seán Mac Réamoinn writes in the sleeve notes to Gael Linn's 2011 three-CD set, *The Essential Seán Ó Riada Collection*) 'an old tune for a new age'.

The author would particularly like to credit Nuala O'Connor's chapter on Seán Ó Riada in her book Bringing It All Back Home *for background information on this entry. See bibliography for further details.*

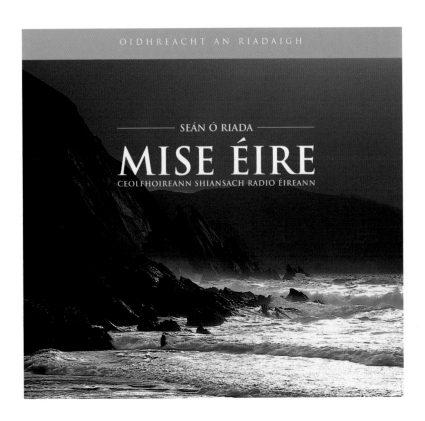

SEÁN Ó RIADA

MISE ÉIRE

CEOLFHOIREANN SHIANSACH RADIO ÉIREANN

Released: 1959
Record Label: Gael Linn Records (George Morrison documentary score), Shanachie (album score)
Producer: Gael Linn
Recorded at: Phoenix Hall, Dublin
Sleeve Design: Steve Averill, Four5One

Tracks:
1 Mise Éire: Múscailt 1:52
2 Cogadh Na MBórach 0:51
3 An Asgard Agus Sochraid Bachelor's Walk 3:17
4 Cois Uaigh Dhiarmuid Uí Dhonnabháin Rosa 1:49
5 Óglaigh Na HÉireann 1:21
6 Luan Cásca 1916 1:17
7 Cathair Bhriste 2:36
8 Tomás Ághas: Sochraid 1:34
9 Mise Éire: Caithréim 2:01

DECLAN O'ROURKE

MAG PAI ZAI (2011)

'*Mag Pai Zai* is a collection of songs that I would say were almost cathartic in their delivery to me, if it weren't for the fact that the experience was so enjoyable. They came in a flourish after a couple of years of adjustment to a new period in my life, and after the death of an old one, so it is filled with the giddy lightheadedness of healing and rebirth, and a little mourning on the side. Of course, that all sounds very heavy, but it's much more fun – and much darker than that, too, haha! Because of the way the music industry is going, and the way the world is right now, money-wise, there seems to be this surplus of goodwill around. Because the record was self-funded, everybody that worked on it cut really good deals, added something, and became a part of it because they wanted to be a part of it. That made it so much easier to work with them, and I was much more appreciative of the creativity they were giving of themselves. When I listen to the album, I hear that. I hope that even a hint of that goodness, that mood, is captured.'

Declan O'Rourke – a late starter on the Dublin singer-songwriter scene of the late nineties/early noughties – is an example of how quality control can work in your favour; he hones songs quietly and assiduously until they are just right, and he never seems in any mad rush to put out material. But why listen to someone who has little of relevance to say, anyway?

Mag Pai Zai is O'Rourke's third album (his haunting debut, *Since Kyabram*, was released in 2005; his lesser second, *Big Bad Beautiful World*, in 2008), and sees him bounce back after the comparative inadequacies of *Since Kyabram*. There are songs here that are as rich as dark chocolate melting into your brain; songs sung in a resonant, reflective voice that will bring tears to your eyes and make you contemplate important matters such as life, love, what makes the world go round, and whether what you get on the swings is really (honestly?) equal to what you get on the roundabouts. In other words, the kind of decent things that good singer-songwriters do in order to help you negotiate life, love and, well, what makes the world go round. Can you detect a theme here?

There are also more than several songs on *Mag Pai Zai* that would win awards, but the two that repeatedly pull at your sleeves like kids in a supermarket are *Langley's Requiem* and *The Hardest Fight*. The former is a wonderfully wrought tale of two New York-based brothers who, through various circumstances, fall foul of society and end up living in secluded OCD squalor amid 'umbrellas and an old X-ray machine, a dozen grand pianos and a rusty spring, a hundred and eleven tons of other things'; the latter song is a lifetime relationship explored by O'Rourke in such an intuitive, poignant and direct way ('in my heart I know what's true – that you loved me and I loved you'), it puts your emotions through a wringer.

'No animals were harmed during the making of this record,' it says in the CD sleeve notes. Maybe so, but your heart . . . Well, your heart, quite simply, will be bruised through and through.

Declan O'Rourke
MAG PAI ZAI

Released: 2011
Record Label: Rimecoat Records
Producer: Declan O'Rourke
Recorded at: The Factory, Windmill Lane Studios, Dublin
Sleeve Design: Swollen

Tracks:
1 Slíeve Bloom **4:31**
2 Time Machine **4:24**
3 A Little Something **4:22**
4 Be Brave and Believe **5:30**
5 Lightning Bird Wind River Man 3:18

6 Langley's Requiem **4:42**
7 Dancing Song **5:50**
8 Caterpillar DNA **4:24**
9 Orphan Wind Song **2:49**
10 The Hardest Fight 3:59

GILBERT O'SULLIVAN
'ALONE AGAIN (NATURALLY)' (1972)

'You could argue that I'm an English songwriter. When I was initially successful, the Irish embraced me, but critically I irritated them. There was nothing Irish about my songs, and there never will be.'

The secret of success is the capacity to survive failure. Noël Coward said that. Smart guy, Noël Coward.

The maxim, of course, could be applied to all areas of life, but with perhaps more relevance in the cutthroat, cut-and-thrust world of pop music. Gilbert O'Sullivan knows all about that particular world, having been managed in the early and mid-1970s by Gordon Mills, a person he once implicitly trusted, but whom he has since described as 'a misguided businessman surrounded by crooks and yes-men'.

In other words, it all went pear-shaped very quickly for Waterford-born O'Sullivan, whose success in that period was such that he rivalled Elton John as the UK's most commercially successful pop star. Unusually for someone who regards himself as Irish (his family moved from Waterford to Swindon in the early fifties), O'Sullivan forged a career based on a songwriting talent that was singularly British.

To say that O'Sullivan stood out like a sore thumb in the pop and rock landscape of the era is an understatement: his song topics ranged from genteel, fond and punning songs (lyrically, he was influenced by Spike Milligan) about love, girls, marriage and childhood to death, suicide and the existence of God. On the latter subjects, none of his recordings was more poignant and brilliantly self-pitying than 'Alone Again (Naturally)'. His fifth single (and his first UK Top 3 hit), it is one of the most introspective pop ballads ever written. It relates the central character's plans to commit suicide after being jilted ('In a little while from now, if I'm not feeling any less sour, I promise myself to treat myself and visit a nearby tower, and climbing to the top will throw myself off'); it also goes into the death of the central character's parents ('I remember I cried when my father died, never wishing to hide the tears'; 'when she passed away I cried and cried all day').

As autobiography, 'Alone Again (Naturally)' is redundant. As a pop song, it was completely against the grain, yet intensely affecting, its subject matter as odd an antidote to prog and glam rock as one could imagine.

It could also be argued (without too much fuss) that O'Sullivan was one of pop music's first true miserabilists, and that – spurious though it might sound – lurking in a suburb in Manchester, someone by the name of Steven Patrick Morrissey (his love of New York Dolls notwithstanding) was humming along to the likes of this one, as well as 'Nothing Rhymed' (which he once covered), 'Clair' and 'We Will'.

Whatever about his other songs, O'Sullivan is fiercely protective of 'Alone Again (Naturally)': in 1991, he successfully sued hip-hop artist Biz Markie for sampling it, and also refused an offer of £500,000 for the song to be used in an American television commercial for washing machines.

For such a perfectly distressing song about loneliness and abandonment (and one that, ironically, enjoys worldwide radio play), it's no surprise at all that its writer keeps it so close to his heart.

Gilbert O'Sullivan – © Hulton-Deutsch Collection/Corbis.

Released: 1972
Record Label: MAM
Producer: Gilbert O'Sullivan, Gordon Mills
Recorded at: Audio International, London
Duration: 3:37

THE OUTCASTS
'SELF CONSCIOUS OVER YOU' (1979)

MARTIN COWAN 'Our best songs were recorded when we couldn't play well enough to do them justice, but then we weren't making music to be analysed years later. It was all about now, throwing out all that went before and having our moment in the spotlight. My favourite review is one in *NME* that said even before we'd started to play, we looked and moved like a real band.'

Scary blokes, naughty boys, The Outcasts. Northern Irish punks that looked the part and who got the name of their band by being turned away from five nightclubs in less than two weeks. They formed in Belfast in early 1977; their early gigs were disasters (sometimes self-inflicted, as the drummer, Colin Cowan, had a tendency to smash up his drum kit after the third or fourth song), and forced them into hiring rooms in venues for 'private parties' – which quickly turned into mini-brawls, before the management realised what was happening and pulled the plug. And banned The Outcasts. Again.

Viewed very much as a punks' punk band (their avid fans were once described as kids who fought their way out at night and fought their way home again), The Outcasts took months to grasp musical techniques. But their innate ability to capture basic adolescent moments in gritty but eminently melodic songs thrust them head and shoulders above other shouty punk acts of the time.

Early songs such as 'You're a Disease', 'Justa Nother Teenage Rebel', 'The Cops Are Comin'' and 'Love Is For Sops' appeared in quick succession, ensuring the band a run of localised hits, signed as they were then to Good Vibrations, the Belfast-based indie label (and record shop) that was pivotal to many bands of the era getting heard on the radio and gaining a fanbase.

It was with the 1979 single, 'Self Conscious Over You', however, that The Outcasts made people really sit up and listen. Like pretty much every punk-rock single of the day, it unashamedly borrowed from prime-time sixties pop – albeit with a twist. It starts off appropriating The Monkees' 'Last Train to Clarksville', immediately segues into a lift from Television's 'Marquee Moon', and then continues with lyrics straight out of a girl's teen magazine ('First time I saw you walkin' down the street, knew I had a crush on you right away. It's really embarrassin' at school, when the teacher asks me what I'm doin' . . . and my mother's always naggin' me, why don't you finish your tea?') before it boils over into a rumbling, hand-clapping banger of a song that has you doffing the cap to the gods. And then? Well, how about a sax solo before the teen-angst lyrics continue ('I see her every day on the bus, and I dream of askin' her out, but I turn red, sweat drippin' down my face, and I'm feelin' such a freak . . .')?

The song (also the title of The Outcasts' debut album, which was also released in 1979 on Good Vibrations) sounds as rough and ready to rumble as the band did in their heyday, yet it remains a textbook example of teenage romance – the fear, the clamminess, the mortification, the excitement – delivered with no pretentions whatsoever. Would they reach such heights again? No, but with a song this good, they'd never need to.

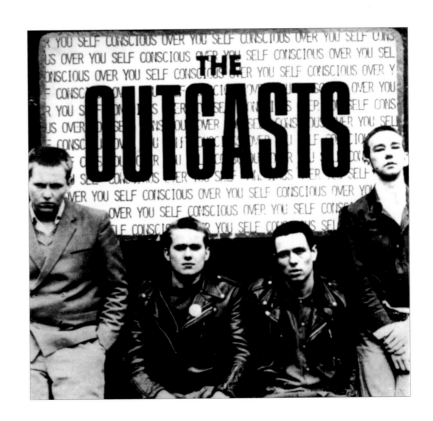

Released: 1979
Record Label: Good Vibrations
Producer: Terri Hooley, D. Smyth
Recorded at: Wizard Studios, Belfast
Sleeve Design: Brian Burrows
Duration: 3:09

PLANXTY

PLANXTY (1973)

'Making music with Dónal, Andy and Liam was as good as it gets. I'd have happily settled for gigs in Slattery's of Capel Street [in Dublin], but it seemed like the world wanted to hear us. Anytime I happen to hear this album, I feel that it has aged very well. I still like it. Andy and Dónal weaved a magic spell, and Liam's playing was thrilling . . . We were flying.'

Dónal Lunny, Andy Irvine, Liam O'Flynn, Christy Moore. Rule-breakers all. Yet before they were Planxty, they were friends, circling around and dovetailing into each other – until the inevitable happened. It started in 1971 with Moore's second album, *Prosperous* (1972), when the four musicians realised that the empathetic connection they generated in its making was worth pursuing in an ensemble band format. And so in 1972, they formed Planxty, creating a band that, many would claim (and few would argue with them), revolutionised Irish folk music.

The reasons why the unit created something so special are manifold. Firstly, they were playing to a younger Irish audience, many of whom were exposed, via the influx of radio and television, to a weightier form of rock music, and a new form of instrumentation. Secondly, Planxty had within its ranks musicians that eschewed the strictly traditional musical configuration of tin whistle, bodhrán and uileann pipes; added to these were guitar, mandolin and (from Irvine's avid admiration of eastern European music) bouzouki. The mixture of strings with fail-safe, if standard, instruments was as exciting as it was groundbreaking – they even recorded a John Peel Session in the months prior to the album being released.

With Lunny as de facto musical director, the track listing for *Planxty* (also known as *The Black Album* due to its monochrome cover shot, taken by Tom McIlroy at a gig in Dublin's National Stadium) slowly took shape. As a statement of intent, it's difficult to get any better than the opening (song-tune segued) track, 'Raggle Taggle Gypsy/*Tabhair Dom Do Lámh*'. The first part was learned by Moore from singing Roscommon traveller John Reilly; the segue, at 2 minutes 30 seconds, from the song into O'Flynn's uileann pipe tour de force of *Tabhair Dom Do Lámh* (originally a tune composed by the seventeenth-century Derry harper Rory Dall Ó Catháin) was virtually unprecedented, and gave the album an incredible kick-start, which became a defining moment for both album and band.

There are superb songs here ('Arthur McBride', Ewan MacColl's 'Sweet Thames Flow Softly', Irvine's 'The West Coast of Clare', 'Only Our Rivers'), but it's the instrumentals that charm the knickers off you: two Turlough Carolan tunes, 'Planxty Irwin' and '*Sí Bheag, Sí Mhór*' (the former sweet and easy, the latter poignant and pithy) are handled so brilliantly by O'Flynn that you'd wonder how he does it without you knowing. Two other doozies are the traditional Kerry slide 'Merrily Kissed the Quaker' (which O'Flynn douses with his innate mercurial playing) and the final track, 'The Blacksmith', an old English folk song sung by Irvine that (symmetry ahoy!) segues into a boisterous, amplified Balkan knees-up underpinned by some of O'Flynn's most dexterous phrasing.

A new chapter in Irish traditional music had begun, and what's the betting that in London a young man called Shane MacGowan was reading it?

Released: 1973
Record Label: Shanachie Records, Polydor
Producer: Phil Coulter
Recorded at: Olympic Studios, London
Sleeve Design: Richard Rockwood, Tom McIlroy (cover photography)

Tracks:
1 Raggle Taggle Gypsy/Tabhair Dom Do Lámh **4:28**
2 Arthur McBride **2:52**
3 Planxty Irwin **2:16**
4 Sweet Thames Flow Softly **4:11**
5 Junior Crehan's Favourite/Corney Is Coming **2:38**
6 The West Coast of Claire **5:34**
7 The Jolly Beggar-Reel **4:23**
8 Only Our Rivers **4:06**
9 Sí Bheag, Sí Mhór **3:34**
10 Follow Me Up To Carlow **2:21**
11 Merrily Kissed The Quaker **2:41**
12 The Blacksmith **4:09**

THE POGUES

RUM, SODOMY & THE LASH (1985)

PHILIP CHEVRON

'What fascinated me, coming on board as I did late in the making of this album, though having been a part of the greater Pogues family for a little longer than that, as a producer, mate and cheerleader, was how they arrived at the point at which Shane's writing went pretty much anywhere it wanted to, a freedom which would, quite soon, leave open the possibility of a "Fairytale of New York" or a "Rainy Night in Soho". Although Elvis Costello did not, I think, always fully grasp the scale of the band's musical ambition, he could not but recognise that MacGowan was a major writer who had not yet, for whatever reason, fully come into his own . . . Elvis understood that what counted was people should hear MacGowan's songs in a relatively unadorned form, so there could be no misunderstanding their brilliance, no allowances made for studio enhancement or sweetening.'

'Their music is like the brandy of the damned,' wrote Tom Waits in the sleeve notes for the re-issue of this album in 2004. No arguments there, then . . . Despite most of their members having been born in the UK (and one, original bassist Cait O'Riordan, born in Nigeria), The Pogues are quite likely the most definably Irish band in this book, and this album – their second – one of the most instinctively hard-wired into the Irish psyche. From their start in 1982, there was little about them you could sit on the fence about: The Pogues were either hated or loved for their bastard hybrid of punk rock and traditional Irish music.

In the blue corner huddled a collective of die-hard Irish traditional music fans, tut-tutting over what they perceived to be a form of cultural desecration. In the red corner gathered a hybrid all of its own: Irish people, weaned on traditional music, who had grown weary of the pearl-laden presentation box it was kept in, bored of the finger-against-mouth shushes whenever they dared to speak aloud in pubs. If The Pogues' 1984 debut album, *Red Roses for Me*, shook a bloody fist at the blue-corner community, then *Rum, Sodomy & the Lash* kicked them up the arse. Big time. Seconds away, round two . . .

Such a commotion might have disappeared if the songs had been anything less than amazing, but the album was full of the kind of songs that would, eventually, go down in history as pioneering classics of their type. Some were just unashamedly terrific ('The Sickbed of Cúchulainn', 'The Old Main Drag', 'A Pair of Brown Eyes', 'Sally MacLennane'), others were class folk songs given a Pogues makeover (Eric Bogle's And 'The Band Played Waltzing Matilda', Ewan MacColl's 'Dirty Old Town', Phil Gaston's 'Navigator'), and others still were trad/arr tunes instilled with ramshackle reverence and due diligence ('I'm a Man You Don't Meet Every Day', 'Jesse James', 'The Gentleman Solider').

It was Shane MacGowan's lyric writing, however, that not so much raised the bar as burned it down. Death and booze are everywhere here, as is sex, vomiting, war, rent boys, religion, and the shattered dreams (and swallowed drams) of a certain generation of London Irish. It would be another album or two before MacGowan's magic would drown in alcohol, but on *Rum, Sodomy & the Lash* he was virtually untouchable. (The 2004 reissue comes with extra tracks, including 1986's *Poguetry in Motion* EP, which features another two bona fide classic Pogues songs: one of their sweetest, 'Rainy Night in Soho', and one of their rowdiest, 'The Body of an American'.)

Released: 1985
Record Label: MCA, Stiff, MEA International
Producer: Philip Chevron, Elvis Costello
Recorded at: Elephant Studios, London
Sleeve Design: Frank Murray (concept),
J. L. A. Gericault (original painting), Peter
Mennim (heads), Lilly Lee (hand lettering)

Tracks:
1 The Sick Bed of Cúchulainn 2:59
2 The Old Main Drag 3:19
3 Wild Cats of Kilkenny 2:48
4 I'm a Man You Don't Meet Every Day
   2:55
5 A Pair of Brown Eyes 4:54
6 Sally MacLennane 2:43
7 A Pistol for Paddy Garcia 2:31
8 Dirty Old Town 3:45
9 Jesse James 2:58
10 Navigator 4:12
11 Billy's Bones 2:02
12 The Gentleman Soldier 2:04
13 And the Band Played Waltzing Matilda
   8:10

PONY CLUB
POST ROMANTIC (2008)

MARK CULLEN

'Most rock 'n' roll is aimed at finding your true love, or telling your object of desire that nobody could possibly love them more than you. That's great when you're fifteen, hormonal and don't appreciate your own company, but I wanted to write something for all those who got the girl (even if it wasn't exactly the one you would have really hoped it would be), got married, bought the house, had the kids and weren't sure where to go from there.'

He's been in hyped/hotly tipped Irish bands (Bawl, Fixed Stars), has written songs for Kylie, is known to all and sundry as Pony Club, and is highly regarded for being the type of songwriter who can deftly tile around kitchen-sink dramas.

When the major-label-band scenario for Fixed Stars went belly up (at the end of their term with a major label, the band was in debt to the merry tune of about £750,000; they couldn't even pay back £50,000 of it), Mark Cullen stopped wondering why love-bombing from the majors went from sweet to sour, and signed to Setanta, the London-based label that specialised in providing a home to many Irish acts in the 1990s. But what to write about?

Among the many things Cullen has pondered is why all dysfunctional families need to have their stories told. He dissected the subject succinctly enough to make Pony Club's 2002 debut, *Home Truths*, sound like shoulder-shrug whimpers from the terminally victimised. Two thousand and four's *Family Business* did exactly what you'd think the title refers to. *Post Romantic*, however – with its indie/electro throbs and tunes recorded, so the sleeve tells us, 'in various bedrooms, parlours and landings'– is a different kettle of stinky fish.

For starters, it's written from the point of view of someone who is no longer in the first flush of youth, who has, perhaps, been knocked sideways by life, love and encroaching middle age, and who has been punched in the face by the drain of a certain type of domesticity. There is no teenage angst here, no *oh-my-God!* dramas of the boy-meets-girl-and-then-gets-dumped variety. *Post Romantic* is all about the reality, the pain, the drudgery, the distinction between the drabness of people's lives and the little victories that humanity can offer up in the wake of disappointments.

On 'I Still Feel The Same', Cullen siphons misanthropy out of a bottle of bile as he touches on loss of spirit: 'Strummer and Mike Leigh were my reasons for living, but now the only songs I like are on "Lite FM"'; 'would you remind me that once I would get upset with the whole bleeding world and every person in it'. On 'Anthony', with its chipper forty-three year old central figure, the owner of an SUV with Basement Jaxx in the music player, he sings 'Congratulations, now we're middle class', but it sounds more like an insult than praise.

Still holding on to the Mike Leigh aesthetic of ordinary lives going through heartbreaking times and saying devastating things, Cullen incisively fashions a dozen songs that ring true. Gifted glam pop with a drop of acid in the centre has rarely sounded so vital or vicious.

PONY CLUB
POST ROMANTIC

Released: 2008
Record Label: Hum Records
Producer: Martin Healy, Darren Cullen
Recorded at: 'Various bedrooms, parlours and landings'
Sleeve Design: Niall McCormack, Dominic Turner (photography)

Tracks:
1 Welcome **2:15**
2 I Still Feel The Same **4:19**
3 Diplomat **3:06**
4 Last Bus **2:50**
5 People Need Others **2:49**
6 To Tell The Truth **2:50**
7 Anthony **3:17**
8 Ideal Man **3:04**
9 The World Didn't End **4:23**
10 In Your Dreams **5:04**
11 Anthony Coda **0:38**
12 What Are You Angry For? **4:16**

POWER OF DREAMS

IMMIGRANTS, EMIGRANTS AND ME (1990)

CRAIG WALKER

'Like most bands' first albums you're just writing songs for the sheer love of it and the chance to play them live. We had a mountain of songs going in to record the album that had been written over a two-year period prior to recording. The Beatles, of course, were a huge influence on us, as were The Smiths, and also Dublin's A House, who made great guitar-driven pop music with social commentary that was unique at the time. Does the album still work for me? Yeah, I still love it and feel very proud of it. People keep telling me that if it were released today it would be a huge success, so I'll take their word! I think Ray Shulman, the producer, did an amazing job, and when I hear tracks on the radio today from it they still sound fresh – the joy of being eighteen comes rushing back to me.'

Power of Dreams received early encouragement from Setanta Records, a London-based indie record label that wilfully championed what seemed to be every decent Irish band that was making music in the late eighties and early nineties. In 1989, the band released their debut EP on Setanta, *A Little Piece of God*. Such was the critical response to it (both *Sounds* and *Melody Maker* made it their Single of the Week) that UK major labels started a bidding war, and in jig-time the band had signed to Polygram. They released their debut album, *Immigrants, Emigrants and Me*, a year later on Polydor.

There were loads of bands around this time that were well able to balance great melodies with psychotic intent, and Power of Dreams were easily one of the better examples. The fact that their music is rooted in a recognisable rock prototype (guitars, rhythm section, vocals) assisted them, but within this framework it is experimental without being too esoteric or radical. Remember, too, that they emerged a year or so before Nirvana broke through; while they were certainly comin' to getcha with all guns blazing, there was nonetheless a smoothness to their music that would soon give way to a roughing up, in general, of pop culture. So, there is no angularity here, no dishevelment, just classy rock music (irrespective of the fact that some of the songs were written with no intention that they would land a place on the album) played by teenage Dubliners with heads of unruly hair.

One of the most remarkable aspects of this album is how simultaneously angry, frustrated and optimistically wide-eyed it sounds. While songs such as 'The Joke's On Me', 'Stay', 'Never Told You', 'Never Been to Texas', 'Where Is the Love', 'Bring It Down' and '100 Ways To Kill a Love' bristle with brutally strategic riffs and clear-headed tunes, singer/songwriter Craig Walker delivers lyrics that enable the listener to get off on words that ponder topics such as loss of love, mortality and ambition.

It isn't all jangling guitars and riffs to smash windows to, though: the rockabilly rumble of 'Much Too Much' comes as something of a surprise, as do the nostalgic reflections of 'Had You Listened' ('Do you remember, remember the bus? Sitting on the top deck, well we talked so much, mainly about the future and about the state, and how we'd really like to get away some day'). What really comes through, however, is the complete lack of indulgence: in essence, *Immigrants, Emigrants and Me* is a youthful, stubble-free zone – as tight and lean as the band members' twenty-eight-inch waists, and as bright as their belt buckles.

Released: 1990
Record Label: Polydor Records
Producer: Ray Shulman
Recorded at: Master Rock Studios, London
Sleeve Design: Abrahams Pants, Bill Doyle
(front cover photograph, courtesy of
Irish Society for Prevention of Cruelty to
Children)

Tracks:
1 The Joke's on Me **2:58**
2 Talk **2:58**
3 Does It Matter **3:28**
4 Much Too Much **2:36**
5 Had You Listened **3:07**
6 Stay **3:12**
7 Never Told You **2:54**

8 Bring You Down **2:48**
9 Never Been to Texas **2:24**
10 Where Is the Love **3:13**
11 Maire I Don't Love You **3:27**
12 100 Ways to Kill a Love **3:51**
13 Mother's Eyes **2:37**
14 My Average Day **3:03**

PUGWASH

ELEVEN MODERN ANTIQUITIES (2008)

THOMAS WALSH

'My obligatory artistic vomiting spewed forth another batch of tunes against my will – which is always the case, and something I can do nothing about. *Eleven Modern Antiquities* became the baby that was unplanned, but one you love with all your heart and soul, regardless. In one last fuck-you of artistic bravado to myself, I managed to put together a collection of songs that I'm immensely proud of, and that are amongst the most preferred pop-powder that stokes the Pugwash canon of songs. Tosh Flood, my right-hand man for all sessions, says it's his favourite Pugwash album. That's good enough for me.'

The first record that Pugwash's guiding light Thomas Walsh bought, from a Dublin market stall, was one by Electric Light Orchestra; an obsession with ELO followed. When his mother asked him on 8 December 1980 which famous musician had been shot dead, young Walsh beseeched her not to tell him it was Jeff Lynne.

What we have here is, essentially, an argument for the abolition of the sensitive singer-songwriter type. Imagine actually wanting to be Jeff Buckley, wanting his trauma, his depression, implies a querulous Walsh on *Eleven Modern Antiquities* – which is such a hybrid of ELO and The Beatles that it hardly qualifies as Irish. What we also have here is, ultimately, another argument – this time for the decapitation of the alt-folk/nu-folk brigade, and the incarceration of experimentalists who think that singing out of tune is edgy.

Thus far, Walsh has led a life of music fanaticism and being ignored by people who consider him little more than a pastiche artist (at best) and a plagiarist (at worst). He bypassed the Dublin band scenes from the mid- to late eighties onwards, preferring to make music on a four-track recording unit in his garden shed (à la XTC's Andy Partridge, another musical icon of Walsh's).

Come 1993, and Pugwash, as we now know it, was formed. The mission? To hone the collected works of ELO, The Beatles, XTC and numerous other US and British pop/rock acts into a distinctive, direct hit to the senses. The result? Nothing.

Yet from their debut album (1999's *Almond Tea*) onwards, Pugwash have slowly transcended their influences, making what was once obviously referenced into something that has a dynamic core all of its own. Accusations that they are overly influenced by the likes of XTC, ELO and other exponents of the perfect pop art-form are rightly shrugged off by Walsh. Ultimately, he couldn't care less. As he writes on the inner-sleeve thank-you notes of his debut album, 'If we forgot anyone, you obviously mean nothing to us.'

On *Eleven Modern Antiquities*, Walsh is assisted in varying degrees by the likes of XTC's Andy Partridge and Dave Gregory, Michael Penn, Jason Falkner and Divine Comedy's Neil Hannon (who, with Walsh, in the guise of The Duckworth Lewis Method, released a self-titled album in 2009 that was subsequently nominated for an Ivor Novello Award).

Is it ground-breaking? No. Is it a wonderful variant of psychedelic pop music unmatched by any other musician from Ireland – created by, no less, a large, bearded man from Drimnagh? Yes.

Released: 2008
Record Label: 1969 Records, Ape House
Producer: Thomas Walsh, Keith Farrell
Recorded at: The Bunker, Dublin; The Glebe, Dublin
Sleeve Design: Emagine Media

Tracks:
1 Take Me Away **3:37**
2 Cluster Bomb **2:28**
3 Here **3:16**
4 It's So Fine **3:27**
5 Song For You **2:53**

6 My Genius **4:08**
7 Limerance **3:48**
8 Your Friend **3:11**
9 The Cannon and the Bell **1:50**
10 At the Sea **3:21**
11 Landsdowne Valley **5:28**

THE RADIATORS

GHOSTOWN (1979)

PHILIP CHEVRON

'The idea of making a pop album based upon a series of imaginative adolescent rambles through one's native city, however much it grandly aspired towards its perceived literary antecedents, however much it attempted to make a virtue of the recent past seen through the prism of the recent present, and however much it hoped to transcend its apparent parochialism, was not undaunting. It was a concern well-founded, as the subsequent critical and commercial indifference to the record in the UK illustrated, in the short term at least. I can't really imagine a British writer or band doing anything comparable to *Ghostown* – Pete Townshend, I suppose, though he did at least have the benefit of cultural references more immediately accessible to British listeners.'

Underappreciated, overlooked, a lost classic, a missed opportunity and a shocking example of how a truly great and ambitious collection of songs can become entangled in music industry trends – *Ghostown* is all this and more.

Following their 1977 debut, *TV Tube Heart*, the one-time Radiators From Space shortened their name, moved to London and started to write and rehearse the material that would become *Ghostown*. Like most second albums, it reflected perhaps a more truthful approach to their environment, which is why the guitar-driven, anthemic attacks of *TV Tube Heart* (best exemplified by the early punk rock bootboy-kick of 'Television Screen') were replaced with intentionally literate and highly melodic songs of the calibre of 'They're Looting in the Town', 'Million Dollar Hero', 'Kitty Ricketts', 'Who are the Strangers?' and 'Song of the Faithful Departed'.

Such juxtaposing of James Joyce (whose disaffected spirit imbues *Ghostown* from start to finish), Seán O'Casey and Irish actor and comedian Jimmy O'Dea with The Beatles, Marc Bolan and David Bowie went completely over the heads of UK critics and audiences, who, perhaps to the punk-manor-born, scornfully dismissed the change of creative direction. Added to this was a year-long delay in getting the album released, which acted as another nail in the band's coffin.

Ghostown also stiffed, leaving The Radiators adrift and smarting at the album's rejection.

It was and remains one of those albums that has always found the listeners it needed to (even if there weren't many of them – main songwriter Philip Chevron once described the band's audience as 'elitist . . . the people who came to see us because The Boomtown Rats were so uncool.'). In many crucial ways, irrespective of its total lack of commercial success, *Ghostown* influenced part of the process that gave rise to The Pogues (a band that Chevron would go on to join) in that it touched on Irish themes in a contemporary way.

Unlike Horslips (see page 108), whose album, *The Táin*, was itself something of a cultural touchstone for *Ghostown*, and who referenced Ireland's mythology, and unlike Thin Lizzy (see page 196), who added rock 'n' roll glamour and sex to the equation, The Radiators wrote of inner-city dramas enmeshed with religion, doubt and social atrophy.

The music on *Ghostown* is emblematic of a time when people dared to make a difference. Even from this distance, it remains a special record that – akin to Harry Potter-like wand lore – has to choose you and not the other way around.

Released: 1979
Record Label: Chiswick Records
Producer: Tony Visconti
Recorded at: Good Earth Soundhouse, London
Sleeve Design: Philip Chevron, Jimmy Crashe, Steve Averill. Still image of Max Shreck from F. W. Murnau's Nosferatu (1922)

Tracks:
1   Million Dollar Hero   **3:06**
2   Let's Talk About the Weather   **4:19**
3   Johnny Jukebox   **2:46**
4   Confidential   **2:51**
5   They're Looting in the Town   **4:01**
6   Who are the Strangers?   **3:13**
7   Ballad of Kitty Ricketts   **3:55**
8   Song of the Faithful Departed   **4:44**
9   Walking Home Alone Again   **3:05**
10   Dead the Beast, Dead the Poison   **3:25**

THE REDNECK MANIFESTO

CUT YOUR HEART OFF FROM YOUR HEAD (2003)

MATTHEW BOLGER

'Cut Your Heart Off from Your Head was recorded less than a year after our first album, *Thirtysixstrings*, and is seen by us to be a companion piece. Listening back to this record for the first time in years, I feel that we've progressed greatly as a band, but the original energy and freshness is still there, and as strong as ever. We all feel very fortunate to be part of this group, and see no end to it.'

The Redneck Manifesto appropriated their name from a book by US social tract iconoclast Jim Goad. If you haven't read it, you should. Goad tackles an important theme: that America's white underclasses do not fail because of individual character defects; rather, they have been handed socio-economic straitjackets at birth.

While it would be handy to cross-reference such themes with a similar strain of grubby anarcho-satire from this Dublin band, it would also be wrong. The Redneck Manifesto – formed in 1998 from the vital organs of four Dublin hardcore/underground bands, from which they utilise elements and temper them with agile wit and touches too elegant to dislike – buck various trends.

For starters, they have little interest in the verse-chorus-verse aesthetic; they do not have that endearing, enduring staple of popular music, a lead singer; ergo, they have no lyrics, allowing their music alone and of itself to state its case, to formulate the ebb and flow of whatever emotions the listener is experiencing at any given time. Taking this intransigent approach to music as a reasonably credible gauge, it seems The Redneck Manifesto are not for compromising.

We have heard this 'not for compromising' thing many times before, of course, but the belief system intrinsic to TRM is solid: what you create must be followed through to the maximum of its ability.

Cut Your Heart Off from Your Head is an album that proves that Irish rock music has finally severed its own umbilical cord, terminating communications between the doting mothership of Irish rock and its many mewling infants. Yet while the hard-core aesthetic bubbles under in the band's debut 2001 album, *Thirtysixstrings*, its presence is less obvious in *Cut Your Heart Off from Your Head*, which is a far more pastoral piece of work.

From the off, the band's ingrained characteristics (trust your instincts, experiment musically, be open to suggestion) are presented. Book-ended by the subtle natures of opening ('Cut Your Heart Off . . .') and closing ('. . . From Your Head') tracks, the album becomes an even more absorbing experience through tracks such as 'Part Monkey Smart Stallion', 'Please Don't Ask Us What We Think Of Your Band', 'Make Yourself Comfortable' and 'The Dillon Family Dancers' (a particular highlight that thrills via an incremental sweep of guitars that fair does your head in).

A short album (the job is complete in just over half an hour) that just can't outstay its welcome. There aren't too many of those out there . . .

Released: 2003
Record Label: Red F Records, Greyslate
Producer: Alan O'Boyle
Recorded at: Family residence
Sleeve Design: Matt Bolger

Tracks:
1 Cut Your Heart Off . . . **5:30**
2 Please Don't Ask Us What We Think Of Your Band **3:12**
3 You Say Tomato, I Say Tomato **3:47**

4 Make Yourself Comfortable **5:15**
5 The Dillon Family Dancers **3:40**
6 Part Monkey, Smart Stallion **4:18**
7 . . . From Your Head **6:03**

FIONN REGAN

THE END OF HISTORY (2006)

'I wrote in the album booklet that making *The End of History* was like building an ocean liner with a butter knife. I am part mule, and have tended to choose an unconventional path in order to avoid making music by committee. This route inevitably throws up its own challenges and restrictions, but in making my first album I found a way of using my restrictions to my advantage. I didn't realise it at the time, but I was laying the foundations for my modus operandi. Learning to use that butter knife proved invaluable. I have my initials on it now.'

It comes as no surprise to discover that, at the start of the noughties, Fionn Regan released an EP (*Slow Wall*) under the moniker of 'Bilbo'. It might be rather fanciful to point out that Regan wouldn't look out of place in the world of J. R. R. Tolkien, but there's a hint of truth in it. The mischievous features, the slim stature, the elfin-like demeanor, the pixie-like looks – Regan has them all.

He jettisoned Bilbo, however, and struck out on his own, transforming into quite a tidy creative proposition. A few more EPs filtered out in the early-to-mid-2000s (including *Reservoir* and *Hotel Room*, on the small Brighton-based indie label Anvil), but Regan's first proper calling card was *The End of History*. Garnering a fistful of praise, plaudits and award nominations (including Britain's Mercury Music Prize and Ireland's Choice Music Prize) that fresh-faced singer-songwriters would sell their acoustic guitars for, the album introduced him to a far wider audience. More or less immediately after the album's release, Regan embarked on a promotional tour that would see him relentlessly traverse Europe and America. And subsequently come, for a time anyway, a cropper.

Is Regan misunderstood? By some, yes. One perception is that he's a bit of a ditherer; another is that he's a space cadet who purchased a one-way ticket for a journey to Jupiter on the Starship Enterprise. One more view is that he's a very fine songwriter with a marked tendency for abstraction, and who occasionally leans towards the doleful side too much, which can therefore be viewed as a default setting. He once said, in that signature circuitous way of his, that creativity is like falling into a hole on a dark and stormy night. For Regan, though, songwriting is surely the journey back towards the light, and his music the proven evidence of the journey.

He's a deceptive songwriter, too: behind the wafer-thin appearance lies a musician of stealth and strength. He's folk, yes, and he carries with him the literacy of Nick Drake and the disdain of early Bob Dylan, but on *The End of History* he can be as breathtaking as a kick to the groin. He also deftly avoids the trap that most 'sensitive' singer-songwriters, almost willingly it would seem, fall into: despite their best efforts, they sound insincere and self-conscious. Regan, on the other hand, with songs like 'Be Good or Be Gone', 'The Underwood Typewriter' ('Step out of your dress and I'll wear you like a hood, for a hood is a home for someone who lives alone'), 'Bunker or Basement', 'Put a Penny in the Slot' ('good company and grief sit like a dock leaf sits beside a stinging nettle') and 'Hey Rabbit', effortlessly achieves directness and believability. His acoustic guitar playing here, also, is simply superb – so nimble you have to listen to it twice for verification. All told, a collection that is a sheer delight from start to finish.

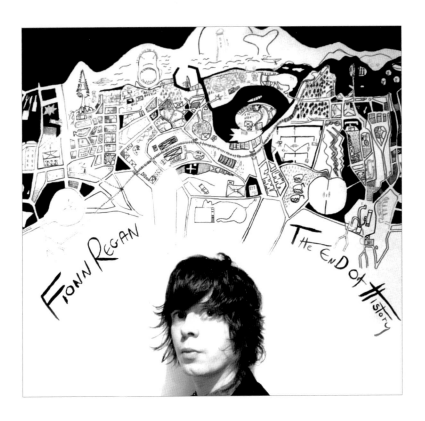

Released: 2006
Record Label: Bella Union (UK), Lost Highway Records (US)
Producer: Fionn Regan
Recorded at: 'a number of locations . . . barns, living rooms, etc'
Sleeve Design: Rossi & Rory at Swollen, Fionn Regan

Tracks:
1 Be Good or Be Gone **3:20**
2 The Underwood Typewriter **3:03**
3 Hunters Map **3:39**
4 Hey Rabbit **3:33**
5 Black Water Child **3:00**
6 Put a Penny in the Slot **4:02**
7 The Cowshed **3:32**

8 Snowy Atlas Mountains **4:14**
9 Noah (Ghost in a Sheet) **3:40**
10 The End of History **4:39**
11 Abacus **2:36**
12 Bunker or Basement **6:26**

THE REVENANTS
HORSE OF A DIFFERENT COLOUR (1993)

STEPHEN RYAN

'This was my first experience of writing an album on my own, so I had no quality-control procedure whatsoever: anything that was completed made it (apart from the title track, which ended up as a B-side somewhere) . . . There was no real difference to working with The Stars of Heaven; I just came up with words/chords, basic arrangements, took it to the band, and we worked it up in rehearsal. But context is important: with The Stars there was a desperation to succeed, whereas with The Revenants it was more of a fun thing, so I think that helped a lot.'

It's all about tunes and guitars, wistful voices and smart lyrics, getting drunk, falling down, falling in love, getting up, getting back. The man you can blame, if you want to, is Stephen Ryan. He was a guiding member of The Stars of Heaven (see separate entry, page 186), a band about which great things were written and even greater things expected. We are poorer for their loss, etc.

The Revenants, however, weren't so much a different kettle of fish (or, now you come to mention it, a horse of a different colour) as a continuation of excellence. Unlike Stars of Heaven, though, The Revenants came on a bit tougher, a bit more rowdy. There was no denying the innate quality of the band's songwriting abilities, and it's hardly stretching a creative analogy to say that this band (Stars of Heaven, too, actually) were to Ireland what The Go-Betweens were to Australia: a responsive, emotionally adept unit thoroughly in tune with the country's inner melancholy, underlying sense of trauma, and drinking habits.

Released in the summer, it deserves to be in a book called *101 Records You Must Listen to in June/July/August*, due to its general aural demeanour of calm climes, rockin' songs and a louche cragginess that wouldn't get within an ass's roar of Mount Rushmore. The Go-Betweens were mentioned earlier, but the band have possibly more in common with their American counterparts, the The Replacements: what we have here is a type of unfussy country rock, but in much the same way as Stars of Heaven were years ahead of the pack with their own take on Americana, so The Revenants evoke music of a previous era yet sound so far advanced that it's positively, spooky.

You could put such a prescient approach down to Ryan's songwriting, which is classic in its style; also, despite the album's occasional delightfully clanging chords, there's a level of softly spoken self-deprecation about the subject matter (wine and women – what else?) that is often beguiling and never throwaway. While the likes of opening track 'Let's Get Falling Down' is all boisterous, Bulmers and brilliant (its opening guitar figures are like REM's Peter Buck arm-wrestling with The Replacements' Paul Westerberg), so many of the other tracks dignify themselves with a sensibility that reflects Ryan's sad explorations of the heart. If you think it's mostly Nashville mournfulness, you might be right, but here's the thing: for every tear-in-the-beer sentiment, there is a liquefied solo that has you tracing it on an imaginary guitar.

Ultimately, it's just so rapturously, euphorically melodic: 'Marry Money', 'Ted's Tune', 'You For Whom Silence', 'William Byrd', 'Capercailye' (the latter two sung quite enchantingly by Eileen Gogan) and 'Speak Slowly' capture the mismatches of love and life. The album ends as softly as it began loudly – with the piano instrumental 'Forbidden Mourning' a figurine of a tune dancing by itself to music no one else can hear. Perfect.

THE REVENANTS

HORSE OF A DIFFERENT COLOUR

Released: 1993
Record Label: Hunter S.
Producer: Chris O'Brien
Recorded at: House of Mediocrity Studios, Dublin
Sleeve Design: Works Associates, Dave Farrell (front cover photography)

Tracks:
1 Lets Get Falling Down 4:43
2 Marry Money 2:59
3 Ted's Tune 3:23
4 You For Whom Silence 3:01
5 Sympathy 3:57
6 William Byrd 3:33
7 The Drinking Side of Me 3:56
8 Capercailye 4:04
9 Xmas Card 3:39
10 Speak Slowly 3:21
11 Doctor Said 3:25
12 Forbidden Mourning 2:05

DAMIEN RICE

9 (2006)

'*9* was a lesson in how not to make a record: pull the fruits from the trees before they're ripe, add too many ingredients, with too many chefs stirring an over-hot pot. The result: burnt vegetarian chicken soup.'

It would be very easy to see Damien Rice's criminally underrated second album as merely an extension of his groundbreaking 2002 debut, *O*. Each record is sparsely produced, and each contains songs that will be – and are – loved and loathed in equal measure. Rice has a distinct knack for dividing opinion – even among his committed fanbase. For those people who aren't fans, the mere mention of his name brings them out in hives: for this crowd, Rice is a byword for preciousness. The music?

O was a slow-burning bolt from the blue (towards which Rice gravitated following a spell in a band called Juniper, which morphed into Bell X1 – see separate entry, page 26), gaining ground in leisurely but certain fashion to the point where it has made Rice a very rich man. *9*, however, comes from a consolidated, perhaps more intuitive, place. Like the material on *O*, the songs here seep into you, and, aside from one significant, puzzling error – 'Me, My Yoke and I', the self-indulgence of which will provide all of Rice's most ardent critics with enough ammunition to continue to gun him down – the remaining tracks contain some of the most honest expressions of emotional intensity you're likely ever to hear.

There is actually little of Rice's perceived hippie-dippy preciousness here; reality checks have clearly been placed on red alert, with the likes of hard-line songs such as '9 Crimes', 'The Animals Were Gone' ('I know I've been a liar and I know I've been a fool . . . I know that I've left you in places of despair'), 'Rootless Tree' ('So fuck you and all we've been through; I said leave it, it's nothing to you, and if you hate me then hate me so good that you can let me out'), 'Coconut Skins' ('You can like between her legs and go looking for . . . tell her you're searching for her soul') and Grey Room ('Have I still got you to cross my bridge in this storm? Have I still got you to keep me warm?').

All of these are robust studies of emotional issues. As such, a theme emerges: the often frustrating, and joyous, experiences of happenstance. If most of the aforementioned songs could easily soundtrack Richard Linklater's *Before Sunrise*, then 'Accidental Babies' (which is tangentially referenced in 'The Animals Were Gone') could have been especially written for the sequel, *Before Sunset*. The song is a brilliantly insightful distillation of hard knocks and difficult choices ('Do you come together ever with him?'), the wear and tear of a relationship's what-ifs, maybes and whys ('Do you feel like you belong?') and who-knows-how-it-will-all-end ('Do you really feel alive without me?').

The album starts brilliantly ('9 Crimes') and finishes on a freaky, ambient note ('Sleep Don't Weep': listen out for the 'hidden' lengthy tone-poem). In between is, by and large, the best confessional and most candid album ever released by an Irish songwriter.

Released: 2006
Record Label: Warner Bros.
Producer: Damien Rice (assisted by Shane Fitzsimons, Lisa Hannigan, Vyvienne Long, Tom Osander)
Recorded at: 'A home studio in various places & spaces in Celbridge, Foxrock, Donard, Los Angeles, and County Wicklow'
Sleeve Design: Damien Rice, Fred & Daisy (paintings and drawings)

Tracks:
1 9 Crimes 3:39
2 The Animals Were Gone 5:41
3 Elephant 5:57
4 Rootless Tree 4:22
5 Dogs 4:11
6 Coconut Skins 3:45
7 Me, My Yoke and I 5:57
8 Grey Room 5:43
9 Accidental Babies 6:34
10 Sleep Don't Weep 21:54

RUDI
'BIG TIME' (1978)

BRIAN YOUNG

' "Big Time" always has a special place in my heart. I was seventeen at the time, it was our very first band, we were the first punk band in Belfast, it was one of the first songs we wrote, and it was recorded the first time we ever set foot in a recording studio. It was also the first 45 on what became Northern Ireland's best-known home-grown label. Overall, on reflection, it's not a bad start for a bunch of no-good teenage troublemakers from east Belfast. For my money, too, it's easily the best 45 that ever came out on Good Vibes, and the best punk 45 that ever came out on an Irish label. Bar none. But, then, I am biased . . .'

Rudi might have turned out to be the band that time well and truly forgot if it hadn't been for the release, on the Good Vibrations label, of 'Big Time'. The song matches (indeed, on certain days, in certain moods, at certain times, it kicks the teeth out of the mouth of) 'Teenage Kicks' as the best-ever single released by an Irish band. Rudi (the name came not from The Clash's 'Rudi Can't Fail', or from David Bowie's 'Star', but from The Jook's 'Oh Oh Rudi'), however, didn't exactly fit the usual profile.

A gang of teenage layabouts from east Belfast tethered to the logic of the homo sapien hybrid that was Marc Bolan, David Bowie, New York Dolls, Slade and fifties rock 'n' roll (in essence, glammed-up proto-punk that mixed erudition, working-class smarts and primordial nudges and winks), Rudi started in 1975 as a covers band, their nascent career as rock stars kick-started by the band's fifteen-year-old singer and songwriter Brian Young meeting Bolan at a T Rex gig on the Isle of Man.

By early '76, a band of sorts was started, playing instruments that were begged, borrowed and (literally) stolen, and as the months passed so Rudi progressed, hiring function rooms in local dives that would soon fill up with fellow underage drinkers and malcontents. Rehearsing in a loyalist band hall in Glenmore Street, Rudi wrote all their songs together, galvanised as much by the thrill of the new as by the shock of the fact that they could actually write basic pop/punk tunes.

One of these was, of course, 'Big Time'. Rudi had written and played many original songs by this point (one such, 'Cops', with its authority-baiting intro/outro chant of 'SSRUC', and chorus of 'We hate the cops', quickly attained local punk-anthem status), but with 'Big Time' the band knew they had hit on something special. Written specifically about a former friend of the band who had notions far above his station, the song's guitar riff was initially inspired by Chuck Berry. Played sloppily and noisier, and you nabbed the Johnny Thunders approach; played faster and louder, and you had The Damned by your side. Played even more ham-fistedly, recalls Young, 'on a tenth-hand Antoria SG through a cheapo Carlsbro Stingray amp with the "suzz" switch full on, and you have the intro'.

The first single to be released on Good Vibrations, 'Big Time' was recorded on begged (if not borrowed and stolen) minutes in Solomon Peres's recording studio in Templepatrick on 7 Feb 1978. Rudi had never before set foot in such an environment, and left after two hours, worrying that the song wasn't going to sound noisy enough. Two months later, a classic pop/punk tune, a bona fide grade-A belter, was unleashed. It remains a template of many things, not least how naiveté and youthful dreaming can create something that is as important a cultural artefact as anything positioned on a plinth in a museum.

Released: 1978
Record Label: Good Vibrations
Producer: George Doherty
Recorded at: Hydepark Studios,
Templepatrick, Antrim
Sleeve Design: Karl Freund
(cinematographer/image of Boris Karloff in
The Mummy)
Duration: 2:46

SAVILLE

NOSTALGIA (2008)

TONY 'TOSH' FLOOD 'We always thought that you weren't a proper band unless you released three albums, at least. This one was the third Saville album. So job done.'

We all know of bands like Saville. Now split up (it happens all the time, apparently), Saville were one of those acts that, despite having more talent in their dandruff than many other acts have in their whole head, would – we just knew in our bones – go the way of the dodo. You know the score by this stage: they were a band riveted to evocative songwriters (Pete Townshend, Ray Davies, Paul Weller) yet with a contemporary edge, not in the centre of the radar screen, living virtually a hand-to-mouth existence, great songs, sporadic gigs, cool image (the Mod aesthetic taken to a different level), and certain critics' favourites.

Saville released *Nostalgia* five years after their second album, *Somnambular Ballads*, and eight years after their debut, *Is Anybody Happier Today*. So clearly they weren't a band in a hurry, but rather a bunch of blokes who worked their collective ass off in order to make money to pay for recording stints. What marked out *Nostalgia* from the previous pair was its sharp rise in songwriting quality: quite simply, it's the sound of a band where everything just fell into place, an album where kismet and The Kinks looked at each other and swooned.

With a bunch of excellent songs that reference Dublin, Small Faces, James Joyce, Squeeze, first love, The Who, sex and the single boy – as well as a sense of sentiment without wallowing in teary contemplation – Saville created a finely wrought, thematic album that utilises classic pop/rock ('It Don't Feel Right Anymore'), mild psychedelia ('Stop Telling Lies', which marries ringing Byrds motifs with The Who's 'Pictures Of Lily'), Mod/soul hints (the title track teases with a Curtis Mayfield swagger; 'I Can't Do Anything To Ease Your Pain' references the Motown strut of Brenda Holloway's 'Every Little Bit Hurts') and a singularity all of its own ('The Lonely Ghost' and 'Flares').

Main songwriter and vocalist Ken O'Duffy (assisted occasionally by co-songwriter and guitarist Tony 'Tosh' Flood) pitches rose-tinted memories against present-day concerns and conflicts with deft lyrical strokes, all the while underpinning such musings with a focused, steely reserve and an effortless, stylish manner. Throughout, the rhythm section (Vin Duffy, bass; Joey Fitzgerald, drums) contains the energy of the songs, emulating a pressure cooker that safely keeps the lid on.

One of the best 'lost' albums released by an Irish band – no question – and a record that contains two of the most gorgeous-poignant pop songs ever written by an Irish songwriter (O'Duffy) – 'Seventeen' and 'Everything Flowers In Her Garden'.

Oh – one more thing – *Nostalgia* boasts one of the best cover images in this book. The front-cover shot, of band friends Dandelion and Jannette Flood, was taken by noted 1970s rock music photographer Laurie Lewis, at the Good Mixer pub in Camden, in 1995. Cheers!

Released: 2008
Record Label: Reekus Records
Producer: Keith Farrell, Stephen Farrell;
co-produced by Saville
Recorded at: The Bunker, Dublin
Sleeve Design: Polly Brady, Laurie Lewis
(front cover photography)

Tracks:
1 And The Star Turns Red 3:26
2 Nostalgia 3:35
3 It Don't Feel Right Anymore 3:32
4 I Can't Do Anything To Ease Your Pain
   2:37
5 Seventeen 3:45
6 Symphony Of Sound 4:46

7 Everything Flowers In Her Garden 3:19
8 Am I Foolin' Myself? 3:39
9 The Only One For Me 3:03
10 Stop Tellin' Lies 3:15
11 The Lonely Ghost 2:51
12 Sweet Music 2:23
13 Flares 3:22

ANN SCOTT
WE'RE SMILING (2006)

ANN SCOTT

'When I was compiling the songs for *We're Smiling*, I remember wanting to emphasise the idea of parallels and plurality in everything. I was seeing layers, looking for double meanings, and presenting dual personalities; where there was "good", there had to be "bad"; where there was "one", I wanted "two", and where there was "me", it became "we". I wanted to balance the ideas and characters with their alternatives – even down to the artwork, for which we used mirrors to create reflections of things. I'm a naturally indecisive person, so I always consider every side to a story. The moral of the story, to me, is less important.'

The aim was just to make a record that she liked, and that some people other than her would like too. There were other objectives, of course, but one of them certainly wasn't to make a record that would get played on the radio. In the latter department, we must congratulate Ann Scott on a job well done. In the former area, she has excelled.

On the initial independent release of *We're Smiling*, Scott claimed that she wasn't in a hurry to stake her claim as one of the best of the new batch of clever Irish female singer-songwriters. This turned out to be both smart and prescient, as she remains (at the time of writing) one of the lesser-known examples of this most endangered species. This is not her fault, of course: in the natural scheme of things, maturity should always allow giddy impetuosity to give way to some form of strategic, operational methodology.

Scott also doesn't seem like the type of singer-songwriter to adopt a stereotypical getting-it-together-in-the-country vibe – a vibe that, while all well and good in some ways, has nonetheless caused some highly talented people to stumble. A sense of discipline, then, informs her work, but you can surely guess by this stage that *We're Smiling* is all about the casual requirement to weld the 'vibe' to the orderliness.

So the name might not be too recognisable, but the music is as slow-burning a blend of narcotic, soothing rhythms and gracefully delivered lyrics as you can welcome into your home with a smile and an offer of a cup of tea. There is also something of the pragmatic about her music. You often read that the writing of songs is a nebulous thing that, like certain deities, moves in mysterious ways; Scott's songs are more assured in their intersection of strange, impressionistic and accessible, and she nails this again and again on tracks such as 'Feather for Feather', 'Jealousy', 'For a Dream', 'Skin Deep' and 'Farewell Henrietta' – all of which are authentic creative statements derived from the Aurora Borealis swirl of ideas in her head.

Chancers, no-hopers, interlopers, loopers and (yes, really) nutters abound in the land of the singer-songwriter. For many of these people, there is always an incentive to start a song, but not always to finish it. Ann Scott knows this, and negotiates the path from A to Z and back again with ease. *We're Smiling* is the certifiable proof of it.

ANN SCOTT
WE'RE SMILING

Released: 2006 (Ireland), 2008 (UK)
Record Label: Raghouse Records
Producer: Ann Scott, Karl Odlum
Recorded at: Temple Lane Studios, Dublin;
other locations in Dublin, Kerry and Wicklow
Sleeve Design: Martin McCann, Alex
McCullagh (photography)

Tracks:
1 Hot Day 4:13
2 Mountain 4:14
3 Feather for Feather 4:29
4 Down at the Parlour 3:14
5 She: Jubilee 6:01
6 Imelda 3:23

7 Jealousy 3:24
8 100 Dances, 1, 000 Stars 3:32
9 For a Dream 3:01
10 Skin Deep 3:30
11 Shark Water 3:34
12 Farewell Henrietta 4:41

SI SCHROEDER

COPING MECHANISMS (2006)

'*Coping Mechanisms* was the sound of me tentatively finding my voice after years labouring with instrumental music. I'd grown up in love with the colourful chaos of psychedelic-era Beatles and their fellow travelers, and had been spurred to make my own music by contemporary versions of that derangement in the late-eighties guitar noise of Sonic Youth and My Bloody Valentine. But I'd become lost in technology, hoping I could create my own version of that beautiful disorientation through samples and beats alone. One emotionally charged night, while toying with a backing track, the lyric and song "C4" emerged like it was there, waiting to be found. That accident released me from the burden of electronica to shape the songs on the album. The languishing instrumentals all found their focus lyrically, and the words unconsciously reflected back at me the craziness of those times – the early years of the twenty-first century, where souls at home and abroad all seemed to be lost and despairing. I'm very proud of the record, and despite all its ghosts, I'm always reassured when people tell me how uplifting they think it is. I've often felt that music is an arm around my shoulder, and so mine should be for those who listen to it.'

We're not sure why, but electronica from Ireland contains some of the sweetest, oddest sounds. *Coping Mechanisms*, the debut solo album from Simon Kenny, was released with a few vapour trails of fanfares and hurrahs, yet quickly disappeared from view. A shame, really.

Coping Mechanisms is something else altogether, however. Made on a wish and a prayer (yes, it is yet another labour of love: thank God for the obsessive types of this world), the album is as multi-layered as an Elizabethan wedding dress but nowhere near as heavy. Opening track 'The Reluctant Aviator' spins on an axis of gloopy droplets, thoroughly wonky guitar lines, and an enveloping fog of noise. Nice work if you can get it.

The amazing 'Lavendermist', meanwhile, is all goth-electro. Throbs so deep that they resemble Black Sabbath suffering from a panic attack underpin the track; there's a lull at just after five minutes, and you think it might be all over, but then Schroeder comes back with gently plucked acoustic guitar and a surge of Driving Miss Hazy-Daisy rhythms. And is that flute we hear lifting the tune even

higher? If it's not, it should be . . . The album continues its upward trajectory: 'C4' is soft vocals, abrupt brass and swish-drums; 'Eyes Wide' is a little bit Laurie Anderson, a little bit Sci Fi; 'Elaine's Porsche/Poor Hélène/Céline Pours' is a simple Beckett-referencing tune that drifts into areas often cited as gorgeous, while 'Duck!' starts off as a genuinely pretty song that slowly becomes spiked by a mixture of sound/noise that ends in a honeyed, if abrupt, tone. After the fine, quietly triumphant closure of final track 'Here, After . . .', space is made for an untitled hidden track that comprises two minutes of a child's word game.

It's a self-indulgent (if also warm and loving) ending to an album that brims over with loads of electronic pulses and fistfuls of heart and soul; it is the latter that distinguishes *Coping Mechanisms* (the title is surely self-explanatory) from electronica's usual run-of-the-mill frills. It's quiet, it's loud, it's turmoil, it's oblique, and it's a few things in between. Above all, it's human.

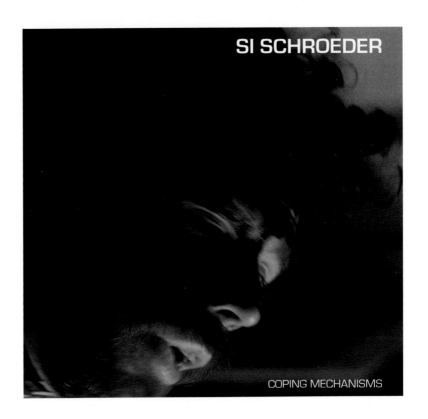

SI SCHROEDER

COPING MECHANISMS

Released: 2006
Record Label: Trust Me I'm A Thief
Producer: Jimmy Eadie (with Si Schroeder)
Recorded at: schroedersound MK I-V and
Asylum Studios, Dublin
Sleeve Design: Dara Ní Bheacháin, Garrett
Phelan (photography)

Tracks:
1 The Reluctant Aviator **4:22**
2 Lavendermist **7:06**
3 C4 **4:32**
4 Eyes-Wide **3:34**
5 (Apology) **0:28**
6 Elaine's Porsche/Poor Hélène/Céline
Pours **4:30**
7 Duck! **5:17**
8 A Little More **7:37**
9 Here, After . . . **9:32**

SNOW PATROL
'CHASING CARS' (2006)

GARY LIGHTBODY

'Songs such as "Chasing Cars" come out, simple as that. Uncoerced. I always say that love songs are the hardest ones to write, yet it's the build-up that is the hard bit. It's months of knocking the melody around, and then the lyrics come out at once – rather than a line of a lyric a day. Somebody asked me once did I ever engineer relationship problems in order to write songs. Certainly not, and the very thought that people actually think that is worrying. What I'm aiming for is to write love songs without resorting to clichés. I work very hard to try to look at love, the idiosyncrasies of love and the difficult moments of love, in a way that is sensible and not twee.'

It is easy to be swept away by mainstream success, especially if your head is in the clouds and not focused on the right kind of longevity. The irony surrounding this kind of success is not lost on Gary Lightbody, the lead singer, main lyricist and primary focal point of Snow Patrol.

In the late nineties, Lightbody was a struggling artist in a struggling rock band, coming and going between Belfast and Glasgow, resigning himself to the idea that he and his fellow musicians would never sell a million records, would never emulate or tour with the likes of U2 (see pages 204-209), would never have a hit single, and would never sell out major venues. Back then, Lightbody was all about the indignation of how Snow Patrol weren't massively successful. Because of this, he got slightly lost.

Luckily, before Snow Patrol had a hit song he had realised that most people's perceptions of success – fame, fortune, celebrity, and so on – didn't really matter to him. In 2002, he had made his peace with being in a band that would never hit the big time. Within a year, this peace was shattered.

What happened was this: in 2003, Snow Patrol released their major-label album debut, *Final Straw*. It followed two previous albums, neither of which bothered the music charts. Something clicked with *Final Straw*,

however. There followed in quick succession a series of hit singles ('Run', 'Chocolate', 'Spitting Games'), the album taking up residence in many charts, and the band breaking through the usually resistant American market by selling over a quarter of a million copies there (and over three million worldwide).

Come 2006, their next album, *Eyes Open*, was released; not only did it end up selling over six million copies worldwide, but it heralded a new kind of song, in the heart-shaped form of 'Chasing Cars'.

Pop songs of and about romance are as cheap as chips, and come wrapped in layers of insincerity that are as pungent as vinegar. But 'Chasing Cars' – which rolls out with glistening guitars followed by a slow build-up that transforms into a muted explosion – is as unaffected as a newborn baby. It is, quite simply, one of the most honest and purest love songs ever written.

It is also a rarity that – if you actually take the time to listen to it, rather than casually dismiss it just because you've heard it as background music hundreds of times – makes you stop for its duration. It makes you think. *Really* think. How unusual and brilliant is that?

Released: 2006
Record Label: Fiction, Interscope
Producer: Garret 'Jacknife' Lee
Recorded at: Grouse Lodge Studios, County Westmeath
Duration: 4:25

SOMETHING HAPPENS
STUCK TOGETHER WITH GOD'S GLUE (1990)

TOM DUNNE

'*God's Glue* was conceived under the ever-present threat of the "drop" from Virgin. "No one is waiting for the next Something Happens album", our A&R man told us, and he was right. The decision to resign from Aer Lingus was suddenly looking rash. One day, late for rehearsal, I wrote the lyrics to "Hello Hello . . ." in my mother's front room in Drimnagh. A few weeks later, Ray Harmon bought a piano. I had an idea for a song with a backing vocal that went "Take a parachute . . . " and I tried to fit it to his first-ever piano composition. I did that in my first-ever flat, while my girlfriend was at work. Those two songs changed everything. We were in a songwriting hot streak. Even the B-sides sounded good. We flew to LA to record the album. My abiding memory is the smell of cinnamon-flavoured coffee that would greet us each day in the studio. We were still nervous that we might not do the songs justice, but gradually we could hear that what was on tape was sounding very good. Excitement replaced nervousness. We had something we wanted people to hear. Beer was had. One night we even went out. Relief was felt in Dublin, LA and London.'

There was initially a relaxed, happy-go-lucky attitude about Something Happens – formed in 1984 – that successfully hid bucketloads of ambition.

Prior to signing with Virgin Records in 1988, the *Two Chances* EP (featuring a cover design by future Father Ted co-writer Arthur Mathews) had been released, and even at this early point it was obvious that the band were on to a winner. While their 1988 debut album for Virgin UK, *Been There Seen That Done That*, set out their stall, the band's follow-up sold everything on display. In fact, it isn't hyperbole (honest . . . and neither is the mind playing tricks) to state that *Stuck Together with God's Glue* ranks as one of the finest albums of the 1990s.

Unusually for any album praised to the hilt, there isn't a duff song here. From über-radio-friendly tracks such as 'Parachute', 'Brand New God', 'Esmeralda', 'Room 29' and the razor-sharp precision rock of 'Hello Hello Hello Hello Hello (Petrol)' and 'Devil in Miss Jones' to the emotional charge of 'Kill the Roses', 'Skyrockets' and 'What Now', the album positively zings with the kind of perfectly executed pop/rock that is as exhilarating now as it was then. Also, just so you're aware of it, 'What Now' remains one of the most eloquent and honest pop songs ever written about infidelity and insincerity. ('Words come easy, I can't give them respect. I put so little into them and then watch the effect. I choose them easy, I know the shape and size, to give some kind of meaning to any pack of lies.')

The group's success in Ireland notwithstanding (helped to no end by the band being a box of Christmas crackers on stage), the album nosedived, in part through an ill-considered singles-release sequence (which in turn brought about a deterioration of the band's relationship with Virgin Records) and BBC Radio's ruling on the unsuitability of playing the eminently tuneful 'Parachute' during the Gulf War. It was also (probably) too sharp-dressed for its own good: too melodically pristine for America's grunge phenomenon and Britain's Madchester fixation. Another magnificent album caught between the crossfire of industry dictates, cultural zeitgeists and plain old happenstance? Heads are still shaking in disbelief.

Released: 1990
Record Label: Virgin Records
Producer: Ed Stasium, Mick Glossop, Chris O'Brien, Something Happens
Recorded at: American Recording, Rumbo Recorders, Grey Room, Los Angeles; Ropewalk Studios, Dublin
Sleeve Design: Steve Averill for Works Associates, Something Happens (concept), David Rooney (illustrations)

Tracks:
1 What Now **4:16**
2 Hello Hello Hello Hello Hello (Petrol) **3:27**
3 Parachute **4:30**
4 Esmerelda **2:35**
5 I Had a Feeling **4:23**
6 Kill the Roses **4:33**
7 Brand New God **2:35**
8 Room 29 **3:56**

9 The Patience Business **2:46**
10 Devil in Miss Jones **4:01**
11 Good Time Coming **3:37**
12 I Feel Good **5:19**
13 Skyrockets **1:48**

THE SPOOK OF THE THIRTEENTH LOCK

THE SPOOK OF THE THIRTEENTH LOCK (2008)

ALLEN BLIGHE

'I suppose it shouldn't really matter where the album fits in, but it does go against the grain of most of what is going on. In the local music scene that I'd be familiar with – and even the more commercial, fashionable circles – I'd see a lot of trends out there, some of which are quite good. Not copying our contemporaries was uppermost in our minds, and the album does seem to confuse people, which is a good thing. Some of the reactions we have received have been mad.'

Surprise, surprise: an Irish band that isn't afraid to wear its indigenous influences on its sleeve. Not only that, but an Irish band willing to steer away from clichés and the usual commercial conceits that come with wanting everything right here, right now.

From their name onwards, Dublin band The Spook of the Thirteenth Lock aren't your usual bunch of wannabe Irish rockers. They are, for starters, named after a poem about a haunted canal lock; the music on their self-titled debut album is similarly infused with long-lost ghosts (Virgin Prunes), abiding spirits (My Bloody Valentine) and other spectral presences (post-rock, psych-folk and no-nonsense, heads-down Irish traditional music). The brainchild of Sligo man Allen Blighe, The Spook of the Thirteenth Lock lay somewhere between unhinged, untethered and downright liberated.

Formed in 2006 following the demise of Blighe's previous band, Holy Ghost Fathers (and yes, we're detecting an eerie theme here; 'I have an interest in darker folk themes', he has said – no kidding), the *raison d'être* behind Thirteenth Lock was to seek an expressive outlet for Blighe's new-found love for traditional Irish music. Factor in his passion for Nirvana, My Bloody Valentine and Lift to Experience, and you might just find yourself with a new, fresh musical hybrid.

What makes *The Spook of the Thirteenth Lock* such an intriguing prospect is the way in which the music and lyrics interlock: on tracks such as 'Pimlico' and 'The Hare', lyrical themes of national identity/struggle, loss of faith, and a nagging sense of socio-cultural discontinuity weave their way through the music like a watertight stitch your grandmother used to make.

And the music itself, the fusion of folk idioms with post-rock, prog-rock and psych-rock? Where the blinkin' hell did that come from? Why, good Irish traditional music tunes, of course, within which you'll discern an underlying droning note. The key of the fusion element here is the sound of the uilleann pipes, which has a depth of tone that resembles experimental and unconventional loud guitar rock.

There are few pieces of music created by an Irish act that have as much gobsmacked disturbance as the album's closing track, 'The Ragged Rock', which at its base takes the *sean nós* tradition and swathes it in a howl of feedback and Krautrock freak-out. As they might not say in Dingle: yowsa!

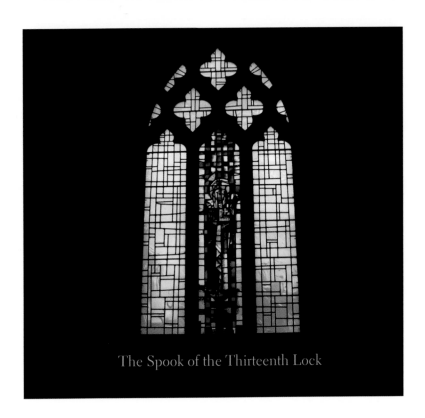

The Spook of the Thirteenth Lock

Released: 2008
Record Label: Transduction Records
Producer: Enda Bates, The Spook of the
Thirteenth Lock
Recorded at: Westland Studios, Dublin
Sleeve Design: Brian O' Higgins (hare
drawing)

Tracks:
1 The Hare **4:21**
2 In Country Dark **4:21**
3 The Partisan **2:48**
4 Christchurch, 6 Bells **3:20**
5 The Lord's Prayer **6:14**
6 The Spook **4:13**
7 Canal Lock Blues **1:48**
8 Down Comes the Bridge **5:36**
9 Pimlico **5:39**
10 The Ragged Rock **8:09**

STARJETS

GOD BLESS THE STARJETS (1979)

TERRY SHARPE

'Having a more objective viewpoint on the album now, I think there really are some very good tunes on it, and some of it's quite clever. Of course, I'd like to remix it and rearrange the track listing – I'd have brought "War Stories" up closer to the top of the album – but in a sense you're never satisfied. Some bits make me cringe – a different vocal or a different song might be needed – but I really think it stands up because of the strength of the songs. The only thing I was miffed about when the album was released was the production – we had two producers; we were influenced by the energy of punk but we loved pop music, so I also think we should have decided what kind of band we were before we went into the studio.'

In the late seventies, up Northern Ireland way, there were more brilliant punk/pop bands per square yard than anywhere else in the world (FACT!). The list is lengthy, and the reasons behind such an outburst of self-expression seem obvious, but, honestly, you couldn't walk the length and short breadth of Great Victoria Street without bumping into a potentially brilliant punk band armed with a batch of spiky, perfectly polished tunes. That the bands tended to have a lifespan approximating the duration of their songs was neither here nor there: Belfast and environs at this time was a breeding ground for the type of creative sparks that wouldn't come around again for many years.

Formed in west Belfast in 1976, Starjets were as well versed in pop music as they were hip to what was happening in London and New York. Like many more of their ilk in their locale, they could only play gigs if they agreed to mix their own material with covers, which is why they ended up playing material by The Beach Boys, the Beatles and The Archies in their sets, and why they supported the likes of Bay City Rollers and The Glitter Band.

Come late '77, it was clear that Starjets had to take some decisive career choices (with some resentment hanging in the air from other Belfast bands such as The Outcasts – see page 148), so they headed over to London. Here, they were promptly signed to Epic Records (by Muff Winwood, subsequently one of the music industry's most famous A&R gurus and multi-million-selling producers and, latterly, Mr Shania Twain), and released, in jig time, their debut (and only) album, *God Bless the Starjets*.

If there is a glittering prize for guitar-driven, infectiously catchy punk/pop that sounds as if it should soundtrack the kicking-in of switched-on television sets, then it should go to this album. 'Schooldays' is pumped-up rifferama, complete with whining guitar solos and an anthemic chorus so fist-pumping it borders on masturbatory. 'Run with The Pack' borrows from The Radiators' (see page 160) 'Television Screen' and at least one Bay City Rollers song. 'Smart Boys' blends wonky guitar lines with a pure pop tune, and 'War Stories' ('Sergeant Fury! Captain Hurricane! Johnny Red! – this is it, this is it!') is so crammed with the best type of ludicrous sloganeering pop lyrics ('Young men heed the call!', 'Battle stations!', 'Hope & Glory', 'We're in sight of victory!') that you're like an eejit repeating them to the end of the song.

Despite being the only Northern Irish punk/pop band of their era to have appeared on *Top of the Pops*, *Juke Box Jury* AND *Crackerjack* (*Crackerjack!*), Starjets and *God Bless the Starjets*, with their A&R pundit and their major-label backing, with their frothy irrepressibility, died a quiet death. But what a life they had. Oh, crikey, what a life.

Released: 1979
Record Label: Epic Records
Producer: Muff Winwood
Recorded at: Manor Studios, London
Sleeve Design: Roslav Szaybo (CBS art department), Terry Lott (photography)

Tracks:
1 Schooldays **3:20**
2 Any Danger Love **2:55**
3 Ten Years **3:29**
4 Run With The Pack **3:17**
5 What A Life **2:56**
6 Smart Boys **3:27**
7 It's A Shame **3:57**
8 I'm So Glad **4:09**
9 War Is Over **3:13**
10 War Stories **2:55**
11 Sitting On Top Of The World **3:21**

THE STARS OF HEAVEN

SACRED HEART HOTEL (1986)

STEPHEN RYAN

'I can't really remember much about *Sacred Heart Hotel* . . . It was exciting hearing the BBC stuff live on the airwaves on broadcast night; that's my happiest memory. I think we were serious and believed in what we were doing in a naive and earnest way, but maybe we should have loosened up a bit. We had a lot more fun recording stuff when we knew in our hearts the band was doomed.'

For the sake of clarity, this particular entry focuses on the original seven-track mini-album (released by Rough Trade in 1986, the first four tracks are from the band's debut John Peel BBC Radio 1 session: 'Sacred Heart Hotel', 'Talk About It Now', 'Moonstruck', 'So You Know') as well as the four tracks from the band's *Holyhead* EP ('Never Saw You', 'Before Holyhead', 'Widow's Walk', 'Someone's Getting Tired of You'), which was released a year later. The mini-album and the *Holyhead* EP were subsequently combined and released by Rough Trade in 1987 as *Rain on the Sea*. In 2005, it was re-released by Dublin-based label Independent, under the 'new' title *Sacred Heart Hotel*, complete with sleeve notes from the band and friends/ associates/music critics. But we're getting ahead of ourselves. Steady on. Hold your horses. Backtrack.

Around the first half of 1983, The Stars of Heaven formed, honing their peculiar craft in the basement of member Stan Erraught's house. Musically, The Byrds were there, as were Velvet Underground, Richard Thompson, Alex Chilton/Big Star. Gram Parsons, The Dream Syndicate, New Riders of the Purple Sage, too. For all that, The Stars of Heaven were (at the very, very least, in Irish terms) a once-off. You could argue that they pre-dated the vogue for Americana by some years (not that the band ever really thought about such things), but even in the pleasure of winning such an argument, you'd also have to acknowledge that punk rock's DIY approach played a part in the end results. The band's debut single, 'Clothes of Pride', found its way to John Peel; he played it more than once, invited Stars of Heaven over for one of his famous 'sessions', and then the band signed to Rough Trade. Which is pretty much were we came in.

But, oh Christ, this record. It may not have been formally conceived as an album 'proper', but its sheer elegance and quality belies such a patchwork job. The songs are steeped in country-music tropes: aching melodies, guitar harmonics, lilting vocals, basic arrangements, lyrics bemoaning (rarely extolling) love, alcohol, emigration, religion, unemployment. 'Dublin in the mid-'80s,' writes Erraught pithily in the sleeve notes, 'was a kip . . . Nobody had any money, and if you were still here after your twenty-fifth birthday, you might as well walk around with a white flag – you were defeated.'

The yearning title track sets the tone: a zigzag intro quickly followed by a sweet, spiralling guitar lick, a low-key vocal (by Stephen Ryan, one of the band's main songwriters; Erraught was the other one) and a guitar motif that simply lifts the spirits. 'Talk About It Now' is so sophisticated in the rhyme and melody departments that you'd wonder how such a small song (three minutes, and not a second wasted) could hold so much. And there's more: the country sway of 'Never Saw You' is so divine it could administer the Last Rites; instrumental 'Before Holyhead' is so slim and slender it almost shouldn't exist. 'Widow's Walk' is melody incarnate. And so on.

An effortlessly graceful band. Delicate, often dainty works of art. A different time and a different place. Still worth your while. Still worth visiting.

THE STARS OF HEAVEN

SACRED HEART HOTEL

Released: 1986
Record Label: Rough Trade Records,
Independent Records (2005 reissue)
Producer: Phil Ross, The Stars of Heaven
Recorded at: BBC Studio 5, Maida Vale; Lab
Studios, Dublin
Sleeve Design: Conor Horgan (front cover
photography), Niall McCormack
 (reissue design)

Tracks:
1 Sacred Heart Hotel **3:39**
2 Talk About It Now **2:55**
3 Moonstruck **2:46**
4 So You Know **3:18**
5 You Only Say What Anyone Would Say
 3:40
6 Folksong **2:22**
7 Man Without A Shadow **2:18**

STIFF LITTLE FINGERS
'ALTERNATIVE ULSTER' (1978)

JAKE BURNS

'It was a song written in the classic punk mode about having nothing to do. Because that was the overriding reality of life in Belfast for a teenager in the mid-seventies. Not the fear of riots or bombs or whatever. It was the sheer tedium of having nowhere to go and nothing to do when you got there.'
Guardian, 24 January 2003

Working at an accounts office in Belfast stamping statements and sending out invoices isn't exactly punk rock, but that's what Jake Burns – soon-to-be singer with Stiff Little Fingers – did for a living in the mid-seventies. At this time, he was a member of a covers band called Highway Star (so named after a Deep Purple song), but was soon galvanised, as so many were, by the emergence of punk rock in London and New York.

Taking their new name from a song of the same title by UK punk act The Vibrators, Stiff Little Fingers gradually ditched the covers (which by this point had evolved into renditions of songs by The Clash and The Damned) and entered into what many of their critics have termed something of a Faustian pact with two journalists, Gordon Ogilvie and Colin McClelland.

Ogilvie's suggestion that they write material based on their life in Troubles-era Belfast was after the fact, as Burns had already written a semi-autobiographical song called 'State of Emergency'. Yet when Ogilvie produced a finished lyric of a song called 'Suspect Device', the die seemed cast, and so, for better or worse, SLF were subsequently accused of using the Troubles as a sensationalist starting point for their career.

Such accusations and arguments (every time, for example, The Undertones would slag off SLF for luridly dramatising the conflict in Northern Ireland, SLF would slag off The Undertones for ignoring it), however, were trumped by the strength of the material. First, the single, 'Suspect Device', and its B-side, 'Wasted Life', were raw-knuckle, raspy punk rock. The band's second single would (irrespective of politics and perceived career practices) thrust them into the pantheon of punk rock greats by being, quite simply, one of the best punk rock songs ever written.

Asked by local punk fanzine 'Alternative Ulster' to write a song for an intended giveaway flexi-disc, the band agreed, writing (for the record, Ogilvie receives a co-writing credit) a song of the same name. When the flexi-disc idea fell through, however, the band, now signed to London's Rough Trade, released it as their official second single.

Direct, in-your-face and frenetic, the song hurtles from start to finish, a clarion call for Northern Irish youth to start afresh ('Get up and grab it, it's yours, ignore the bores and their laws, be an anti-security force, alter your native land'), mixing righteous social realism with a copper-fastened melodic intensity that easily matches other early agit-punk songs by The Sex Pistols, The Clash and The Ruts.

The truth of conflict? An object lesson in class struggle? A tune that takes your breath away? Ulster says yes.

Released: 1978
Record Label: Rough Trade Records
Producer: Ed Hollis
Sleeve Design: Milton Haworth (cover photography)
Duration: 2:42

TASTE

TASTE (1969)

DONAL GALLAGHER

'Rory had to go through a fairly cruel three-month farewell tour with Taste, a tour that had been booked by the record company, and that he had to do because he was flat broke. And following the demise of Taste, a sort of depression had set in . . . Things got better, though, due to a management connection with Peter Grant, and so Rory went into the studio for this album with much more confidence and a lot of baggage left behind. There's a sense of innocence in the songs, a sense of optimism. The album is by a person who had the shackles taken off.'

Power trios in the 1960s were a common enough sighting. It's a pity that making money for the bands wasn't. This was a time when, if they were lucky, musicians would be on a weekly wage of £30: rent money, some food, some alcohol. The real money, bands were told by management, was being 'invested'. In other words, any musician worth their salt didn't join bands for the money, but for the sheer pleasure of playing.

Formed in Cork in 1966 by Rory Gallagher, a short time after he completed his musical apprenticeship with The Fontana Showband (starting in 1963, ending in 1965, with Gallagher cannily transforming them within his tenure from a pop song covers act into a kind of R&B band called The Impact), Taste toured around Ireland, and held down exciting but energy-sapping residencies in Belfast. Here Taste would support the likes of John Mayall's Bluesbreakers and (blues-oriented) Fleetwood Mac. Come 1968, Gallagher broke up the original line-up (bass player Eric Kitteringam and drummer Norman Damery, formerly of Cork band The Axels) and brought in two Belfast musicians, drummer John Wilson (formerly of Them) and bass player Richard 'Charlie' McCracken.

The first cue: a repositioning of the band, primarily in the UK, that gained them a number of fans with a series of near-legendary shows in London's Marquee Club, as well as support slots with Cream (at their farewell concert at the Royal Albert Hall) and, subsequently, with Cream offshoot 'supergroup' Blind Faith, on their North American tour. It seemed as if nothing could go wrong: here was a great band, playing incendiary gigs, having signed to a major label, and strategically placed to take over from Cream as the powerhouse blues/rock trio of the era. All they needed to do was release a debut album that matched, if not shattered, expectations.

The second cue: they released a debut album that matched, if not shattered, expectations. *Taste* begins with a complete and utter blast: 'Blister on the Moon' is as raw and visceral a blues-rock song as you can imagine, with something like a masterclass in guitar work. Other original tracks, such as 'Born on the Wrong Side of Time' (guitar-solo bliss), 'Hail' (cool, scattish folk/blues) and 'Same Old Story' (chug-chug blues/rock saved by yet another pinprick solo) provide further evidence of Gallagher's superlative guitar style. Covers include Hank Snow's 'I'm Moving On' (light as a feather country/skiffle) and Huddie Ledbetter's 'Leavin' Blues' (flinty blues par excellence), and showcase Gallagher's influences.

Although marred somewhat by the overwrought trad/arr 'Catfish' (eight minutes of proto, blues-weighted heavy metal), *Taste* was the first, and best, of a mere two studio albums from a band that could have and should have but, perhaps inevitably, didn't. Gallagher, a guitarist's guitarist, would go on to make more advanced and adventurous solo records, but for a primer in no-tricks/no-frills blues rock, this is the effin' A-bomb.

Released: 1969
Record Label: Polydor, Universal
Producer: Tony Colton
Recorded at: DeLane Lea Studios, London
Sleeve Design: Paragon Publicity

Tracks:
1 Blister on the Moon **3:26**
2 Leaving Blues **4:16**
3 Sugar Mama **7:15**
4 Hail **2:37**

5 Born on the Wrong Side of Time **4:01**
6 Dual Carriageway Pain **3:13**
7 Same Old Story **3:33**
8 Catfish **8:04**
9 I'm Moving On **2:28**

THAT PETROL EMOTION

BABBLE (1987)

DAMIEN O'NEILL

'Despite having a major label push (Polydor) and fairly healthy radio play for the song 'Big Decision', and an appearance on the Tube, the single still only reached number forty-two in the charts. The album certainly contained all the elements of a hit record – poppy melody, great guitar hook and intelligent lyrics. Alas, it wasn't enough, and has always had us pondering over the subsequent years,"what if" . . .'

From fresh-faced Derry teenagers singing spritely pop songs about girls, chocolates, teenage kicks and perfect cousins, to men in their twenties influenced by Afrika Bambaata, Captain Beefheart and Can, singing about the conflict in Northern Ireland, and getting singles banned by the BBC. You could say with a degree of certainty that The Undertones (see page 202) were very much a thing of the past.

When The Undertones split up in the summer of 1983, there was initially a hint of what-in-the-name-of-God-comes-next from the creative core of brothers John and Damien O'Neill. What came next was something that no one expected – on-edge, questioning, politicised individuals (the O'Neill brothers 'gaelicised' their names) that severed all musical connections with their previous band, and presaged a new kind of music (as the title of their 1986 debut, indie-label album would have it, a *Manic Pop Thrill*) that acted as a trail-blazer for both Britpop and the so-called 'Madchester' scene. While the first single ('Keen') and the first album positioned That Petrol Emotion as cautious, possibly incongruous contenders (*Rolling Stone* magazine described them, incorrectly, as a mixture of The Clash and Creedence Clearwater Revival), their 1987 follow-up (and the band's major-label debut) was a straight-up success.

Babble thoroughly avoided easy-peasy categorisation by spiking sugary and hook-laden pop with odd tunings and declamatory lyrics that run the gamut from personal to political. The first talking point is 'Big Decision'. The first single from the album, it landed just outside the UK Top 40, yet its swirling, swerving blend of rock, dance and hip-hop (it was one of the first songs in the rock/pop genre to integrate call-to-action rap – 'Agitate, educate, organise!') bestowed onto 'Big Decision' a reputation that hasn't diminished.

Other tracks spin a fine web, too: 'Swamp' (from the opening seconds, you're besotted with an all-encompassing rave tune, nicely completed with crunchy dual guitars from Séan Ó Neill and Reamann Ó Gormain, and a pop melody that snags), 'Static' (a churning two-note riff that builds intensely), 'Creeping to the Cross' (a mini-epic that starts with looped sampled vocals from Steve Mack and ends with a big-sloppy-kiss crescendo), 'For What It's Worth' (say hello to a prowling mantra), and 'Inside' (never mind the claustrophobia, feel the angst) prove that the band were, in quite a vital way, that most rare thing in rock music: pioneers not settlers.

Released: 1987
Record Label: Universal, Polygram, Polydor
Producer: Roli Mosimann
Recorded at: Jam Studios, Livingston Studios, London
Sleeve Design: George Doherty, Steve Double (photography)

Tracks:
1 Swamp **3:20**
2 Spin Cycle **2:05**
3 For What It's Worth **3:50**
4 Big Decision **2:42**
5 Static **3:36**
6 Split! **1:38**
7 Belly Bugs **2:43**
8 In the Playpen **2:32**
9 Inside **4:12**
10 Chester Burnett **2:41**
11 Creeping to the Cross **4:42**

THERAPY?

TROUBLEGUM (1994)

ANDY CAIRNS

'The main spark for the direction of the album came from the song 'Screamager'. We'd tried to do our own take on Ulster punk with the tune, albeit adding a touch of Helmet-style riffage to bring it closer to our orbit, and we'd enjoyed the process. With the lyrics, I wanted them to have a brevity that would have the same impact as punchlines. For me the aesthetic uniformity of the album means that its currency still resonates with fans of agitated guitar music of various stripes.'

Andy Cairns, guitarist/singer of Therapy?, has blood dripping out of his mouth from eating a mound of raw meat. By his side sits a naked woman in a lopsided Shirley Temple wig; she has lines of cocaine arranged like chevrons on her lightly tanned stomach. Beside him, a battered flight case lies open to reveal wads of $1,000 bills, a DVD pack of animal porn, scrunched up blackmail letters from the 'pretty one' in an internationally famous boy band, and a scorched Faustian pact signed by Cairns and the Devil, and witnessed by a music industry lawyer. Where did it all go wrong, you might ask? Andy looks at you with glazed, red-tinted eyes, and a feral sneer, and spits: 'Enough of your landscapes, tell me about the worms.'

With the exception of Cairns quoting the line from Samuel Beckett's *Waiting for Godot*, the above paragraph is a tissue of lies predicated on the perception that certain people have of metal bands. Other perceptions? That members of metal bands are connected to the last vestige of the outsider, and are the kind of people who have lived a dysfunctional life, or want to. Obviously, the truth is more prosaic and lies closer to refinement and civilisation than we would like to believe.

Therapy? started in 1989, released their first single ('Meat Abstract') in 1990, released their debut album (*Babyteeth*) in July 1991, their second (*Pleasure Death*) in January 1992, their third (*Nurse*, their major-label debut) in November 1992. Clearly, Therapy? had things to do, and made sure they did them very quickly indeed. Turns out they were only just starting . . .

In February 1994 (following a year when they cracked the UK Top 40 a few times, leading to, of all things, appearances on *Top of the Pops*), Therapy? released their fourth album, *Troublegum*. From the cover to the music, an unsettling, provocative, desolate yet highly individual atmosphere abounds – it's metal, it's punk, innately melodic (Therapy?'s less obvious but always winning default setting) and lyrically incisive. Finding it impossible to squeeze into the various moulds their record company wanted for them (they didn't wish to adopt the perceived nihilism of Nirvana, they didn't want to be the European version of Metallica), Therapy? stuck to their guns and clung to their hero worship of the likes of Husker Dü and Steve Albini. With three 1994 UK Top 30 singles ('Nowhere', 'Trigger Inside', 'Die Laughing'), it must have, ultimately, irked their record company that the band refused to adapt.

Therapy? had the last laugh, however: *Troublegum* was listed for the 1994 Mercury Music Prize (it wasn't the first Irish album to be nominated for the prize, and neither was it the last, but it was definitely the loudest) and proved that buzz-saw guitars, stop-start riffs, direct songs and a twisted raw power could matter more than you had ever thought possible.

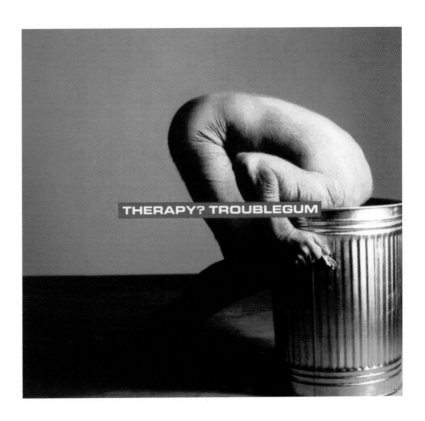

THERAPY? TROUBLEGUM

Released: 1994
Record Label: A&M Records
Producer: Chris Sheldon
Recorded at: Shipping Norton Studios,
Oxford; RAK Studios, The Church, London
Sleeve Design: Simon Carrington, Jeremy
Pearce, Valerie Phillips (photography),
Nigel Rolfe (art direction, photography)

Tracks:
1 Knives **1:56**
2 Screamager **2:36**
3 Hellbelly **3:20**
4 Stop It You're Killing Me **3:50**
5 Nowhere **2:26**
6 Die Laughing **2:48**
7 Unbeliever **3:28**

8 Trigger Inside **3:56**
9 Lunacy Booth **3:55**
10 Isolation **3:10**
11 Turn **3:49**
12 Femtex **3:14**
13 Unrequited **3:03**
14 Brainsaw **3:58**

THIN LIZZY

JAILBREAK (1976)

BRIAN DOWNEY 'We were a little bit apprehensive going in to record *Jailbreak*, because the other studio albums hadn't exactly burned up the charts. So we pinned our hopes on it. It was towards the end of recording, when the reactions of some of the record company people made us sit up and listen, particularly their comments about 'The Boys Are Back In Town', which to me was just another album track. I had no idea it was going to be one of the band's biggest hits! And *Jailbreak* was our biggest album hit; I like the feel you get off it – 'Angel From The Coast' isn't a track that too many people remember, but it's a great song. There were a few different styles on the album. Phil's versatility comes across, and that's what makes it for me – it wasn't just your regular hard rock/metal album.'

Thin Lizzy had been slogging away for years, having formed in the late sixties, and having gone through various incarnations, but always with founding members Brian Downey (drums) and bass player/singer/songwriter Phil Lynott (see page 122) at the fore and at the helm.

Until the release of *Jailbreak*, however, the band was perceived – at least in terms of a chart act – as a one-trick pony. While no one could deny their appeal on the live circuit, the chart figures speak for themselves: only one hit single (the wholly unrepresentative UK Top 10 hit 'Whiskey in the Jar'), and one placing in the UK albums chart: a mediocre number 60 for their 1975 (and fifth) album, *Fighting*.

At such a point in a band's career, it's either do or die, and with the way the music industry worked at the time, the 'do' part was all about selling singles and getting into the charts. And so Lynott began to take note of American songwriters such as Bruce Springsteen, who, thematically at least, wasn't a million miles away from Lynott's localised songs of street cred and romantic associations.

To say the album hit the charts with a bang is something of an understatement; the album sailed to the UK number 10 spot, while the first single, 'The Boys Are Back in Town', reached number 8. America, too, loved the album, but seemed to take the single to its collective heart. The inherent and bare-faced Friday-night strut of the single, in particular, was enough to establish Thin Lizzy as the major breakthrough rock act of the mid-seventies. It wasn't all about one song, though: 'Emerald', 'Cowboy Song', 'Warriors', 'Angel from the Coast' and 'Running Back' all added to the sense of *Jailbreak* being one of those albums where pretty much everything goes according to plan.

Musically, the rockers were propelled along by the achingly macho guitar work of California's Scott Gorham and Glasgow's Brian Robertson (whose output set a benchmark for twin-guitar assaults in mid-seventies rock). Mellower tracks, such as 'Running Back', 'Romeo and the Lonely Girl' and 'Fight or Fall' displayed Lynott's flip-side – the place in his heart where swagger is replaced with swoon, aggression with friendship.

As utterly believable (Running Back's sad-sack singing 'just leave me by myself, I'll be all right here on my own') as it is ridiculously enjoyable ('Cowboy Song's protagonist in a border town in Mexico 'busting broncs for the rodeo' and 'running free with the buffalo'), *Jailbreak* amounts to a terrific album (all thirty-six minutes of it!) and arguably marks the birth of melody-driven metal.

196

Released: 1976
Record Label: Vertigo (UK), Mercury (US)
Producer: John Alcock
Recorded at: Ramport Studios, London
Sleeve Design: Jim Fitzpatrick

Tracks:
1 Jailbreak **4:01**
2 Angel from the Coast **3:03**
3 Running Back **3:13**
4 Romeo and the Lonely Girl **3:55**

5 Warriors **4:09**
6 The Boys Are Back in Town **4:27**
7 Fight or Fall **3:45**
8 Cowboy Song **5:16**
9 Emerald **4:03**

THE THRILLS
SO MUCH FOR THE CITY (2003)

CONOR DEASY

'*So Much For The City* had a slow birth. Though we signed with a small Irish independent label in 2001, it would be a good two years before it was released. We had some of the songs at that point. "Santa Cruz (You're Not That Far)" was even more convoluted then it would end up being. "One Horse Town" was still a ripped-off Belle & Sebastian melody. And "Big Sur" was two different songs. Despite all of this, we thought we were ready to make the album. And then we got dropped. And then our drummer moved down to Cork to play in a wedding band. It wasn't a high point. But it proved to be something of a catalyst. I do think the American influence on the album is a little predominant, and that made things difficult for us later on. But I still think there are some great songs on it, and that we got close to what we set out to do.'

Artists can, of course, leave a bad impression on certain people when they see acres of positive press and magazine covers too soon. The theory goes that if you haven't got the songs to back the coverage then the naysayers can always turn around, wag their fingers, and say I told you so. But even if you make a good record, it's not enough for some people. *So Much For The City* isn't just a good record, though – it's a sublime one. The Thrills' one-time detractors, who denounced the band for having the audacity to forego schlepping around Ireland's minor venues for a few years (aka the local-hero thing), had another bone to pick, however: they sounded nothing (and we really mean *nothing*) like an Irish band.

In Europe and America, people seem not to mind about the background of bands once their records are good. In the UK, and particularly Ireland, there's an overriding preoccupation as to where a band has come from and what they've been doing for the past few years. Anything that isn't vernacular is somehow suspect; anything the public can't put their finger on is deemed unworthy. That's *So Much For The City* knocked out cold, then, yes?

Well, no. For some, the album is perfectly judged retrospection with its blend of California dreaming, late-sixties folk rock as blueprinted by Neil Young and The Byrds, and Brian Wilson hooks. The five-member band spent about four months in and around San Diego in 2002, hanging around and picking up tales of love, loss and longing that would make their way into highly romanticised and sun-tanned songs. With every other band in the early 2000s wanting to be The Strokes, the five musicians were hardly jumping onto any passing bandwagon, and with songs as beautifully bittersweet as 'One Horse Town', 'Santa Cruz (You're Not That Far)', 'Your Love Is Like Las Vegas', 'Don't Steal Our Sun', 'Just Traveling Through' and 'Big Sur', what rings true from start to finish is a certain naive charm that captures melancholic, mellow and unselfconscious moments.

The album was strategically released in the summer, and acted as the perfect soundtrack for beach bums, beach buggies and beach barbecues any time the sun shone (or threatened to). Inevitably, such wistful bliss wasn't to last. Following the release of their third album, *Teenager*, in 2007, The Thrills were dropped by their record company; they remain on 'indefinite hiatus', which sounds suspiciously like a euphemism.

A very special record, then, from Dubliners with a temporary Californian accent. Yet for all its pleasures, *So Much For The City* self-defined and placed the band into a box they could not escape from.

Released: 2003
Record Label: Virgin Records
Producer: Tony Hoffer
Recorded at: Sound Factory, Los Angeles;
Strongroom Studios, London; Area 51
Studios, Dublin
Sleeve Design: Ben Drury

Tracks:
1 Santa Cruz (You're Not That Far) 4:13
2 Big Sur 3:07
3 Don't Steal Our Sun 2:50
4 Deckchairs and Cigarettes 4:58
5 One Horse Town 3:14
6 Old Friends, New Lovers 4:01
7 Say It Ain't So 2:44
8 Hollywood Kids 5:33
9 Just Travelling Through 3:21
10 Your Love Is Like Las Vegas 2:23

TWO DOOR CINEMA CLUB
TOURIST HISTORY (2010)

KEV BAIRD 'Our songs are pretty short in themselves, so it would have been hard to make a long album. But it was conscious as well: we could have had more tracks on it, but it didn't seem right. All our songs are pretty short and to-the-point. We didn't want to overload the album: we just wanted ten really good solid tracks, just short and sweet, like our songs are in general. I think when you have a short album like that, it's pretty easy for someone to listen to it often. It's not like you have to take an hour out of your day to listen to it.' *entertainment.ie*, February 2010

Roaming around the world, there are misguided souls who claim that guitar-based music is dead. These people clearly haven't heard *Tourist History*, and they clearly haven't seen a gig by Two Door Cinema Club. The fact that the album is such an unadulterated pleasure from start to end is not too surprising, but something else is afoot here.

Frankly, indie kids that are as bright, smart and cherubic as Two Door Cinema Club's Alex Trimble, Sam Halliday and Kevin Baird surround us. They look, it has to be said, like a myriad of other such Topshop/ Abercrombie & Fitch bands: Ivy League preppy types, skinny jeans, tight shirts, hair this way, cheeks that way, and the music they play isn't too far off the blueprint of what goes down most weekend nights at your indie disco.

Inevitably, something as vague as 'too far off' indicates the differences between generic and genius, and it is these very differences that form the several unique selling points of TDCC. Not for nothing was *Tourist History* named album of 2010 by *Nylon* magazine (edging out the likes of Arcade Fire, Kanye West and Vampire Weekend); not for nothing did *Tourist History* sell over 100,000 copies in the UK alone in its first year of release.

Impressive statistics these figures may be, but they would count for little if the music were dressed-up punk/ pop tat, which it most certainly isn't. 'Do You Want It All?' is buoyed by thrillingly optimistic opening guitar chords and the kind of lyrics that speak slowly and clearly to the band's youthful fan base ('We're low in our hearts, we're low in our heads, but all in good time, we'll take charge'). 'This Is The Life' (another staccato burst of enthusiastic idealism here, with it's 'feel something right and feel something good' line) cracks open a bottle of sonic bubbly with such ferocity that you'd swear it sprays all over the song's digital code, while indie-pop nuggets such as 'What You Know' ('I can taste it, it's my sweet beginning') and 'Come Back Home' ('You'll hit your target some day') balance old-school melody lines, new-fangled angularity and those superior teenage kicks lyrics in such a clever way that you end up – whatever age you are – smiling like the proverbial Cheshire cat.

So – an album whose pint-sized thirty-two and a half minutes pass by like three and a third. Biff! Bam! Pow! Splat! Take that, sucker! Guitar music? It's alive and kicking very hard, indeed, thank you very much.

Released: 2010
Record Label: Kitsune Music (UK), Glassnote (US)
Producer: Eliot James
Recorded at: Eastcote Studios, London
Sleeve Design: MEGAFORCE

Tracks:
1 Cigarettes in the Theatre **3:34**
2 Come Back Home **3:24**
3 Do You Want It All **3:30**
4 This Is the Life **3:31**
5 Something Good Can Work **2:45**

6 I Can Talk **2:58**
7 Undercover Martyn **2:48**
8 What You Know **3:12**
9 Eat That Up, It's Good for You **3:45**
10 You're Not Stubborn **3:11**

THE UNDERTONES

THE UNDERTONES (1979)

DAMIEN O'NEILL 'I always thought the Derry journalist Eamon McCann summed up "Teenage Kicks" the best when he called it "A beautiful sound coming from an ugly place". For me, it's a beautifully written innocent rock 'n' roll song (The Shangri-Las could have covered it in '64) performed by five determined young people whose timing was right and who certainly had nothing to lose.'

They looked no more like punks than the Bash Street Kids, but for many people, Derry's Undertones epitomised so much more than just a London/NYC-dominated music scene. With their flares and their parkas, their early gigs in schools, parish halls and Scout huts (lead singer Feargal Sharkey was a Scout leader, after all), and their distinct lack of natural sophistication and studied cool, The Undertones unwittingly championed the revenge of the ordinary. With no image to speak of, the music had to matter.

Formed in 1975, galvanised by punk rock in 1976, composed original material in 1977, signed to a major record label in 1978 – if three years went by in a flash, it didn't faze the lads. Nineteen seventy-eight, though, was their year. Early that year, they recorded a demo tape, sent copies of it to record labels, and music industry movers and shakers, only to receive (at best) letters of rejection or (at worst) nothing. Not from BBC Radio 1 DJ John Peel, though, who, liking what he heard, funded a recording session in Belfast. With a budget of £200 or thereabouts, the band recorded four songs: 'True Confessions', 'Smarter Than U', 'Emergency Cases' and 'Teenage Kicks'.

All four were smarter-than-smart, pinprick pop/punk, but the latter track – one of those catch-all, simple enough tunes that seemed to have composed itself – would go on to catch fire. Released on Belfast's Good Vibrations label (overseen in piratical fashion by Terri Hooley, the proud owner of one eye, hence the spelling

of his first name) and played in what seemed like quick rotation, first by John Peel and then other DJs, the song quickly attracted the attention of the very people who had previously ignored it. By September 1978, the band had signed to Sire Records.

Six months later, in May 1979, the band's self-titled debut album was released (it was re-released five months later with extra tracks 'Teenage Kicks' and 'Get Over You'; nit-picking parked, brakes on, engine off, doors locked, that's the album we'll get excited about here), and within the space of a medium-length Pink Floyd track, it proceeded to lay waste to any naysayers who may have considered the band lightweights.

With ne'er a political comment to be discerned, songs such as 'Jump Boys', 'Male Model', 'Get Over You', 'Jimmy Jimmy', 'Here Comes the Summer', 'Teenage Kicks' and 'I Gotta Getta' burst from highly sprung traps like foxes after rabbits. Mostly written by John O'Neill (who was helped along the way by his brother Damien, Mickey Bradley and Billy Doherty), the album tracks, honed to near-perfection by regular gigs, were recorded in less than two weeks.

More was to come (the band's second album, 1980's *Hypnotised*, is another box of crackers), but here, in flawless, childlike wonder and tatty polo-neck jumper, was where it started.

THE UNDERTONES

Released: 1979
Record Label: Sire Records
Producer: Roger Bechirian
Recorded at: Eden Studios, London
Sleeve Design: Bush Hollyhead (design), Larry Doherty (photography)

Tracks:
1 Family Entertainment 2:37
2 Girls Don't Like It 2:19
3 Male Model 1:54
4 I Gotta Getta 1:53
5 Teenage Kicks 2:25
6 Wrong Way 1:23
7 Jump Boys 2:40
8 Here Comes the Summer 1:42
9 Get Over You 2:44
10 Billy's Third 1:57
11 Jimmy Jimmy 2:41
12 True Confessions 1:52
13 (She's A) Runaround 1:49
14 I Know a Girl 2:35
15 Listening In 2:24
16 Casbah Rock 0:47

U2
BOY (1980)

'I wasn't even thinking about lyrics – they're just sketches. I'm definitely the person who let that album down. It's one of the best debut albums ever. And if I'd sung in my own accent and finished the lyrics, it might have been really good.' *Mojo*, July 2005

After a couple of years of building up a profile in Ireland and the UK, the young U2 – formed as Feedback in the autumn of 1976 at Mount Temple Comprehensive School, known for a while as The Hype, and given their reluctantly accepted new name by designer/musician Steve Averill – signed with Island Records in March 1980. Within six months, the band's debut album would be rehearsed, recorded and released (the quickest turnaround time for any U2 record).

Early critics of the band were less than excited by the notion, never mind the reality, of a debut album. Some singles had been released – notably the band's second single for Island, 'A Day Without Me', a piercing, declamatory track that bode well for the future – but the band's live shows were primarily what people based their opinions on, and these, for the most part, were often ragged affairs, full of bluff and bluster from lead singer Bono, yet saved in part by the crystal-clear fluidity of guitar player Dave Evans (aka The Edge).

'A Day Without Me' had been produced as a suck-it-and-see exercise by Steve Lillywhite, who got on with the band so well that he was asked to oversee *Boy*. Many of the songs earmarked for the album were from the live set the band had been refining throughout 1979 and the first half of 1980, so (perhaps for the first and only time) U2 entered the recording studio with a full set of album tracks effectively rehearsed to within an inch of their respective lives.

The album cover was very much intended to portray a story of innocence and gradual development, while thematically, the album itself hit a few raw nerves with its overall concept: the anxiety of adolescence gradually coming to a close, the emblematic conflict of maleness, the nature of male bonding, and associated questions about spirituality and sexuality.

The music, however (even for those who had seen them live many times up to this point), was something else – revelatory, even. An amalgam of Edge's mercurial guitar lines (terrifically effective, volatile almost, on 'I Will Follow', 'Out of Control', 'An Cat Dubh' and 'A Day Without Me'), Bono's impressionistic lyrics, and Lillywhite's empathetic production (which blended tension, dynamics, fragility, atmosphere and aggression) created the kind of album that only comes around once in a lifetime.

The subject matter alone was, for its time, unique. To marry such topics with music so realistically measured and, often, so intriguing, was to listen to a band aiming for a lot but achieving so much more.

Released: 1980
Record Label: Island Records
Producer: Steve Lillywhite, Chas De Whalley, U2
Recorded at: Windmill Lane Studios, Dublin
Sleeve Design: Bono/Rapid Exteriors, Hugo McGuinness ('Boy' photographs)

Tracks:
1 I Will Follow **3:36**
2 Twilight **4:22**
3 An Cat Dubh **4:47**
4 Into the Heart **3:28**
5 Out of Control **4:13**
6 Stories for Boys **3:02**
7 The Ocean **1:34**
8 A Day Without Me **3:14**
9 Another Time, Another Place **4:34**
10 The Electric Co. **4:48**
11 Shadows and Tall Trees **4:36**

U2

THE JOSHUA TREE (1987)

BONO

'The significant thing about *The Joshua Tree* is that I had to "come clean" as a word-writer. Instead of trying to capture the elusive message of the music, which is what I'd normally try to do with my words, I wanted to speak out specifically, but without a placard, and without my John Lennon handbook.'
Propaganda, 1987

Following 1984's *The Unforgettable Fire* – which was shaped by producer Brian Eno's creative direction of forging musical landscapes rather than structured songwriting – U2 set about flipping the switch. The Unforgettable Fire tour clocked out at Tampa, Florida, in early May 1985, and very shortly afterwards, the band convened at bass player Adam Clayton's Dublin house.

It was a loose arrangement, by all accounts; at the starting point, there were no new songs written, but the general consensus was that the new songs had to be more concise, more hook-laden. Alongside this, was the geographical and cultural broadening of the band's own horizons.

If the languor of *The Unforgettable Fire* was mostly European, then the new album looked to America for its influences. Parameters, although still in operation, increased significantly, and as the songwriting took shape it became apparent that everything about *The Joshua Tree* was geared towards embracing the strengths and, occasionally, weaknesses of America.

At least half of the tracks here are omnipresent by this point: the album, U2's most commercially successful, went on to become a multi-million seller. In their stage shows, meanwhile, they still make a feature of songs such as 'With or Without You', 'I Still Haven't Found What I'm Looking For' and 'Where the Streets Have No Name' – the latter, in particular, having taken on its own iconographic status within U2's world. For all its success, though, it is the album's less-played tracks,

such as 'Running to Stand Still', 'In God's Country', 'Trip Through Your Wires' and 'One Tree Hill' that potently counteract the often detrimental ubiquity of its best-known songs.

While there's no doubting the emotional push and pull of the likes of 'With or Without You', 'I Still Haven't Found What I'm Looking For' and 'Where the Streets Have No Name', there seems somehow a far greater urgency to songs such as 'Running to Stand Still' and 'One Tree Hill'. The former has its lyrical touchstones in Dublin's heroin-bruised northside, while the latter (a tribute to a close associate of Bono's who had been killed in a motorbike accident in Dublin) is not just a song of true spiritual balm but also contains a vocal performance that no one would have thought Bono capable of.

The enormity of U2 (and after *The Joshua Tree* they would join the pantheon of the world's biggest rock acts) would not yet become a hindrance; for now, though, they had fashioned an utterly confident, mature and often spine-tingling cinematic album that mixed gospel, grandeur, soul, artistry, ambience, bluegrass 'n' blues, and understatement in equal measure.

Released: 1987
Record Label: Island Records
Producer: Daniel Lanois, Brian Eno
Recorded at: Windmill Lane Studios, Dublin
Sleeve Design: Steve Averill, The Creative
Dept. Ltd, Anton Corbijn (photography)

Tracks:
1 Where the Streets Have No Name
   5:38
2 I Still Haven't Found What I'm Looking
   For **4:38**
3 With or Without You **4:56**
4 Bullet the Blue Sky **4:32**

5 Running to Stand Still **4:20**
6 Red Hill Mining Town **4:51**
7 In God's Country **2:57**
8 Trip Through Your Wires **3:33**
9 One Tree Hill **5:23**
10 Exit **4:13**
11 Mothers of the Disappeared **5:12**

U2

ACHTUNG BABY (1991)

LARRY MULLEN JR 'It dawned on us after *The Joshua Tree* that the bigness of U2 had become a distraction. I remember thinking that we were in a position where we really didn't have to do anything any more . . . The only thing we could do was to split up or pour all our confusion into the music. In some ways, *Achtung Baby* is the sound of a band fighting for its musical life. To me it's like a first album, the beginning of U2 Mark 2.' *The Face.*

Good buzz-words: 'industrial', 'sexy', 'throwaway', 'dark' 'trashy'. Bad buzz-words: 'linear', 'righteous', 'earnest', 'sweet', 'polite'. If a song took you on a journey, or made you think that your sound equipment was broken, that was good. If a song reminded you of U2, that was bad.

Coming off the final dates of their Rattle and Hum tour, rocking their American-preacher-man look and pitching up tent at Dublin's (then) Point venue, U2 finished their final show by stating that they had to go away and dream it all up again. In truth, they absolutely *had* to dream it all up again: themselves, their music, their general demeanour. The downside of *The Joshua Tree* and *Rattle and Hum*, in particular, had seen them wallow in such levels of aching sincerity and earnestness that they (Bono, specifically) had become virtual caricatures.

And so, from November 1990 to March 1991, the band and producers (Daniel Lanois, Brian Eno, Flood) decamped to Berlin's Hansa Studios, from where they wrought, often rancorously, the batch of songs that would provide enough artistic ammunition to save their career.

The arguments landed due to the radical new ideas being lobbed back and forth by guitarist Edge, Bono and the Lanois/Eno axis, with drummer Larry Mullen Jr and bass player Adam Clayton initially unconvinced as to the worthiness of the songs – particularly the noise collages of opening track 'Zoo Station', the harsh metallic funk/rock of 'The Fly', and Bono's change of tack in lyric writing. Mullen Jr, perhaps in particular, felt that his input was being diminished by the extensive use of drum machines. The early sessions were, as per usual in the band's recording history, riven by lack of rehearsals and preparation. And so it continued.

Yet *Achtung Baby* is, in most respects, an album of birth, rebirth and change, of what was initially a positive thing being switched at the most inopportune moments: Bono's daughter Eve was born in July 1991, while in the lead-up to the album being recorded, Edge and his wife, Aislinn, were separating.

Joy, tiredness, elation and unease bled through the music, which gradually began to gel. The result was another close shave of an artistic triumph, albeit one that the band's more traditionalist fans took some time to mull over. Yet with songs as beautiful as 'One', as exhilarating as 'Who's Gonna Ride Your Wild Horses', as slow-buring as 'So Cruel', and as bitter as 'Acrobat', it slowly took hold.

For an album that did everything U2 weren't supposed to do, *Achtung Baby* did just fine. Formula was upended by chemistry. Job well done.

Released: 1991
Record Label: Island Records
Producer: Daniel Lanois, Brian Eno
Recorded at: Hansa Ton Studios, Berlin;
Dog Town Dublin; STS Studios, Dublin;
Elsinore, Dalkey; Windmill Studios, Dublin
Sleeve Design: Steve Averill, Shaughn
McGrath (Works Associates), Anton Corbijn
(photography)

Tracks:
1 Zoo Station **4:36**
2 Even Better Than the Real Thing **3:41**
3 One **4:36**
4 Until the End of the World **4:39**
5 Who's Gonna Ride Your Wild Horses
 5:16
6 So Cruel **5:49**
7 The Fly **4:29**
8 Mysterious Ways **4:04**
9 Tryin' to Throw Your Arms Around the
 World **3:53**
10 Ultraviolet (Light My Way) **5:31**
11 Acrobat **4:30**
12 Love Is Blindness **4:23**

VILLAGERS
BECOMING A JACKAL (2010)

CONOR O'BRIEN

'The songs were written, primarily arranged and demoed in complete isolation. Some of them arrived almost fully formed, others were more like jigsaw pieces of pre-written musings or emotional outbursts that duly went through many different phases, the goal of which was to seemingly make use of as many different cognitive techniques I could pull from my otherwise puny brain. The other aspect of the whole process is far more ethereal and mysterious and, as such, it would be a waste of time to try and express it in text form. But it also happened. The addition of Cormac (Curran)'s masterful string arrangements, Tommy (McLaughlin)'s astute engineering and co-production, Ben (Hillier)'s sympathetic mixing skills and Bunt (Stafford Clarke)'s old-school mastering techniques (he toured Africa with Nina Simone in the mid-sixties!) helped me realise that it was all worth it. The results are accomplished. I'm proud of it. I think it's a good album. The next one will be better.'

The one prerequisite is silence. Actually, make that two – silence and solitude. Which is interesting and curious, because with Villagers (aka sole songwriter Conor O'Brien and a crack team of friends/musicians), the shtick is all quite intense in a nervy, preppy, Talking Heads-'Psycho Killer' kinda way. Offstage, O'Brien is incredibly polite, reserved, utterly attentive. On stage, he's a mixture of thousand-yard-stare and focused therapist, picking out the words to his songs like Veruca Salt choosing sweets from Willy Wonka's chocolate factory: assiduously, full of concentration, but with no small level of excitement and just a little bit spoiled-rotten. It is no surprise to discover that intelligent lyrics (some might say ponderous, some might say pretentious) are central to O'Brien's songwriting process.

O'Brien's talent first came to light as a member of The Immediate, a highly rated band whose sudden split was due to 'existential differences'. O'Brien carried on regardless, swiftly moving his talents across to Cathy Davey's band (as well as contributing strategically to Davey's *Tales of Silversleeve* (see page 62) and giving over time to hone his own formidable songwriting. Cue Villagers.

Becoming A Jackal caught many by surprise; the erst-while Kinks/Radiohead hybrids of The Immediate were jettisoned for something rather more rarefied, narrative-driven and cerebral. 'Have you got just a minute? Are you easily led?' O'Brien asks at the start of the first track, 'I Saw The Dead', and from there we're glued to, clued into to next forty-five minutes. You could, if you were of a mind, describe the music here as existential pop: there are the dread nightmare scenarios of the aforementioned 'I Saw The Dead', the bitter glance at relationships in 'The Meaning Of The Ritual' ('my love is selfish and it cares not who it hurts. It will cut you out to satisfy its thirst'), the precise, clipped lyrical pronunciations of the title track, and the shared experience of a bus breaking down in 'Twenty-Seven Strangers' – perhaps the album's oddest, best song. Today, anyway.

Through it all, O'Brien borrows from this, that and the other (a little of bit of Leonard Cohen, and gentle reminders of other 1960s/70s singer-songwriters the world has long since forgotten), delivering a song suite that combines his favourite things: the twisting and turning of lyrics, discovering characters, layering stories, creating context within the songs with arrangements, repeating imagery, and narrative tricks. Difficult to categorise? That's part of the pleasure.

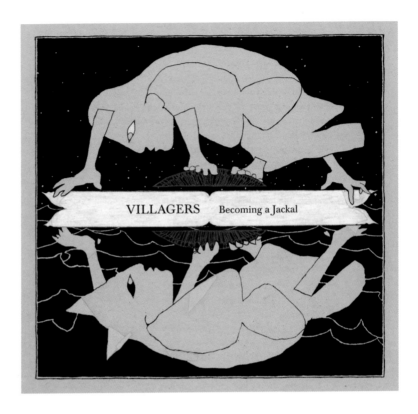

Released: 2010

Record Label: Domino Records

Producer: Conor J. O'Brien, Tommy McLaughlin

Recorded at: Attica Audio, County Donegal; Miloco, The Pool, London

Sleeve Design: Matthew Cooper (design), Conor O'Brien (artwork)

Tracks:
1 I Saw The Dead **5:04**
2 Becoming A Jackal **3:19**
3 Ship Of Promises **4:36**
4 The Meaning Of The Ritual **3:14**
5 Home **4:41**
6 That Day **3:10**
7 The Pact (I'll Be Your Fever) **3:28**
8 Set The Tigers Free **3:22**
9 Twenty Seven Strangers **3:24**
10 Pieces **5:25**
11 To Be Counted Among Men **4:43**

VIRGIN PRUNES
. . . IF I DIE, I DIE (1982)

GAVIN FRIDAY

'The record is split in two parts/sides – Blue and Brown. The blue side, musically, came from our confrontational punk/pop/noise fixations, whereas the brown side, musically, came from our take on spiritualism via Celtic *sean nós* and tribalism . . . Overall, the brown side holds up the strongest – our dabblings in ethnic/Celtic/*sean nós* seem way ahead of their time, and prove we were a lot more Irish than the eye could see way back then. As for 'Caucasian Walk' and 'Theme For Thought' – one would have to have grown up in repressed '70s Ireland to come up with these gigantic rants, and they still sound powerful and believable . . . Ultimately? It's a fucking great album . . .'

Formed in the late seventies, out of the naively creative 'Lypton Village' community that gave the world U2 (The Edge's brother, Dik Evans, was also a member), the band seemed to thrive on controversy for controversy's sake. Given their monikers through membership of teenage fantasy concoction Lypton Village, Fionan Hanvey (Gavin Friday; see separate entry, page 84) and Derek Rowan (Guggi) utilised a singular type of cathartic performance/music that was viewed by some as guttural, exciting art-terrorism, and by others as high-minded, pretentious art-wank. Whatever way the Virgin Prunes were perceived (and they didn't just divide opinion, they rent it apart), there was no doubting one thing: they were absolutely, terrifically unique. But how to transfer on-stage purgings full of Victoriana misgivings, Miss Haversham ravings, and primeval blood, muck and guts to the confines of an album? The answer is that they couldn't, but within the parameters of . . . *If I Die, I Die* they came pretty damn close to a sonic approximation.

It starts with a twist: the dinky instrumental 'Ulakanakulot' segues into 'Decline and Fall's opening tribal whistles and Friday's soft/declamatory vocals. 'Sweethome Under White Clouds' sets the mad ball rolling, however, and it continues with 'Bau-Dachöng' (covered ever so differently on *Songs of Love and Death*, by Emm Gryner – see separate entry, page 90) and 'Dave-Id

Is Dead', which, featuring a lead vocal from band member Dave-Id Busaras, is simply grist to the mill for those who claim that Virgin Prunes took perverse delight in weirding people out. And yet, despite the oddities dotted throughout, there are moments of sheer delight, which are, just as plainly, grist to the mill for those who claim there was much more to the band than art pranks.

The guitar/piano tune 'Fádo' is as pretty and delicate as porcelain, yet retains a worrying atmosphere akin to a child playing in an attic where some unspeakable evil resides. 'Pagan Lovesong' and 'Baby Turns Blue' are, effectively, the 'hits', while 'Ballad of the Man' (again featuring the unconventional singing voice of Dave-Id Busaras) is like Bruce Springsteen with a migraine.

The album finishes with a flourish: 'Walls of Jericho' (with Dik Evans' guitar pings referencing the style of his brother), 'Caucasian Walk' (a boot-stomping screech-out between Gavin and Guggi), 'Theme for Thought' (a *sturm und drang* tune occasionally mollified by a pixie-dancing contribution from saxophonist Keith Donald), and 'Chance of a Lifetime' (think the *Blair Witch Project* compacted down into aural form) and 'Yeo' (Fádo, Part Two, except here the demon appears and whispers 'Boo!').

Here we go, then: focused post-punk fun 'n' games (with a strong hint of Celtic shriek-back) that in turn confounds, intrigues, amazes, perturbs, camps it up and stamps it down.

VIRGIN PRUNES
...IF I DIE, I DIE

Released: 1982
Record Label: Rough Trade Records
Producer: Colin Newman
Recorded at: Windmill Lane Studios, Dublin
Sleeve Design: Slim Smith, Ursula Steiger
(photography)

Tracks:
1 Ulakanakulot **2:26**
2 Decline and Fall **4:52**
3 Sweethome Under White Clouds **4:43**
4 Bau-Dachöng **5:51**
5 Pagan Lovesong **3:28**
6 Dave-Id Is Dead **4:17**
7 Fádo **1:59**
8 Baby Turns Blue **3:42**
9 Ballad of the Man **3:32**
10 Walls of Jericho **3:09**
11 Caucasion Walk **4:43**
12 Theme for Thought **5:44**
13 Chance of a Lifetime **2:55**
14 Yeo **4:49**

WHIPPING BOY

HEARTWORM (1995)

FERGHAL MCKEE 'I just put Whipping Boy into a corner and forgot about them. That was my way of dealing with it. Then you have friends you meet often, and they keep on playing the album to you, and saying things like, "what are you doing? Why don't you get back together again?" These questions would slowly drill their way into you, and it took me about five years to listen to *Heartworm* again. Is it brilliant? I don't know – but it seems to have stretched across the generations.'

Whipping Boy, as anyone who negotiated their way around the Irish music scene in and around the late '80s will tell you, were the contrarians of the bunch (says Ferghal McKee, lead singer: 'I was just having the craic. Some people might not have known I was having the craic, but why would I want to tell them? I take that privilege as an entertainer.'). Perhaps matched only in the unpredictability stakes by Microdisney's/Fatima Mansions' Cathal Coughlan (see entries on pages 52 and 128), McKee is up there as a guy with a creative logic so twisted it occasionally had to be restrained by a straitjacket (sometimes literally). Words like 'surprise' and 'danger' are thrown about with reckless, ridiculous abandon when it comes to describing the live-act shenanigans of rock bands, but in Whipping Boy's case you genuinely didn't know what was going to happen before, during or after the songs.

Unlike most of the other also-rans from the late '80s and early '90s onwards, Whipping Boy refute the oft-expressed notion that the memories were stronger than the songs. The band's first release was a cassette-only album called *Sweet Mangled Thing*, and if ever there was statement of pure intent then by God that was one. A second, very strong album, *Submarine*, was released in 1992, and although mentioned in dispatches as a classic Irish rock album, it's really 1995's *Heartworm* that clinches the title.

Heartworm remains the record that most people remember Whipping Boy for. And for good reason, as it's a dizzying, intense, exhilarating experience, full of songs that feature singer/lyricist Ferghal McKee at his most heart-warming ('When We Were Young': 'shifting women, getting stoned, robbing cars, bars and pubs, rubber johnnies, poems'), charming ('Twinkle': 'she's the air I breathe, not too pure for me'), borderline paranoiac/abusive ('We Don't Need Nobody Else': 'I hit you for the first time today, I didn't mean it, it just happened . . . Christ, we weren't even fightin', I was just annoyed. That really hurt me, you said. Yea? And you thought you knew me!'), ruthlessly pragmatic ('Personality': 'people grow old, they get bored, they forget to take a risk') and tender/tense ('Morning Rise': 'let the morning rise like our heart's desire, I can't help thinking that I love you'). Even the 'secret' spoken word track ('Natural') shifts and shudders via a traditional music motif that is mugged by guitar chords.

Imbued with the kind of thrilling, weirded-out, high-anxiety pop music that sounds as pitch-perfect today as it seemed out of place when it was first released, *Heartworm* balances anger, poignancy, distress, self-loathing and passion without so much as breaking sweat. Yours, for the price of a cappuccino, from a bargain bin near you.

whipping boy

Heartworm

Released: 1995
Record Label: Columbia Records, Sony
Producer: Warne Livesey
Recorded at: Windmill Lane Studios, Dublin
Sleeve Design: Works Associates, Brendan
Fitzpatrick (photography)

Tracks:
1 Twinkle **5:02**
2 When We Were Young **2:51**
3 Tripped **3:44**
4 The Honeymoon Is Over **3:38**
5 We Don't Need Nobody Else **4:16**
6 Blinded **3:54**
7 Personality **4:26**
8 Users **3:55**
9 Fiction **3:25**
10 Morning Rise **4:52**
11 A Natural **3:47**

WILT
MY MEDICINE (2001)

CORMAC BATTLE

'With *My Medicine* we felt it was time to ramp things up, as endless toilet tours of the UK and Europe, although fun, were getting a bit wearing. So without selling our souls we wrote songs with highly addictive melodies and welded them to short sharp punches of guitars. Things really took off – MTV had us on high rotation – and we believed our time had finally come to move into the big league. On returning from a video shoot in New York, however, we found out that a major label had bought Mushroom and, in the transfer, flushed us down the toilet. A week later I was doing a government-sponsored Desktop Publishing course. Rock 'n' Roll is a risky business; the road is strewn with great albums that could have made a difference . . . I believe *My Medicine* is one of them.'

Thousands of people in thousands of rock bands are in relentless pursuit of something, and, if they're honest with themselves, they're never certain if it's to sell millions of records, or to achieve some notional level of success (the definition of which is subjective, anyway).

The members of Wilt used to be those people; able-bodied souls (two of whom, Cormac Battle and Darragh Butler, were in a fine, tough rock band called Kerbdog) prostrating themselves at the altar of mammon in return for weekends of freedom. In the early 2000s, however, they were bold Irish men with guitars resting at their sides, tunes tightly wrapped around their midriffs, melodies darting forth from their chests like strikes of lightning. In short, Wilt made a strong case for the apparent unending stream of punk/pop that made its way from the pages of *Kerrang!* towards less exclamatory publications.

The band, however, were smart enough to hone their exceptional brand of literate punk/pop while others around them snagged their surfer-dude cut-offs on nu-metal and the like. If Wilt's 2000 debut album, *Bastinado*, heralded forth an Irish talent intent on making the world safe from Blink-182, then *My Medicine* looked set to propel them from relative obscurity to definite contenders. What differentiated Wilt from the rest of the pack, though, was their value for the more fragmented cerebral concerns of their fans. Helped in this regard by Battle's documenting of his own problematic experiences of mental health, the songs have an edge that simply wouldn't be there if there was any pretence on display.

Anxiety and neuroses go hand in hand with fighting your way through the mire of the music industry – but you need chronic self-belief, too, and throughout *My Medicine* Wilt prove their mettle via songs such as opening tracks 'Distortion' (do not adjust your volume – that's a piece of helpful advice as well as a warning) and 'Understand' (think of REM as a collective of bodybuilders just before they capitulate to years of ingesting steroids). Other songs such as 'Take Me Home' (music versus muscle – it's a draw), the propulsive, guitars/strings title track ('God, I'm not feeling well, you're right, but you can nearly feel it as well; and take my temperature tonight cos I can hardly get out of bed with all this medicine inside . . .') and closing track, 'The Plan' (what Rocky might call a bone-cruncher, albeit one wrapped up in a cloak of jangling, jabbing guitars) generate the kind of Pavlovian responses that come with a liking for staccato, quiet/loud and supremely finely-tuned, intelligent rock music.

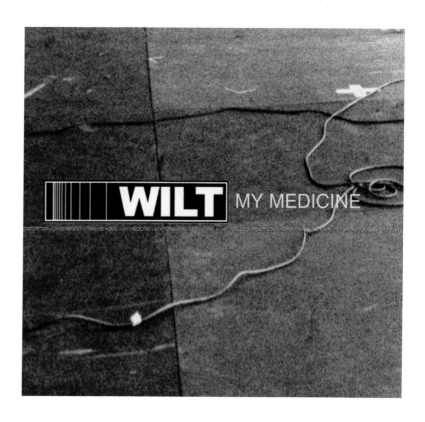

Released: 2001
Record Label: Mushroom Records
Producer: Dave Eringa
Recorded at: RAK Studios, London
Sleeve Design: Craig Gentle

Tracks:
1 Distortion 3:28
2 Understand 3:50
3 Take Me Home 3:47
4 My Medicine 3:42
5 Stations 2:41

6 Dave You Were Right 3:25
7 Tell You Too Much 3:53
8 Family Man 3:55
9 Wait a Minute 3:34
10 Broken Glass 4:09
11 The Plan 3:52

THE WOULD BE'S
'I'M HARDLY EVER WRONG' (1990)

EAMONN FINNEGAN

'*I'm Hardly Ever Wrong* was written during a serious bout of idealism brought on by the belief (mistaken or otherwise) that we could all make our lives much more vital and rewarding if we could just somehow remember all the little lessons we learn every time we hear a wonderful song that has a very simple but devastating home truth that makes you really think, but alas, only for a day . . . With this song, as with most of them, we were trying to get a balance between insight into life and a sense of humour about it all . . . it struck the right chord with all the right people, at just the right time in our lives.'

John Peel loved them (number 12 in his Festive Top 50 in 1990). Morrissey loved them (support act at some Dublin gigs). Stephen Street produced them (instant credibility). The Smiths with a female singer. The recipients of one – or was it two? – Singles of the Week in *NME*, in the days when that really meant something.

Some members (notably the Finnegan brothers, Mattie, Eamonn, Paul) burrowed their way out of Kingscourt, County Cavan and nearby Kilmainhamwood, County Meath. The original (and best) lead singer, a slip of a teenage girl called Julie McDonnell, came from a village close to Ardee, County Louth. The band even featured a female trombone and saxophone (and occasional violin) player called Aideen O'Reilly. And they were managed by an older Finnegan brother, James – which, in retrospect, probably wasn't a good idea. Rural. Ireland. God. Love. You.

Formed in the late eighties, from the ashes of a band called The Nobodys, music from The Would Be's first surfaced on local radio in the Louth/Meath area, filtering slowly across the national airwaves, and then across the Irish Sea to London, where John Peel, as much enthused by The Would Be's as he had been thirteen years previously by The Undertones (see separate entry, page 202), went radio ga-ga over debut single 'I'm Hardly Ever Wrong' and its B-side, 'Great Expectations'. In short, he played it off the air. Cue major-record-label scrums, wherein quite a few A&R people flew in from here and there, checked out the band, talked to their brother/manager, only to walk away with a perplexed shake of the head. One can only surmise what took place between the jigs and the reels of managerial and label negotiations, but what transpired is that the band (who first released 'I'm Hardly Ever Wrong/Great Expectations' on the Dublin indie label Danceline) eventually signed to an obscure London indie label, Decoy Records, and effectively disappeared.

What's left, of course, is what the likes of Peel and Morrissey swooned over: that incredibly sweet first single, and its inordinately deft flip-side. It is rightly regarded as the best Irish indie pop single ever released, coming at you from the off with a squiffy guitar build-up and trombone parps, its blend of naiveté and melody, lightness of touch, McDonnell's hide-and-seek voice, and lyrics that, in part, extol the virtues of popular culture (music, books, movies), while simultaneously, dolefully, undermining its worth ('Please tell me why when you're a lover of life you always lose your appetite; you see a film and it changes your ways but only for a day, and a day is not enough').

The band would go on to release a few more tunes, with at least one replacement female lead singer, but this effortlessly sublime tune was their most significant, most adorable moment in the spotlight.

The Would Be's

d Be's

I'M HARDLY EVER WRONG   GREAT EXPECTATIONS

Released: 1990
Record Label: Danceline Records (Ireland),
Decoy Records (UK)
Producer: Eamonn Finnegan, Mattie
Finnegan
Recorded at: Sun Studios, Dublin
Sleeve Design: Aideen O'Reilly
Duration: 2:51

YEH DEADLIES

THE FIRST BOOK OF LESSONS (2011)

ANNIE TIERNEY

'My favourite song on the album is "Disc Jockey Blues". It really sums up what it's like to work nights on your own, feeling like an observer. It can be lonely. I like the line, "I'm tired and you're dreaming, your voicemail just goes beep!" The whole band went to our friend Frank Wade's attic, and we recorded the drums there. Everything else was recorded at home in our sitting room. Johnny and Dave spent evenings and weekends calling over whenever there was a spare hour working out harmonies and adding bits and pieces. Padraig O'Reilly, my husband, spent hours mixing on his own, and we'd all listen back together and decide what to change. Padraig wrote the songs on *The First Book of Lessons*, but I feel very connected to them; they are a soundtrack to a part of our lives together, and I spent a lot of time with them! There is a song about when we first met, "The Present Perfect", which is a pretty straight love song about wanting to be stuck in that moment at the start of a relationship. It's also about the similarities between the feeling of listening to a great pop song and the feeling of being in love.'

Dublin band Yeh Deadlies comprise various members of the capital's Popical Island collective, a crack brainstorm unit designed to nudge the heads of underground sounds over the parapet. What's great about them is that they are unashamedly in love with pop tunes. You can tell this from the off, when tracks such as 'The Present Perfect', 'Magazine' and 'Best Man Speech' are delivered with all the ease and authority of a band at peace with the odder and often gentler elements of 1977/78 punk rock.

Never mind that Yeh Deadlies' music is occasionally naive, ragged, scuzzy, fuzzy and snotty (not necessarily a bad thing - ever). Rather, you have to admire their skills at gathering together on one album (their debut, no less) songs from various eras of guitar-driven Great Pop. Ultimately, it's all about the intuitive genius of stealing, and applying and portraying the swag in ways that interest, intrigue and excite.

It's all about that on *The First Book of Lessons* (the cover of which, as you can see, is like an original Penguin paperback defaced by a second-year secondary-class misfit – all that's missing are 'Boyzone suck' and 'Your mother's a lezzer' scrawls); save occasional references to religion and society, love and marriage, and the saving grace of pop, there is little that is profound to be discovered in the lyrics. In 'Disc Jockey Blues', mention is made of 'the frottage industry', but – and, er, here's the rub - beyond that, anything pertaining to doing, or thinking of, the nasty is sublimated to the rhythms of the music.

Ultimately, *The First Book of Lessons* is an elevator pitch in how to make peer-group pressure dissolve like the inside of a Malteser under gentle probing from a tongue. That its main musical thrust is in respectful thrall to what sounds like the line-up of a show in London's 100 Club, circa 1978 (Young Marble Giants, X Ray Spex, Subway Sect, Wreckless Eric), is only one of its many strengths.

The primary achievement of this very fine album, however, is one that so many bands fail to comprehend, let alone attain: the blending of talent and skill with charisma and charm, intuition with acumen, devil-may-care with commitment. The first lesson of pop? Make it look effortless. With this album, Yeh Deadlies have done just that.

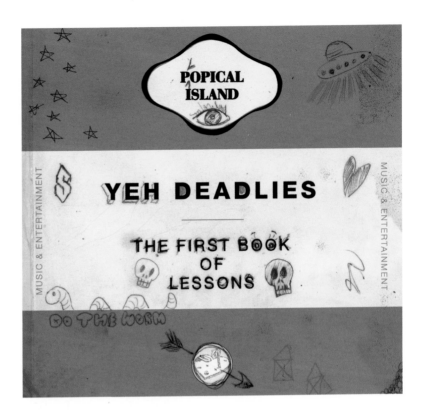

Released: 2011
Record Label: Popical Island
Producer: Padraig O'Reilly
Recorded at: Frank Wade's attic, Annie &
Padraig's gaff
Sleeve Design: Bronwyn Murphy-White,
Ruan van Vliet (Big Wow)

Tracks:
1 The Present Perfect 2:16
2 Magazine 2:18
3 Best Man Speech 2:12
4 Disc Jockey Blues 2:19
5 The Kids In The Band 2:38
6 It Must Be Thursday, Here Comes Ruby
   3:00
7 No Rock 'n' Roll Dreams (In Empty
   Beds) 2:32
8 Sophomore Evil 3:16
9 The First Book Of Lessons 1:59
10 Almost Two 5:14
11 Do The Worm 3:14
12 Superman Song 2:45
13 Learning Chinese 4:55
14 Waiting On The Sun To Rise 1:19

Ham Sandwich – © Kieran Frost.

FURTHER READING & BIBLIOGRAPHY

Beautiful Day: Forty Years of Irish Rock by Sean Campbell and Gerry Smyth (Atrium, 2005)

Bringing It All Back Home by Nuala O'Connor (BBC Books, 1991)

Can You Feel The Silence? Van Morrison: A New Biography by Clinton Heylin (Viking, 2002)

The Complete U2 Encyclopedia by Mark Chatterton (Firefly Publishing, 2001)

The Humours of Planxty by Leagues O'Toole (Hodder Headline Ireland, 2006)

Irish Folk, Trad & Blues by Colin Harper and Trevor Hodgett (The Collins Press, 2004)

Irish Rock: Roots, Personalities, Directions by Mark J. Prendergast (The O'Brien Press, 1987)

Irish Rock: Where It's Come From, Where It's At, Where It's Going by Tony Clayton-Lea and Richie Taylor (Sidgwick & Jackson, 1992)

It Makes You Want To Spit by Sean O'Neill and Guy Trelford (Reekus Music Irl Ltd, 2003)

Listening To Van Morrison by Greil Marcus (Faber & Faber, 2010)

Luke Kelly – A Memoir by Des Geraghty (Basement Press, 1994)

U2 By U2 by Bono, The Edge, Adam Clayton, Larry Mullen Jr, with Neil McCormick (HarperCollins, 2006)

A Woman's Voice by Eddie Rowley (The O'Brien Press, 1993)

Many thanks, also, to irishrock.org and irishmusicdb.com, each of which enabled me to cross some tees and dot some eyes.

PHOTOGRAPHY CREDITS

Page 14

MayKay from Fight Like Apes – © Kieran Frost

Bell X1 – © Paul Bergen/Redferns

Damien Rice – © Markus Cuff/Corbis

Glen Hansard – © Kieran Frost

Sinéad O'Connor – © Darlene Hammond/Getty Images

Gary Lightbody of Snow Patrol – © Buda Mendes /Getty Images

Bob Geldof – © Lynn Goldsmith/Corbis

Gavin Friday – © Brenda Fitzsimons/*The Irish Times*

The Cranberries – © Kate Garner/Corbis Outline